a Different
journey

a Different journey

Brian D'Arcy

Sliabh Bán Productions,
PO Box No 6369,
Fortfield, Dublin 6W, Ireland.

Sliabh Bán Productions
PO Box No 6369,
Fortfield, Dublin 6W.

ISBN 0-9545829-5-0

A CIP record of this book is available from the British Library.

If the publishers have inadvertently overlooked any copyright holders,
we would be happy to make appropriate arrangements.

Photography: Ray McManus, Brendan Moran, Sportsfile
Additional photographs: Sunday World, Pat Lunny, D'Arcy family album
Layout and design: Mary Guinan
Printed in Ireland by Future Print

DEDICATION

For Hugh D'Arcy and Ellen Corrigan.
May they be at Heaven's door to welcome me home
when all my journeys are over.

ACKNOWLEDGEMENTS

It's risky to mention names, but I don't know of any other sincere way to say thanks to so many people who helped me throughout my life, but particularly in the preparation of this book. A special thanks to Brian and Trish Carthy for their constant encouragement over many years to put my experiences on paper. Now through Sliabh Bán publishing company the day has arrived. Thanks to all at Sliabh Bán for all your hard work.

I am grateful to those who helped me put the text together especially Orfhlaith Ní Chonaill, who worked unsparingly to ensure the story unfolded in a meaningful way. Her advice was invaluable and on days when I got lost in the midst of my own life, she was always able to point out where the light might be.

My thanks to Michael Doherty for his incisive and skilful editing, and to Richard Gallagher for his helpful suggestions.

When it came to writing the book the Mercy Sisters very generously gave me the use of one of their houses so that I could have a few days of peace and quiet. I'm forever grateful for their generous offer. If it hadn't been for Albert Reynolds and *The Dancing News* in Longford, I might never have started in journalism in 1966.

My thanks to the *Sunday World*, who have retained me as a columnist for over 30 years and who supported this book at every stage. BBC Radio Ulster and BBC Radio 2 in London have a special place in my life too.

I want to thank Professor Michael Carroll and his wife, Cathy, for their professional advice, encouragement, friendship and patience beyond the call of duty.

The community, staff and voluntary workers at St Gabriel's Retreat, The Graan, without whose help this book could never have been written, know how genuine my gratitude is.

Mary Guinan did a superb job with the design and layout of the book and Ray McManus almost succeeded in making a silk purse out of a sow's ear with his expertise in photography.

Seán McGrade helped with publicity and advice and Kevin Brophy was the one who published 10 books over a 20-year period.

I am grateful to you for buying A Different Journey *because, as with all my books, profits will go to help the poor.*

My thanks to all my Passionist Brothers in Ireland, Scotland, Paris and Africa for their understanding since I first entered on the 1st of September 1962.

Sir Terry Wogan continues to be an inspiration to me and a real friend in time of need. His beautiful words in the Foreword are undeserved and I feel humbled by his kindness to me.

I know you will forgive me if my last word of thanks is to my family, particularly my brother, Gaby, his wife, Maura, my sisters, Marie and her late husband, Pat Brogan, and Joan and husband Kevin, my nephews Des (Deirdre & family), Gerald (Mandy & family) and Adrian. My nieces Eileen (Declan & family), Sinéad (Frank), Carmel and Margaret. Without their love, understanding and loyalty I would be a lost soul.

And thanks to the many hundreds of people who have loved me and befriended me in almost 40 years of priesthood.

FOREWORD

Fr Brian D'Arcy has been there for all the important events of life in the Wogan family: the funerals of my mother and father, the weddings of my three children — and he'll probably see me off the premises as well, because he hasn't aged a day since I first met him.

If ever there was an advertisement for the good life, it's Brian D'Arcy. Not "good" in the modern, hedonistic, materialistic sense; good in the way it used to be: decent, kind, gentle, wise. All the epithets for goodness you can think of — all could be applied to this man, and none would do him justice. For he epitomises everything a man of God should be.

Fierce honesty, straight talking and a reluctance to toe the line have undoubtedly hampered his progress up the hierarchical ladder. Maybe he loves life too much — and music, and sport. But what a bishop he would have made!

Yet, could any priest have achieved more than he has achieved on his "different journey" through life? He has crossed forbidden boundaries again and again in Northern Ireland, risking all to temper hatred and bring tolerance and understanding. He has toiled in the townships of South Africa. He tirelessly travels the length and breadth of Ireland and Britain, succouring the sick, the lost and those in need.

He is devoted to his community in The Graan, Co Fermanagh, and to his flock. He writes for newspapers and magazines and regularly joins me at the microphone for BBC Radio's *Pause for Thought*.

Brian D'Arcy is doing it not for fame or fortune, reward or applause. He's doing it for good.

Thank God for him!

Terry Wogan

INTRODUCTION

I have been writing for the popular press for 40 years. Even though I have compiled 10 very successful books from my *Sunday World* contributions, this is the first time I have attempted a continuous narrative with a specific purpose.

For over a decade, publishers have encouraged me to write an autobiography. I couldn't agree to do it, because I don't believe the life I have lived warrants an autobiography.

On the other hand valued friends took a different approach and insisted that because of the many different lives I have lived – priesthood, journalism, broadcasting, entertainment – I am in a privileged position. They argued that I had stories and experiences which should not only be told, but reflected upon.

I have lived through a period of unprecedented change in Irish society and the role played by the Catholic Church in our society. For example, I joined The Passionist Congregation during the Second Vatican Council; I was a part of the most successful event in the history of the Irish Church, namely the Papal visit of 1979, and I'm still part of an Ireland which has largely turned away from the Catholic Church. Through it all I have been writing for 30 years in the *Sunday World* about these changes and getting grass-roots reaction every week.

How did it happen? Why did it happen? How have I been changed by the events around me? What keeps me going? What sort of Church might speak to the Irish people in the 21st century? Is there a different way we can journey in hope?

For that reason, memoir had more appeal than autobiography for me. I wanted the stories, and how they influenced me, to be the central theme of the book, rather than for me to highlight the unimportant bits and pieces of my life.

Thomas Merton, the Trappist monk, fuelled the spiritual revolution of the 1960s, and is one of the great heroes of my life who appears often in this book. He put words on my dilemma: "If you want to identify me, ask not where I live, or what I like to eat, or how I comb my hair. But ask me what I think I am living for; ask me what is keeping me from living fully for the thing I want to live for" (Thomas Merton 1975).

And so after Easter 2006 on three days a week for six weeks I put down some of the stories I thought relevant and interesting. I had already spent years reflecting on some central themes in my life with the help of spiritual directors and counsellors – a normal and fruitful way to grow up. And here with the help of story consultant Orfhlaith Ní Chonaill, I've tried to shape those stories in a way that might spark a reaction in your life as well as mine.

I wanted most of all to have a readable book and one which would be accessible to the loyal readers of the *Sunday World* as well as to the wonderful people who encouraged me to stay in the Church and in the priesthood throughout our awful recent history. I wanted a book which would encourage those interested in the Church to question constructively and purposefully from within.

What I didn't want was an angry book. And that is why I needed to submit the text to two highly qualified professional psychologists – one a man, one a woman – who assured me that I was focusing positively on whatever justified anger I experienced. It's important not to let anger destroy us.

Since this is not an autobiography, my family, whom I love dearly, and my very close friends do not feature in central roles. In fact when friends and family, a little nervously, quizzed me about the contents of the book, I assured them that hardly any close friends are mentioned. I have written about key events along the way rather than plodding chronologically through the story of a life from the cradle to pretty close to the grave. I wrote as honestly as I could about the struggle to stay a priest in a Church in crisis.

As an immature 17-year-old I left home to join the Passionist Congregation and I believed then that the order I joined would never change and furthermore that the Church I was giving my life to would always stand for morality, honesty and justice.

In fact, in the Western world at least, our order is now downsizing our foundations because vocations have dried up. When it comes to the Catholic Church its reputation is in tatters because of the clerical sexual-abuse scandals combined with its blatant abuse of power worldwide.

I have written about the laboured little journeys I have made, be they right or wrong, fully realising that because of my unique position, mine has been a different journey.

All of us have to make our own choices in life. My journey cannot be yours. But perhaps what I share with you might encourage you to reflect on your own journey and to realise that no matter where it has taken you, your journey has been good. It's good because God welcomes us no matter how many diversions or side roads we've gone down. God understands and accepts us even when Church and society reject us. That's where true hope resides.

Sr Joan Chittister, the prophetic American nun, believes that the deepest spiritual question facing us today is not, Is there a life after death? Rather the deepest spiritual question facing us today is, Is there a life before death?

When we go through life crippled by fear – fear of God, fear of what others think of us, fear of what life after death holds for us – it can be a wasted life. When we allow God rather than our own selfishness to be the centre of our spiritual journey, we live life to the full, using our gifts as God intended. That's making the best of life in a positive way without wasting it worrying needlessly.

I have no doubt there will be different reactions to what I have shared in these pages. Some will be horrified that I have spoken the unspeakable; others will experience a sense of betrayal that I needed to reveal so much about myself and about the sinful Church; still others, I hope, will experience a sense of relief, liberation and hope that a different journey is possible.

As I read through the pages, I noticed two recurring themes – journey and hope. I was aware of the importance of journey but I was pleasantly surprised that I still have a little hope after a life of searching sceptically and sometimes aimlessly.

To all who helped me on my journey with prayers, friendship, love, patience, encouragement, inspiration and trust, I offer a sincere thanks.

I suggest you read through the book at your leisure. The chapters provide natural resting places along the way. I hope you enjoy what you read, that some of it will challenge you, that most of it will give you hope, that you'll have plenty of laughs and even shed a few tears.

Finally, I know that some people may be hurt by what I write here. That was not my intention even though I fully realised it could happen. I hope you will trust me when I say that my main purpose in revising the book numerous times was to edit out whatever might be hurtful. Life is too short and too precious to waste on spitefulness, and if we search with honesty, compassion and integrity, we will each arrive at the same destination even if we each made *A Different Journey*.

I'm not claiming my journey is better than yours – it's just different and it's my journey.

Brian D'Arcy
October 2006

LET IT BE PRINTED

I looked forward to reading Brian D'Arcy's memoirs. Having journeyed a bit of the way with him, I was keen to see if the person behind the professional would come through. It does. Both are there: the man himself and the stories and narratives that go to make up the professional. This is a marvellous blend of story, people, religion, spirituality, critique, vulnerability, faith, doubt, curiosity, wondering and integrity.

It's honest – as I would have expected. It doesn't hold back – as I knew it wouldn't. It's written compassionately – I would have been surprised otherwise. It shocks at times – I am pleased it does. It recommends ways forward – for a new image and version of Church. This book is not about trendy gimmicks to entice or seduce people into the fold – it's about engaging and meeting people where they are, which is the essence of Brian's life.

A summary of the book for me is how to hold integrity in a Church that has disappointed and betrayed and still find a ministry that speaks to many, both in the mainstream and on the margins.

I know there will be varied reactions to this book: horror from some and a sense of betrayal from others who will feel let down by its honesty.

There will also be a wonderful sigh of relief and liberation from those who feel a side of religion and Catholicism not often acclaimed has been captured and at last has been spoken.

Professor Michael Carroll PhD

CHAPTER 1

THE TOWN OF THE FLAGSTONES

My family is an ordinary working-class family. We lived in the village of Bellanaleck (which means 'the town of the flagstones'), about five miles from Enniskillen in County Fermanagh. I lived there with my father, Hugh, my mother, Ellie, my sisters, Marie and Joan, and my only brother, Gaby, in a nice cosy little house. Our house was beside the road and everybody who walked up and down dropped in. Old people, collecting their pensions, would call to my mother on the way home, get a cup of tea, have a rest and head off home restored. That's my abiding image of my mother – always at home, always doing her best to help and to encourage. Everybody who visited trusted her. My mother chatted to them all and she was a kind of a confessor for them. She was a huge influence on me; my way of being a priest comes from her.

Because my father was football mad, our house at night had callers who talked football, local and national. It was a dull night if nobody came in. That's where I learned the art of storytelling and the art of listening. I can still remember stories and characters from that time. Although I didn't know it at the time, it was where I discovered how to recognise and tell a good story. These people were experts who could hold you enthralled from beginning to end. They had rehearsed it and they made sure you never forgot it. They were superb teachers although most of them could barely read or write. Maybe that's why Bellanaleck has produced seven well-known writers and broadcasters – Cormac, Mickey and Seán MacConnell, George and Jennifer Cathcart, Derek Thornton and me.

Even in those days, in the mid-1950s, literacy could not be taken for granted. My father could read and write, and he used his skills to fill in forms for his neighbours. After the Second World War, the Government handed out free shoes to some children and bus passes to other children and meal vouchers, too. You could get free supplies of orange juice and cod liver oil, to build up strong, healthy bodies. The orange juice was lovely but the cod liver oil was a sickening dose. My father filled in the application forms for half the country for these. There were always visitors and they were always welcome. To this day, I love to see people calling for the tea and a chat; it seems a truly Eucharistic thing to do.

My mother baked bread. She'd roll it out on the table and bake it on the open-hearth fire, in an oven hanging from the crook. She'd put a row of coals on the top of it so it baked from the top and the bottom. I can still smell that bread baking. We called it fadge bread and nothing ever tasted as good. While it was still hot we spread butter on it, watched it melt, and ate it as quickly as we could. We caught the chicken out in the field, wrung its neck, plucked it, cleaned it out and cooked it in the pot, in the same way over the big, open fire with the turf flaming round it.

We always had a big, roaring turf fire. We were never short, but we never had anything extra, either. It was a struggle to make sure there would be enough on Thursday to buy what we needed, so that, when the wages came on Friday, we'd be able to start again. Thrift was encouraged, nothing was wasted. But we were no different from any other family in the parish. Working-class people lived close to the breadline.

Being young and Catholic meant I was an altar server and played Gaelic football morning, noon and night. If there was a wake or if somebody was sick, my mother made bread and brought it to them. It was the same for both Protestants and Catholics. Being a good neighbour wasn't sectarian. There was, however, a strict code when it came to religious practice. I remember going to the door of the Protestant church but never entering. It was the same when Protestants came to Catholic funerals. Even then I knew it was stupid.

Hard work was part of the example handed down by my father. He was up at seven, got on his bicycle and started work at eight in Enniskillen Railway Station. He finished at five, was home about a quarter to six, ate spuds and bacon and cabbage and then started another day's work, setting potatoes, and getting as much as he could from five acres of bad land. The day finished at 10 when he'd come inside and get more tea. That's when the visitors came in. It was that kind of house, that kind of life.

In my young days we got one day's holiday a year. We went to Bundoran. My father worked on the railway and we thought it was a wonderful privilege to get a free pass on a train from Enniskillen to Bundoran. We really thought we were special, a step above the ordinary. I used to get so excited about our day out that my family couldn't tell me beforehand. On two occasions, I got, literally, sick with excitement, and the whole family had to stay home. They learned not to tell me about the day out until they were ready to travel.

Suddenly, I'd get a shaking in the bed very early in the morning. "Come on, you have to get up, we're going to Bundoran today." We'd get the eight o'clock bus to Enniskillen and catch the nine o'clock train to Bundoran. Our meal was the sandwiches we brought. There was no such thing as going to cafés, and if you did, you brought your sandwiches with you and bought the tea.

I was nearly drowned in Bundoran on one of those days out. I went walking along the sea pool and slipped in. Nobody saw me, and when eventually they did, none of them could swim. Someone pulled me out and I spent the day wet and shivering. It scared my mother. Another day, my father had me on a boat in Lough Erne and I fell out of the boat. He pulled me back by the hair of the head and, after that, my mother would never let me go near water or swim again. She said, "The third time you'll die." And it meant that I was 35 years of age before I had the courage to go to a swimming pool. I'm still not comfortable in the water, though.

My father was an active officer in the local GAA club. He was a famous footballer himself, who played for Fermanagh for nearly a decade. It's not for me to boast, but those who saw him play reckon he was as good a half-back as ever played for the county. He was a respected man and a capable man, even though he had to leave school early. His constant mantra was, whatever you do, get a better education than I did. The key at the time in the North was the Eleven Plus. I was going to a small, two-teacher school in rural Fermanagh with fewer than 30 pupils in it. In its entire history, nobody had ever passed the Eleven Plus. My father concluded that not every child in this area was stupid, so it had to be the system that was wrong.

I had an aunt in Omagh, my mother's sister, who had a boarding house there. Aunt Maggie came to visit us and obviously heard some cheeky backchat from me. I can still hear her describe me: "That's an ould-fashioned brat there and if I had him I'd put manners on him." That's how I attended the Christian Brothers' school in Omagh. I went down every Sunday evening with my little case. My father brought me five miles on the crossbar of the bike, as far as the train. I got on the train, at nine years of age, went 30 miles to Omagh, got off the train, walked about a mile to my aunt's house and helped with the dishes and got ready for school the next day. I hate Sunday nights to this day. Sunday nights are leaving nights for me.

My aunt was a nice woman who was good to me. She had boarders as well as her own family and the first thing I did when I got up every morning was to set the table for the boarders. She spent her day cooking for them. There was no molly-coddling, no room for emotion. You did the job you were expected to do and there were no excuses taken for not doing it. But Aunt Maggie was good to me and I would have got nowhere without her foresight and the dedication of her son Donal, who taught me.

In Omagh School they had a superb system of preparing for the Eleven Plus. Every Friday we did test papers under exam conditions. When the actual days of the Eleven Plus came round it was just routine. So after two years in Omagh, even I was able to pass the exam. It meant I got free grammar school education.

There is a kind of providence about growing up which, in an unknowing way, directs the rest of our lives. For me it began with being chosen to go to school in Omagh, the loneliness I endured during that time, the preparation for future life which it entailed; all this I can see now as God's providential care. Why was I the one that my aunt's eyes lit on that particular day? If my brother, Gaby, had been the one who answered her back, he might have been the one taken by her and he'd have made a better, safer priest than me. I'd say there's many a bishop who thinks my aunt made the wrong choice and it should have been left to

God, not her. Yet we know it's God who makes the choices and it's not always the most obvious one He chooses.

I came back to Enniskillen and went to St Michael's College in 1957. I was the only one from our whole area in it. That's why there's a part of me that is always lost. When I went to Omagh, I was a country boy, not only moving to a town, but a town 30 miles away. I was struggling all the time, both in Omagh and in St Michael's in Enniskillen.

In St Michael's College, priests ran the school like a junior seminary. The Presentation brothers founded St Michael's but moved out in 1957 when the priests took over. The reason the priests came was to encourage Fermanagh boys to become priests in Clogher Diocese.

As a teenager, I had no real notion of being a priest. I was a normal, reasonably good young fellow who did what I was told, served Mass and tried to live the way my parents taught me. I didn't consider I had a vocation because I didn't think I was good enough to be a priest. My family wasn't wealthy enough to pay for me. At that time, you had to be a boarder in a junior seminary for two years before they'd accept you in Maynooth.

I wasn't the most suitable one in our family to be a priest because I was always interested in music and sport. I always had a variety of interests. I was more like my father and more influenced by him. I was a footballer like him. At 16 I had played in the county championships at all levels.

My interest in pop and popular music goes back to my earliest days. In our wee house in Bellanaleck we always had a wireless. Television was totally unheard of in those days. It sounds as if I'm going back to "old god's time", but it's actually only 50 years, a short enough period as history goes. The wireless was in the kitchen and had a grand shelf all to itself.

Before we got electricity, the wireless ran on what were called wet batteries. They were two glass containers that held some sort of acid. They had a short lifespan and these wet batteries had to be brought to a supplier in Enniskillen who recharged or refilled them and so kept us up to date with the news for another couple of weeks.

Wet batteries were used sparingly. The wireless was put on for the news each night. We all had to be as quiet as mice as my mother and father and whatever visitor happened to be passing our door all gathered as close to the wireless as they could.

Another big occasion was the broadcast of Gaelic games on a Sunday afternoon. If we weren't quiet we were put out to play. Usually five or six men came and parked their bicycles along the tightly clipped hedge on the side of the road. They then proceeded to kick every ball with Micheál O'Hehir as he broadcast in his wonderfully exciting fashion from the mecca itself: Croke Park in Dublin. For me, O'Hehir has always been the voice of the GAA.

Later we got electricity into the house. There were few enough appliances that could run on electricity and we could afford. There was a light in each room which was a godsend; there was one electric fire with two bars which was used sparingly because it was too expensive and a little two-ringed cooker which was more effective for heating water and boiling eggs early in the morning before the turf fire took off. And there was a wonderful Morphy-Richards radio. This meant the wet batteries were gone forever and we could listen to the radio night and day.

That was when I discovered Radio Luxembourg. It had a famous catch-phrase: "208 on the dial". And that's when I began to discover the world of pop music, especially the great Elvis Presley. For me, back in the 1950s, Elvis on Radio Luxembourg was eternal happiness on earth.

From that moment I was hooked on music. The highlight of the week was the *Top Twenty* from 11 to 12 on a Sunday night. The problem was that I had to wait until 12 to find out what was number one. No self-respecting student could dare enter St Michael's College the next morning without having listened to the number one the night before. That was "cool" back then. To get staying up until 12 o'clock on a Sunday night was always a fight. But secretly I think even my parents were interested in pop charts though they constantly berated the "jungle music" of Elvis, Cliff, Bill Haley and Billy Fury.

In St Michael's College it was the custom for priests to visit and give a really good talk about the work their congregation or order did. Then they'd give you a slip of paper asking if you were interested in their work. If you were interested they sent you material. I remember one priest who came and gave a great talk about his work in South America. It was an appealing and idealistic life. He was from The Legionaries of Christ. At the time I showed some interest, so one evening, about a month afterwards, this priest arrived at our house. He was probably Spanish and looked awfully clean with his white cuffs and gold cufflinks. He looked perfect.

My father and I were out in the field working when this strange priest came out to us. He stood at the edge of the field and beckoned my father to come to him; they talked secretly for 10 minutes or more. He never spoke to me at all. I never knew until 30 years later what he said to my father. First, he asked how much my father earned, and when my father told him, he said, "I don't think your family is rich enough for your son to join us. We're not interested." A cousin in whom my father confided told me that long after my father died. My father never told me, but I discovered that he was deeply hurt by this insult. When he came back to me in the potato drill, all he said was, "You won't be joining that crowd anyway."

The founder of The Legionaries of Christ, in the spring of 2006, was silenced by the Vatican for the alleged abuse of young boys, especially young students who entered his order.

Looking back, I understand now why my father didn't want me to be a priest. He always said we weren't rich enough for me to be a priest. Early on he did his best to change my mind. It would be a very long time afterwards before I understood why.

My first meeting with a very quiet Passionist priest in a mystical church attached to The Graan in Enniskillen in 1960 was a different experience. It was a quiet Saturday evening and I had gone there to confession. The priest obviously took time to speak to his penitents. I didn't know who he was then, but I got to know him later. His name was Father Angelo. His family name was Boylan from County Monaghan and he still has two nephews in the Passionist congregation.

Angelo was a quiet man and saintly in a detached sort of way. When he left the world he was quite happy not to rejoin it. At the end of confession he whispered through the wire mesh, "Have you ever thought of becoming a priest?" I answered that I hadn't and that was really the truth. Actually, I hadn't thought about it seriously even at the time of The Legionaries of Christ; I was only vaguely interested then.

He continued whispering through the grille, "I think you should think about it. Could you come down to meet me tomorrow evening?" It sounded a bit rushed to me and anyway I had a football match to play for Kinawley minors the next day. And I told him the truth – that I couldn't do it. But he did make an appointment for the following Saturday. I was really scared of it but felt I had to keep it.

I told him what my parents had said – namely, that I was too fond of music and football to be a priest. I subsequently learned that Angelo had no great love of football although he would have claimed a certain musical ability.

My mother didn't want me to be a priest either, though her opposition was for a different reason from my father's. Maybe she understood the loneliness of a priest's life. My father worked for the parish priest in his local area at one time, so maybe he knew what a priest's life was like, too, and didn't want it for his son.

I mentioned my dilemma to a friend at school, Artie McCann, and he shocked me by admitting he had decided to join the Passionists. His uncle was a Passionist priest. We began our journey together then. The life appealed to me because I heard our neighbours talking about going to The Graan to get blessed or going to The Graan for confessions. The Graan always seemed to be a place that people thought highly of. It was a place where people weren't afraid of priests. Or, if you were in trouble, The Graan had a special place in people's lives. That image of priesthood attracted me.

My mother tried to persuade me not to go. She prayed every day and got the rest of the family to try to persuade me not to go because my interests were incompatible with what they thought a priest should be. She gave in on my last summer in school. I would have been 15, going on 16, and she said to me, "If you come with me on a pilgrimage to Knock, we'll pray there. Then, after that, if you still want to go, I'll not stand in your way."

The parish was running a bus to Knock. We said 15 decades of the rosary on the way, 15 decades while we were there, another 15 on the way home. I had as much praying that day as I ever needed. But it was a lovely place and I still go to Knock once or twice a year, just to top up my vocation, as it were. Because that's where it came from.

About two or three weeks later, my mother asked me, "Do you still want to be a priest?" And I said, "I think I have to give it a try." That's when she agreed to let me go.

It seems providential that out of very ordinary circumstances and out of basic choices, a life journey begins. We have no idea where the little decisions we make today will eventually lead us.

The priests of the diocese didn't want me entering the Passionists because there was a hint of mistrusting religious life. I was told I was making a mistake by joining the Passionists. It would make more sense to be a diocesan priest. The president of St Michael's College, when I asked him for a reference, gave it to me but made his displeasure obvious. I didn't understand it at the time and still don't.

The parish priest, Fr McIlroy, who lived two miles up the road beside the church in Arney, was very good to me. I'd been an altar boy and he knew me well. His advice was simple and reflective: "It takes a good man to enter, Brian, but it takes a great man to leave if it's not made for him." Sound advice.

The next thing was to buy a new black suit. I didn't want my family to be out too much money, so I worked. Peter McKevitt had a pub in Arney and he used to see me going to morning Mass. He'd probably heard I was thinking of going on to be a priest. One day he approached me: "I wonder if you would paint our pub, Brian?" He worked it out that I would get two shillings an hour. And I worked it out that if I painted for 10 hours I could make a pound a day. The suit cost 24 pounds in Tully's. I got the money for it by working for Peter and also by helping out my cousins and getting the odd fiver here and there. So my family weren't out too much money when I joined. Passionists didn't ask for much money from the families. Once you made your profession, you were a Passionist after that and they took care of you.

On the night of the 30th of August 1962, I went to Bundoran to a dance as a kind of a last fling, myself and my brother and a few neighbours.

I went to dances regularly before I entered and I still wanted to hang on to the music. It was a double attraction that night. The Melody Aces were the first band and Butch Moore and the Capitol Showband were the second, in the Astoria Ballroom in Bundoran.

There's a quaint story that gives you an indication of the times we lived in back then. I actually played football for a neighbouring club, Kinawley, at underage level, and they took me onto the senior panel as well. I played in the county senior championship semi-final in August when I came on as a sub even though I was only 17 years old. We won the match and got to the final. But I had entered the Passionist monastery at The Graan before the final took place and I never played in the county senior final. We didn't get letters, papers, visits from people or anything like that while we were in the novitiate. We simply entered a monastery and from day one you became a contemplative monk. One day I was a teenager running around Bellanaleck and the next I was a contemplative monk. I never knew who won the county final until Christmas morning, when we were allowed one letter from my family. That was when I first realised that Roslea, not Kinawley, had won the cup.

The day I entered was a really, really sad day. I spent the day crying and saying goodbye to people, places of interest and even the sad old donkey out in the field. The day before I entered I had a sense of it being the last day of my life. I remember going on a bicycle to Enniskillen, crying because I was leaving home at 17 years of age. It was almost like a death in the family. That was the feeling around the house. My mother and my sisters were crying all day. Somebody had arranged to get a car to bring me to The Graan, which was unusual in itself. All my worldly possessions were in one little case.

The bleakness of The Graan was awful.

CHAPTER 2

PLAYING BY THE RULES

I entered the monastery at six o'clock on a Saturday evening, the 1st of September, 1962. The doors closed behind me and that was it. Other postulants came on the same day from Ireland and Scotland. This group of strangers were preparing to launch out on the Passionists' way of life, for the very first time. Eight of us entered that day as clerics and many more as brothers. Seven out of that eight were ordained, which is unusual. The eighth one, Jim Dougall, went on to become an influential broadcaster with RTÉ and BBC.

My abiding memory now of that evening is one of darkness. A strip of polished lino up the middle of corridors of pitch pine. Unpainted, unvarnished, virgin pitch pine in the rooms resulting in white, wooden floors washed and scrubbed and bare. Just noisy, cold, wooden floors. There was a basic iron bedstead with a hair mattress on it. There were a few woollen blankets on a chair. There was a pillow, just one pillow. A makeshift wardrobe you didn't need because you'd nothing to put in it and, literally, an orange-box standing on its end beside your bed. A crucifix hung on the wall, nothing else. There were well-spaced-out, naked, 40-watt bulbs on long corridors without windows. Just enough light not to bump into things. I often think it was a parable of what I was doing in real life. Enough light to see where I was but no idea where I was going.

On the first night we went to bed at nine o'clock, but sleep never came. We were wakened early the next morning, just to remind us that the easy life was gone for good. We went to Mass, but not in the public church, because we were entering the first phase of withdrawal from the big, bad world. I was now a postulant, and after a month, if I was still there, I'd be a novice. Everything, even the language, was unreal and ancient.

Right at the start, the novice master called us individually into his spartan office. I had to bring him everything I brought with me – watch, pen, clothes, books, gifts I had been given, money. Everything was taken and locked in the novice master's cell. I was then given a simple, black, ill-fitting habit to wear. Underneath we wore a rough, khaki army shirt and funny-looking trousers called "billies". They came to just below the knee and made me itchy all over. Our rooms were called cells, and that's why they were spartan. The message was loud and clear – we were going to prison for a year to test what we were made of. As usual, though, it was given a "religious" name – the novitiate. After three days of softening up, reality hit me and I cried secretly for a week, wondering how I could get out of the place with even a little respectability.

Why didn't I leave? I don't know. Fear of going home was one reason; fear of being a failure was another. One of the reasons why my mother and father didn't want me to enter was the fear that I'd leave and be called a "spoiled priest".

After three days, the routine began. Novices went to bed at nine o'clock. We got up at 2am for an hour's prayer. At 3am we went back to bed and then we got up again at six. I knew before I entered what the routine would be and so too did my family. I learned later that my mother often woke at 2am and wept at the thought of me up praying at that ungodly hour. My sisters let me in on that little secret on the night out we had to celebrate my being 30 years ordained.

There was more prayer for an hour and a half until 7.30, when we were allowed to go for breakfast of black coffee and dry bread, eaten standing up. That may have been fine for a 17-year-old in Italy, where the order was founded, but the Roman model didn't work here. It's why our graveyards are full of 30-year-old priests and brothers who died of TB, because of lack of proper food and a too-rigorous lifestyle that put the emphasis on an unreal asceticism ahead of healthy, mature living. In 1962 we lived the lax version of Passionist life, yet it was a draconian regime. Why didn't we revolt against it? Because every second of the day was accounted for, so there was no time to think.

THE HORARIUM

Faith (Morning)		Hope (Evening)		Charity (Variation) Sundays	
2.00am	Matins	1.30pm	Silence	8.00am	Free Time
6.00	Rise	2.30	Vespers,	8.15	Novices'
6.15	Lauds		Novices' Rosary		Regulations
6.30	Mass &	3.15	Tea	8.30	Spiritual Reading
	Meditation	3.30	Recreation	9.00	Study
7.30	Collation	4.00	Examination of	9.30	Last Mass
8.00	Study for		Conscience &	10.15	Offices &
	Chapter		Life of Saint		Free Time
8.30	Last Mass	4.30	Class	10.45	Solitary Walk
9.00	Chapter	5.00	Study	11.15	Life of Saint
9.30	Examination	6.00	Class	11.45	Stations of Cross
	of Conscience	6.30	The Holy Bible	12.00	Sext
	& Scripture	7.00	Offices	6.45pm	Rosary
	Reading	7.15	Rosary &		& Meditation
10.00	Book on Sacred		Meditation	7.30	Supper
	Passion	8.00	Supper &	8.45	Compline
10.45	Offices		Recreation		
11.15	Free Time	9.30	Matins &		
11.30	Solitary Walk		Compline		
12.00	Sext Dinner &	10.15	Retire		
	Recreation				

After a month we were clothed, which meant we got our own habit and sandals. I also got a new name. It was the rule at that time. The world was bad and I was leaving my "old self" (and that was the phrase, 'old self') behind. I took on this new self which was symbolised by the new name. From that day forward I was called by a different name, Desmond Mary. Desmond after a friend I knew, Dessie Corrigan, who went to be a priest in the Society of African Missions. And since there is no Saint Desmond, they attached Mary to it. After the Second Vatican Council we were allowed to go back to our baptismal names and I once again became Brian D'Arcy, even though one of my nephews was called Desmond, after me.

Thinking and individualism were discouraged. The institution was always right. If you couldn't fit into it, you hadn't a vocation. Vocation killed your own unique spirit and you had to become whatever the institution wanted you to be. It was cloning before its time.

The whole regime was designed to produce a compliant monk who would do what he was told. For example, we weren't allowed to speak to other people, even fellow novices, except for very short periods during the day. We couldn't read anything other than rules and regulations and some spiritual books, chosen to reinforce the system.

There wasn't much formal education involved, except perhaps in spiritual practices: how to meditate, be silent and repeat endless rosaries. We memorised the monk's alphabet, which had quotes like, "I am a worm and no man". It was about killing your self-esteem, even though most of us hadn't much of it to kill. To this day I'm often crippled by my own unworthiness. I have to constantly struggle with self-image.

Every night I had to confess my faults publicly, as had the other novices. I carried a black cross through the refectory and knelt before the rector, the novice master and the whole community. Faults like, "I broke silence", "I didn't mortify my eyes", "I looked at the paper I was using to clean the sanctuary lamp", "I broke a plate at wash-up" were confessed. We then got a penance. It could be a prayer or for something considered serious it could be to eat your supper off the floor. It could be to prostrate yourself on the corridor while all the community walked past and prayed for you. All of those were regular penances. I lived in fear of doing things the wrong way or being caught breaking any of those innumerable and often senseless rules.

One day I was given a great big ball of twine and given instructions how to make scourges of tightly knitted cord. Each of us had five whips about four inches long of this tightly knitted twine with a rope handle long enough to make sure you could beat your backside. After night prayers, three times a week, we went to our rooms and whipped ourselves on the bum for as long as it took to say five Our Fathers, five Hail Marys and five Glorias. I'm ashamed to admit now that I did this for years. When we questioned it, we were told, "You should count yourself lucky. Ten years ago we did it in common." What? "We did it in common. We went into the community chapel and everyone took down their pants and whipped themselves publicly." To do it in the privacy of your room/cell was an advance. Even then it felt sick. Obviously they got sense and stopped the common flagellations in the 1950s. Our self-flagellation lasted all through the 1960s, but most of us knew it was such a sick practice that we gave it up as students. I stopped it when I was close to ordination. Others took it more seriously, and I could hear them whacking and whipping with gusto as I walked through the corridors at night.

Self-flagellation was supposed to be a reminder that Christ was scourged at the pillar. In fact though, we believed the body was bad and had to be beaten into submission.

I'm not saying that the men who enforced this system were bad men. I've lived with many men whose lives were ruined, partly by the system and partly by their own choice. Many blamed the system for their own lack of maturity, but it was a form of training that enabled dysfunctional people to mask their shortcomings in the worst aspects of religion.

My novice master, though, was a good man, a nice man and a friend until the day he died. He was very encouraging, strict, fair, ascetic, and we knew that he himself was attempting to be holy. He wasn't a sadist. He believed in what he was carrying through. Some of the men who were novice masters before him were sadists and they left their mark on the men they put through their hands.

There's a story about a novice from Mayo whose family had money. When he entered, he was better dressed than the other novices. His dressing-gown and shirts were of a fine quality. The novice master at the time, a sadistic tyrant of a man, opened the window on the top floor of The Graan and threw the clothes out the monastery window with the famous dictum, "You're not bringing the dross of the world into the purity of the monastery." That says it all – a sadist mentality in an arrogant man convinced that the world was bad and the monastery somehow "purer".

The practices were meant to test us during that initial year. There was a reasonable aspect to it. If one could survive that first year of virtual imprisonment then there was a good chance you might survive the rest of student life. But it was a test of endurance rather than a test of a vocation. There was hardly any spirituality taught and most of the practices were designed to encourage blind obedience rather than an interior life of genuine holiness.

Most input came from what were called conferences. These were of two kinds – general and individual. At general conferences the master of novices gave talks on the vows of poverty, chastity, obedience and spreading devotion to the Passion, which is the fourth vow specific to our congregation.

All I knew about the vow of chastity at that time was that I could never have sex. That was as much as I knew, and as much as I was taught. The result was that life focused on a negative – make sure that you don't put yourself in danger of breaking your vow of chastity. Even having a "bad" thought at night caused me crippling scruples. So you were forced to suppress and repress all your sexual inclinations at an early stage.

Chastity was the big one. At that time it was the moral law of the Church that when it came to matters of sex there was no "parvity of matter". In other words, if you stole two pounds it would not be serious enough to be a mortal sin because parvity of matter applied. Yet a bad thought was a mortal sin and as damning as rape. It was such an unhealthy view of sex. In theory it was believed that sex was good, but in practice it was always sinful and bad.

Not as much emphasis was put on the vow of poverty. Why I don't know. The vow of obedience was important for control, and it became the greatest criterion of what God's will was for me. If my superior asked me to take on some task, then I accepted that it was what God wanted me to do, even though I felt ill-equipped to carry through the task.

As Passionists we are committed to preach the Passion of Christ. But nobody quite knew what this devotion to the Passion meant. How were you to spread devotion to the Passion? The rest of my life has been an attempt to make the Passion, Death and Resurrection of Christ relevant to my own life and to inspire those called to share His Passion through suffering.

It was pointed out that there were two ways of keeping our vows. The first was the letter of the law and the second, which was much more important, was the spirit of the vow or the virtue each of the vows taught. That was good and is still helpful to this day.

Individual conferences were almost like confession. Not being the perfect novice, I was quickly alerted by the master as to where I was going wrong.

I want to emphasise again that the novice master at the time, Fr Bernard, was a good and kind man and I have nothing but the highest respect for him. What he taught us was outdated but he was handing on what had been taught to him. He was not a man of the world and devoted himself to the spiritual life. That was both a help and a hindrance. It was easy to take correction from him because I knew he was a decent, honest and holy man himself. But I also knew that the life which was so important to him never existed in reality.

Every three months we had to get through a chapter meeting. The community held a meeting to discuss each of us individually. We could have been sent home at any of those, if the community thought us unsuitable. They were a problem because it meant that you behaved externally in a perfect way so as to please the people who could vote against you in the chapter. I tried my best to live as good a life as I could. I found it extremely difficult. What made it even more difficult was that it never made sense to me. It revealed a part of me that I didn't like, namely that I was willing to put up with things so that I could be professed and ordained. I was doing it to get through the system rather than out of conviction. Some would call that hypocrisy and I wouldn't argue with that.

One of the practices that went on in the novitiate throughout my time entailed novices being ordered to do obviously stupid things to test this blind obedience. My inclination was not to do them, but not to do them was seen to be disobedient and therefore a fault for which you could be sent home. It meant that as novices we frequently did things we knew were stupid, but we did them because we were afraid we'd be thrown out. That's what you call blind obedience and it's also the perfect example of brainwashing at its most cynical.

A number of episodes come to mind. One of them happened in January 1963. Those who have long memories will know that was the last time we had a really serious fall of snow. We lived in cruelly cold cells on the top corridor of The Graan monastery. It was not pleasant to walk around in sandaled feet in deep snow.

Matters came to a head one Sunday early in January, when the snow was a foot deep. It was the custom, after Sunday evening devotions, that we would be allowed to play football. But because this was a dark time of year we were given the opportunity of playing football immediately after lunch and before the devotions. The novice master was away and the vice-master asked us in the sacristy if any of us would like to go out snowballing. Remember most of us were 17 at the time and would do anything to get out of the house. So most of us volunteered to go snowballing. I'd never done it in my life.

When it was agreed that most of the novices wanted to go snowballing, the vice-master told us to change for football. We were to put on one light jersey, one pair of togs, one pair of socks and football boots. Like fools we did it. We came to the back door of the monastery and were then ordered by the vice-master to go snowballing in our football gear. We were absolutely frozen and shivering as darkness fell.

One of the novices, unfamiliar with the geography of the garden, fell and broke his nose. But the rest of us had to stay out in the snow for two hours. We got in after two hours because others in the community were horrified to see young novices out shivering in the snow when there was absolutely no need for it. It was cruel and senseless.

Then there is the notorious case of a novice master telling a novice from a farming background to plant cabbages upside down. He knew it was wrong but did it out of blind obedience. Humiliations like that destroyed good young men.

As a result of the snowballing incident, some of the novices, including me, got a severe flu. With me it got so bad that I was brought for an X-ray for suspected TB. There was a shadow on the lung and it meant my future as a Passionist was in doubt. In those days a serious illness was enough for one to be sent home and many good men were sent home from the novitiate because of contracting TB. I survived but still can't donate blood and have an increasingly weak chest.

In the novitiate, we had no contact with our family. But on the 1st of June 1963 my family left me a birthday present at The Graan. It was the big hit record at the time, very appropriately called *Bachelor Boy*, by Cliff Richard.

The novice master was disgusted. He never told me the record was left in but brought it to the priests' recreation room. There one of the professed brothers, Br Aloysuis, breaking every rule in the book, called me aside and told me about my family's gift.

The next Thursday afternoon when I was doing manual work in the garden, he suggested that I should get the job of weeding around the front door of the monastery. When I was well placed down on my knees pulling weeds from the flower beds, he opened the window of the recreation room and played me Cliff's version of *Bachelor Boy*. I thought it was a fantastic record and couldn't wait to get out of the novitiate four months later to hear it again. That was as close as I got to my family's present for my 18th birthday.

On another occasion I had a toothache and needed to be brought to the dentist in Enniskillen. It was one of the most humbling experiences of my life. I was well known in Enniskillen before I entered, mainly through football. I had to walk through the town dressed as a clerical student with a hat, black suit, white collar and black coat. The master held me by the hand, like a child, as we walked through the town. If there had been handcuffs I might have been given them. As we walked up the town we went to a hardware shop in the centre of the town, Dickie's, to buy a hammer.

My father by then was a bus driver, and as he drove the bus through Enniskillen, he saw me walking up the street hand in hand with the "minder". That was the first sighting Hugh D'Arcy had of his son since I left home the previous September. This was now summer of 1963. He got so excited that he drove the bus into the depot and rushed up to see if he could talk to me.

The meeting took place in the door of Dickie's shop. The priest had me by the hand walking out of the shop. My father walked into the shop. We met in the doorway. I was not allowed to speak to him or even look at him. The priest said, "Isn't your son looking well, Mr D'Arcy?" and he chucked me by the hand in case I would touch, speak to or look at my own father. I glanced back as I was being pulled up the street and I saw my father with tears in his eyes looking aghast as I disappeared around a corner.

There were regular meetings to assess if we could continue to "first profession" throughout our first year of novitiate. These were called chapters. The 11th-month chapter, the month before profession, was the most important one. We lived in fear of that because members of the professed community, who didn't know us, voted on our future. How could they know us since we weren't allowed to speak to the professed members of the community? Yet they were observing us all the time. Monastic Big Brother before its time. It was an effective way to make us malleable, and it was designed by the institution to break our will. Conform because you are being watched. We were conforming, not because we wanted to but because if we didn't we wouldn't be professed or ordained. The fact many of us came through this with a reasonable degree of integrity is a miracle in itself.

I was professed as a Passionist on the 29th of September 1963. Our profession ceremony itself was quite elaborate but it was a cruel ceremony for our families. In 1963 I was 18 and a very unworldly, naïve 18 at that. I was asked to commit myself for life to poverty, chastity and obedience and to promote devotion to the Passion. It was emphasised we were taking vows before God, a frightening proposal at 18 years of age and maybe an impossible one.

The whole liturgy was built around the Passion. The Passion was read; death was a major theme and, at one part of it, I carried a cross on my shoulder as I paraded round the church. At 18 years of age, we dressed in a full-length black habit, wore sandals that we made ourselves, rosary beads and a black-and-white plastic sign in the shape of a heart with the words "The Passion of Jesus Christ" written on it. This is the distinguishing sign worn by Passionists. We processed solemnly around the packed church, carrying a cross each and with a crown of thorns on our heads. Real thorns, not driven in, but sitting on top of our heads, uncomfortably.

I remember looking at my mother's face as I walked nervously around the church. She just couldn't understand why this son of hers was doing this. Then I took the cross off and lay down flat on a terrazzo floor. All seven of us lay in a line on the cold floor. A big, black pall, a cloth for hanging over a coffin, a huge pall that covered the entire sanctuary, was spread over us to signify our death. All seven of us lay under this while the Passion was read out. When I got up I glanced at my family and by now my mother was crying.

That memory stays with me to this day. And it haunts me now more than it did then, because my mother understood what I was doing and I didn't. It didn't make sense to her that the son she reared had to die to be good. What was wrong with her rearing? And where did I get my vocation anyway?

I saw my mother at the profession celebration later that day and I saw her alive only once after that.

CHAPTER 3

THE ARGUS CATALOGUE

After profession I moved from The Graan to Mount Argus in Dublin. Our class was lucky to be sent to UCD, even though I didn't particularly want to go because I didn't feel bright enough. It was the best thing ever happened to me. Again, proving that what we want is not always what's good for us. I would have been a very different character had I not gone to university. The concept of university, of broadening the mind, of listening, of challenging, of debating, did eventually outweigh the stifling scholastic philosophy of the time.

A priest, Dr Horgan, was professor of scholastic philosophy in UCD. For him there was a right answer and a wrong answer for every question, which is a contradiction in itself. There was no room for lateral thinking or for living with the pursuit of truth. As (what was termed) "an occasional student from the North", I did a pass course, not honours.

One day I met Professor Horgan on the corridor. He was a friendly man. There were hundreds of clerics, all dressed like little priests, cycling up and down to university. As a professed Passionist with vows I wore a Roman collar, a black hat and a suit at university. Trying to hold your hat on while negotiating a bicycle over tramlines is a rare skill in itself. You should try it some day. Hold your hat on with your left hand, turn your bike with your right and try to jump the front wheel out of the track, before you fall under a car.

Even though we looked the same, Dr Horgan knew most of us by name. I told Dr Horgan that I had a difficulty with Empiricism and the theory of knowledge. I had read "O'Neill's book" and still didn't understand it, proving I was well and truly brainwashed already. He said, "Now, Mr D'Arcy, you tell me what you know." He took the time and the patience to listen. I tried to pick my words well and to explain my difficulties to this dignified old professor. When I was finished he said, "Ho ho ho, Mr D'Arcy you should be doing honours." I felt about six feet tall at least. "You talk very well about it, but I doubt if you know what you're talking about." That's how to raise somebody up and deflate them all in one sentence. It also says a lot about what he thought of honours students.

There was one lecturer in UCD who was entirely different. Fergal O'Connor, a Dominican priest, was the greatest influence for good on me in university without a shadow of a doubt. I went to his class even when I wasn't taking exams and so did many others. I learned about politics, how to think freely and how to be different and have integrity.

He used to be on the *Late Late Show* often. He said this "revolutionary" thing that hit all the front pages in the 1960s. He said that every married couple should have a sofa instead of armchairs in their living room, so that they could enjoy a good cuddle at night. Imagine a priest saying that there should be sex in marriage or that it should be enjoyable! And that was Fergal. He was crippled with arthritis all his life yet died only in recent years. He was a wonderful thinker and a great influence on my formative years. He explored the goodness of the human mind way back in the 1960s when it was unheard of. He influenced generations of politicians and thinkers who were at UCD in his time.

Another great influence was John Jordan, Professor of English, who had an acerbic wit but developed wonderful critical faculties.

The older I get the more I appreciate Fergal O'Connor's gifts and I even wrote to him to tell him so in the mid-1990s. I'd love to have gone to see him but couldn't get the courage to do it. When he died I offered Mass for him because this man sowed a seed of hope and never knew it bore fruit.

Even though we were at university, our superiors believed we needed extra training to be good and servile Passionists. They arranged evening classes in Mount Argus. One of these evening classes was in Passiology – the science of studying the Passion of Christ. There was an English Passionist, Edmond Rankin, teaching us about new theories of the Passion. When did it happen? Did Jesus hang on a cross? Was he nailed or was he tied? It was good but not wildly exciting. We were in class in Mount Argus on a dull November evening when one of the priests knocked at the classroom door, to tell us, "President Kennedy has been shot." Fr Edmond replied, "Oh really? Now, let's get back to the discussing why Good Friday actually fell on Holy Thursday." That was the interest he had in President Kennedy being shot. The class continued as if nothing ever happened.

President Kennedy being shot was totally irrelevant. It's another example of how he had been conditioned to think that the world doesn't matter and shouldn't matter. President Kennedy was shot but our wee world went on regardless. Our training was uninfluenced by the real world. There were answers to questions and you'd better know the answers. In many respects, that's what's happening in our Church today. Rome comes up with an array of wonderful answers to questions nobody's asking. We can still live in an ecclesiastical world as if it is the only world. President Kennedy is dead. Oh really?

I met President Eamon de Valera once when I was a student. I had to look after him when he visited Our Lady's Hospice. At the Nationalist meetings around Fermanagh, where I come from, the phrase "Up Dev" was a mantra. I didn't know much about politics then, but I met Dev, had a great chat with him and was really impressed at his patience and interest. I wish I could remember what we talked about, but I do remember he talked to me as if I were an old man. He advised, "Don't waste your time fighting over insignificant things." I don't remember the exact words but that was the import. He was saying it's prudent to know which fights are worth fighting and leave the rest aside. Let stuff go. The skill is in recognising what is worth fighting for.

When I went to Mount Argus the same strictures applied to listening to the radio and reading papers. There was no TV, of course. As a great concession we got to listen to radio for an hour a week on a Wednesday. We could tune into *Hospitals Requests*. That's when I first heard Terry Wogan,

Mike Murphy, Joe Linnane and Treasa Davidson as they played the hits of the time and read out lists of sick people in hospitals all over Ireland.

One of those hits was a song called *There's a Hole in the Bucket*, sung by the heroic civil rights singer Harry Belafonte. One Wednesday Treasa had obviously mistimed her script. A story song should never be faded half way through – or at all. But all rules take second place when it comes to news bulletins. The 1.30 news loomed closer as Harry was no more than warming up. Treasa had to do the unthinkable – fade the record and introduce the news. And that is how one of the most famous links in Radio Éireann's history was made. "And now as we come to the news at 1.30, I'm afraid we have to leave Harry Belafonte with his hole in the bucket."

So maybe *Hospital's Requests* wasn't as safe as our superiors thought.

When I was a student in Mount Argus, I rarely did anything that was seriously wrong. I was too timid and too scared. But I did once do something utterly mad. I sneaked out of the monastery the night the Beatles came to Dublin.

When I entered The Graan, I had never heard of the Beatles. But when I finished the novitiate and came to Mount Argus, the Beatles had arrived. I loved the pathetically small amount of their music I heard. So when I saw they were coming to Dublin I wanted to see them. Problem was I had no money and would *never* have been allowed to go out to such a worldly event and me out of the novitiate.

That's when the rebel in me took over. On the night they came to town I went to night prayers as usual and when everyone was safely in their cells (rooms) I went to the recreation room and opened the big window on the ground floor. Then I got on my bicycle and made my way to Abbey Street in the centre of the city. I hardly knew where Abbey St was, but the noise and crowds led me there.

It was sheer madness. I bobbed and weaved my way to where the crowds were. I have no idea how close I was to the Adelphi but I could hear the noise of a distant band and the screaming of out-of-control young women. I can't say I saw the Beatles play live, but I did my best to hear them.

After an hour I began to realise what I had done and a cold sweat broke out as I imagined the superior looking for me, or the window having been locked. So off I went and got my bicycle and retreated sheepishly back up Clanbrassil Street, along by Mount Jerome and round the back of Mount Argus. The window was open and in I got, promising never to do another wrong act in my life.

Over the next few days I was a nervous wreck, afraid to go to confessions and unable to go to Communion until I confessed and did penance. Eventually I went to an old priest who was blind. Luckily for me, he'd never heard of the Beatles and wondered how looking at crawly insects could possibly be a sin. I got my absolution.

I never told any student what I did until I was ordained. I still feel slightly guilty even today.

However, I knew that night in Abbey Street that the world in which I was reared was gone forever and would never be the same again. To see young people my own age acting so differently and so freely disturbed me beyond words. Elvis, who was my hero before I entered, did his bit to change the world but the Beatles took us to another world. For good or evil the 1960s were the bridge between the old, safe world and the new, exciting world of free expression.

As students, we never got home but we did get letters. I got a letter from my mother and she hinted that she wasn't feeling well.

I asked permission to go to visit my mother on an Easter Monday. The student who entered with me, Artie McCann, said the two of us would go home that morning as we had to do it in one day. We could not get out of the monastery for even one night. We got on bicycles at Mount Argus on Easter Monday 1965 at 3am and we cycled from Mount Argus out to Blanchardstown. We left the bicycles at the Greyhound Bar. Dressed in our Roman collars and hats, there we were at 4am, two clerics thumbing on the road to Navan. The first car that came along was a Garda squad car. They were wondering what these mad clergymen were doing on the road at an unearthly hour. They thought we were drunk, or worse. We explained to them that we were going to Enniskillen and they drove out of their way to take us to Kells in the squad car. We got out and started thumbing again when some guy in a green mini-car gave us a lift. When we got to Cavan, Artie McCann's brother borrowed a car and brought us home.

My mother was a big, strong, healthy, plump, even fat, woman. But when I saw her this time, she was a wee thin woman and obviously sick. The rest of the family whispered, "She won't go to a doctor, maybe you could persuade her." I had suddenly got powers because I had a Roman collar.

She had great devotion to Father Charles of Mount Argus (of whom much more later), because of what I wrote to her. I also sent her prayer leaflets. She told me, "Well, if you say a novena to Father Charles, I'll make up my mind at the end of it." Here was the same woman who had brought me to Knock to help me to make up my mind, now wanting me to pray for her to make up her mind. At the end of my novena, she went to the doctor and, of course, it was too late.

The next time I saw her was on the night before she died in hospital. I never got over the shock that she was so close to death. At seven o'clock in the morning we got word that Mammy had died. It was Ascension Thursday, the 27th of May 1965. If my mother had lived they were going to amputate her leg. She didn't want that, so luckily for her, she died before the amputation took place. Ever since that, Father Charles has had a really special place in my life.

When I came back to Dublin, I took it badly. I was in my second year at university. I was sent to the doctor because I was quite traumatised by it. The doctor advised me to start smoking, believe it or not. His own wife had died suddenly shortly before, leaving a young family behind her. The two of us shared our grief. He said that once as he walked in Stephen's Green, a lovely thought occured to him. "The other day, it just struck me that the one thing I wanted for her was that she would be happy and I contented myself that now she's happier than I could ever make her." It was a nice phrase that stuck with me and gave me consolation at the time. He advised: "You should ask your mother to help you and she will." And I do to this day. I really am convinced that, had my mother not died, I would not have been a priest. And if I'm any good as a priest it's because of her influence from a better place.

What really kept me sane during these trying years was music. I was an innocent abroad when I sneaked out to see the Beatles. But later as a student I always cycled to the centre of Dublin on our free half day on Thursday to meet and talk with the showband musicians. This time there was nothing underhand. I had permission to meet with them as long as I got back for the night prayer.

I knew some of the showband musicians because I went to school with them – people like the Plattermen, the Polkadots and the Skyrockets. All the bands used to stay in the same Dublin hotel. Barry's Hotel was the in place at one time. The Belvedere Hotel later became our haunt. If you knew one band, eventually you got to know them all.

One day as a penniless student I was passing a free Thursday afternoon walking up and down O'Connell St in Dublin, dressed in Roman collar, black suit, hat, fáinne and pioneer pin, hoping to meet someone who would invite me for a cup of tea or even an ice-cream.

Outside the famous Gresham Hotel, I met Eddie Masterson and two friends. Eddie Masterson was the most famous solicitor in Ireland at the time. He lived in a single room in Barry's Hotel in Denmark St, Dublin, for 17 years. His office was the inside pocket of a heavy grey coat. He usually wore shirts that were once white but were now stained with tea and cigarette ash. He always had a cigarette hanging off his lower lip.

Eddie knew everybody, particularly those in showbands and in sport. He fixed break-ups in bands and wrote hits on the back of Sweet Afton cigarette packets about the current events of the day. When the great Jim Reeves died, Ireland went into mourning and Eddie, spotting the potential, wrote the first of his many tributes. It was cleverly put together and eventually Larry Cunningham and the Mighty Avons recorded it. Larry was a Jim Reeves soundalike and the song went into the British pop charts, the first showband record to do so.

Eddie was a legend. The two men with him outside the Gresham were Jimmy Molloy from Longford and one Albert Reynolds. He and his brother, Jim, owned a chain of ballrooms all around Ireland.

The big pop magazine at the time was *New Spotlight*, a predominantly pop-oriented publication. Albert wanted to set up his own magazine and Jimmy Molloy was to be the editor and printer.

That's when Eddie introduced me to his friends.

"There's a guy who'll write for you," Eddie said to Albert. "He knows the scene and he'll write for nothing."

I protested that I wasn't supposed to listen to radios or read papers, never mind write for them.

"You don't have to tell anybody. Be like the footballing priests and use someone else's name. What's your father's name?"

The next month there were two articles by "Hughie" published in *The Dancing Gazette*.

And that's how my career in journalism began – as simply and as accidentally as that. I wrote every month for the best part of four years under an assumed name, because I would have been sent home if I had been discovered writing without permission. I had entered the seminary in 1962 and this was 1965, the same year my mother died – that's how I remember it. Everyone in the bands knew who Hughie was, but my superiors knew nothing of it. Just before I was ordained, I had to come clean and tell my superiors about my nefarious writings for fear ordination would be invalid. To my surprise they said very little and saw no obstacle to ordination.

My family bought me a small transistor radio. Even though it was against all the rules I had it in my room and used it sparingly to keep up to date with the music scene. The other students knew I had it and often came to me to listen to music or sporting events. Often in life we have to break the mould in a quiet, unrevolutionary way. As the spiritual writer Richard Rohr wrote, "We don't think ourselves into new ways of living, we live ourselves into new ways of thinking." That was the principle behind so many of the reforms in Religious life, which was authenticated by the Second Vatican Council.

The Second Vatican Council went on all through my training. Vatican II was about radically rethinking our attitude to the world. The world is not bad. The world is good and the world is redeemed. The world can teach the Church and the community many things, just as the Church can teach the world something. They're not enemies. They should work hand in hand.

Pope John XXIII died in old age yet he died before the Council ended. Pope Paul VI came after him and trusted the Council, but got caught up in his encyclical *Humanae Vitae*. That was before my ordination. For my examinations I was learning a theology in Latin for the oral examination. Throughout my student days I was living in two different worlds. To be ordained I knew I had to conform to the pre-Vatican II Church, but I also knew I had to be conversant with the teachings of Vatican II if I was to be a relevant priest. I knew I had to change to meet the needs of the world rather than the other way around.

One other classmate thought exactly as I did and we both spent our time reading up on Vatican II so that we'd have something to offer after ordination. We learned what we needed to learn for our examination and studied what we needed to study for our future in our own time. I spent all my student days doing that.

It was essential for examinations to learn off the "right answer", that is, the answer they needed. It was the opposite of being taught to think. If you asked a question in class that was remotely awkward, you were told *mysterium est*. That is a mystery. You weren't supposed to question mysteries. It was a cultic way of training. Most people settled quietly into the system so that they could be ordained. You had to play the game but some of us knew it was only a game.

Religious weren't part of that hierarchical career structure and it gave us a little more freedom. Many of those who went to Maynooth admit that it was a stifling place to be, especially for those who wanted more than membership to a clerical club. Religious had their own taboos that had to be observed and, in Dublin anyway, we had to satisfy the diocesan authority by sitting their exams as well as our own. It was hard to escape the party line.

As a result, many of those with get-up-and-go, got up and went.

On the morning of my ordination on December 20th, 1969, I was surprised to find that a number of people from showbands came to the ceremony in St Michael's College in Enniskillen.

I was surprised because most of them would have been working the night before and made a great effort to be there on a slippery winter's morning for nine o'clock.

I was ordained in St Michael's College because I owed much to them. 1969 was the beginning of change in many areas of the Catholic Church.

One of those changes meant that candidates for ordination had a choice, within limits, of where they could be ordained. Previously, vast numbers were herded together in places that suited the ordaining bishop.

I chose St Michael's College to try to be some sort of healing between the Passionists and the diocese of Clogher. There had been, in the early days, bad feeling between the two, but Bishop Eugene O'Callaghan worked hard at mending bridges.

Bishop O'Callaghan was known for many things. One of them was that he had no time for showbands or dancing. During his time it was a mortal sin for a person in the diocese of Clogher to go to a dance which didn't end at midnight. So, in a way, it was ironic that so many of the bands came to an ordination service conducted by Bishop O'Callaghan.

As it turned out, I was the last priest he ordained. He retired very shortly after that. It has been said on many occasions, only half jokingly, that when he realised what he had done, it's no wonder he retired.

I'm the only priest to have been ordained in the college.

There was a quiet reception afterwards in Derrylin. The music and craic were good and Brian Coll kept us entertained all evening long. Only a limited number attended the ordination because the college chapel was small, and anyway I didn't want to put my family to any more expense.

One of the people who attended was Eddie Masterson. As you can see, he keeps popping up in the most unusual places. Because he was a solicitor he was asked to make a speech on behalf of my friends in showbusiness. He was sitting beside the bishop. The bishop, unconcerned, listened to what Eddie was saying. After all, he had been introduced as a solicitor. That was impressive. Eddie got up in his grey suit and sparkling new white shirt for the occasion, but the ever-present cigarette hung off his bottom lip. As his opening text, spoken slowly as any good parish priest would, he had a quotation of sorts from Scripture. He said ponderously, "What does it profit a man if he gain the whole world and never hear Big Tom sing *Gentle Mother*?" The bishop looked aghast. Most people didn't get the joke. And the 20 of us who did went under the table, partly with embarrassment and partly in admiration at the genius of the man. He got away with it.

CHAPTER 4

CAUGHT IN THE CROSS FIRE

The very first time I ever broadcast on radio – as a priest – was in 1970. I had just become editor of *The Cross* and put the Beatles on the front cover with the caption: *Are They More Popular than Jesus?* That was a little radical for a religious magazine in 1970 and it caused a mini-sensation.

The best-known radio programme on RTÉ at the time was the *Liam Nolan Hour*. Liam Nolan came home from England, where he had worked on all of the top programmes in BBC and ITV. It's true to say he invented morning radio in Ireland.

Previously, Radio Éireann, as it was called, closed down about 10am and opened again at lunchtime. Liam Nolan was brought in to create a programme which would attract listeners, especially women, throughout the morning. He did that more effectively than anybody could have imagined. In later life he became a close friend and I learned about all forms of communication from Liam. I still regard him as a friend and hero.

However, on that first interview for the *Liam Nolan Hour* he almost destroyed me. I was young, nervous and not used to such a searching but fair interviewer. I performed pathetically. Immediately after the programme, Liam realised I'd performed badly but suspected I had more to offer. He instantly recorded a follow-up interview for broadcast the next day. On Tuesdays, the last half hour of the programme dealt with new forms of music. I covered myself in glory on that one and introduced Liam, and many of the people of Ireland, to the lyrics and music of Kris Kristofferson. It was as successful as the previous day's interview was disastrous.

On the Monday after the disastrous interview I went back to the monastery in Mount Argus. The provincial at the time was Fr Valentine McMurray. He was a brilliant man who, as superior, took risks by introducing a better quality of education for Passionist students. He wanted all of the students, as far as possible, to experience a university education. For an order like ours, that was really revolutionary.

It was he who appointed me editor of *The Cross*, but on this particular Monday he was anything but sympathetic. His anger was obvious. In the community room after lunch, before all of the senior members of the community, he told me in no uncertain terms how badly I had done and how much I had let the Passionist congregation down. He also told me that if the Archbishop of Dublin phoned him, he couldn't defend me. And then he added, "I hereby ban you from ever appearing on radio or in public on behalf of the Passionists again." Many of the older priests were delighted. A few of the younger ones were taken aback. I was the "baby" priest in Mount Argus and as such wasn't allowed an opinion. Those who knew him best advised me to go privately to him in the afternoon. In those days one didn't really speak to religious superiors until you were spoken to. This was especially true if you were the junior member of the community, as I was then.

But I had to do something because I had already recorded a programme which was due to go out the next day. Late in the afternoon when I thought he would have cooled down, with great temerity I knocked on the door of the provincial's office. Fr Valentine was an incessant smoker. Sometimes you could hardly see him behind his desk for smoke. He was smoking in every sense of the word that day. I apologised for my bad performance that morning and explained to him that it was due to nervousness. I then told him I had recorded a much better programme to go out the next day, which I hoped he would like.

His humour had improved but he told me that I should ring RTÉ and ask them to pull the programme on his say-so. Even then I knew to do that would cause a bigger controversy than the programme was worth and I told him so. In fairness to him he accepted my view and said, "Well, I'll lift the ban until I hear the programme tomorrow." That's about as close to canonical approbation as I ever got.

Galway County Libraries

When the programme went out the next day I never heard a word from the provincial or indeed from any of the community. And so began a long career in broadcasting and a long friendship with Liam Nolan and a lifetime of respect for Fr Valentine. He had saved me once before. Just before ordination I got a Valentine card. The director wanted my ordination delayed because of the Valentine card. The Provincial didn't agree. He said, "The man received a Valentine card; he didn't send one. My name is Valentine and I get cards every 14th of February. You can't send him home for that." And they agreed to me being ordained.

As soon as I was ordained, I was appointed editor of *The Cross*, the magazine of our order at that time. After the Second Vatican Council, all religious magazines were struggling. None of the experienced priests in our order wanted to be the one to close down this famous magazine. They thought the poisoned chalice would be good for me. They didn't tell me the magazine was struggling. They didn't tell me they wanted it closed. So I worked like a demon to make it a success.

My basic aim was to produce an interesting, readable magazine. Secondly, it had to be entertaining. People would buy it if it had those attributes. If it wasn't interesting and entertaining it didn't matter how pious or how worthy it might be, it would die a death.

I knew a relevant message needed a fresh style, which to me had to be based on pop culture. Right or wrong, it was all I knew. At this point in my life I had good contacts in journalism, all of whom advised me to do a journalism course. My friends in the newspapers used to write for me in the magazine. Michael Hand, Liam Nolan, Mary Robinson and Brian Faulkner all wrote for me. Paddy Devlin of the SDLP did too. It became an influential magazine in the political and social scene. As the months went by, the papers began to lift stories from the magazine. My superiors, to their credit, gave me a free hand and the circulation rose again.

Many of the older Passionists, though, didn't like what I did with *The Cross*. They wanted to see a list of Passionist preaching engagements. I believed that was the function of a newsletter, not a magazine. A magazine must stand on its own, commercially, and refresh the image of the Church.

But there was opposition to it. One senior rector used to throw the bundle of magazines in the fire unopened and unread. It became known as The Ceremony of Burning The Cross in the community recreation room. He was unable to accept change. He had been a writer himself in the bygone era of that florid, verbose style which lost its impact 20 years before. The style dated the message.

In the early 1970s, unions were stronger than they are now. You couldn't write for a newspaper regularly unless you were a member of the National Union of Journalists. My friends in journalism sponsored me to join the NUJ so I made an application to the union. Wages were a major obstacle. Since I had a vow of poverty, I had no wages. The union informed me that unless I was getting a certain percentage of my wages from journalism, I couldn't become a member of the NUJ. I wrote back with an argument I thought logical. What is the difference between my situation and that of a hen-pecked husband? He brings home his wages and hands them over to his wife. I earn the money and it's handed over to my order. They wrote back immediately accepting me into the National Union of Journalists.

That was 1972. I don't know whether it's true or not, I can't make the claim, but they said I was the first priest in Ireland to become a member of the NUJ. That gave me a standing in journalism. I'm still a member of the union and proud to be part of it.

I interviewed Bernadette Devlin back in 1972 when I was editor of *The Cross*. The Archbishop of Dublin, Dr McQuaid, wouldn't give me permission to publish it because he said the content was anti-Catholic. The diocesan censor's office and the archbishop himself said it would be imprudent for me to publish the article, even though they agreed there was absolutely nothing contrary to faith, morals or Catholic teaching in it.

Fr Valentine was the provincial when I ran into the controversy about whether to publish the interview with Bernadette Devlin in *The Cross*. I argued that the question of faith and morals was indeed the prerogative of the archbishop's office, but a question of prudence was an editorial decision. I was the one to decide what was prudent, not the archbishop's office.

I felt that in fairness to the Passionists, I had to ask my provincial what I should do. I gave him a copy of the article and told him what the archbishop's advice was and gave him my opinion. To his eternal credit Fr Valentine handed me the article and said, "I'll leave the decision entirely in your hands." I thought then, and I think now, that it was a brave and independent decision for a major religious superior to take in 1972. Personally it showed that he trusted me to make a mature and balanced editorial decision. On that occasion I most certainly appreciated his vote of confidence. Because of his trust, I tried hard to weigh up all editorial decisions in a balanced way. So I decided to publish the interview. It became the most widely quoted summary of Bernadette's philosophy at the time.

It's not that Bernadette Devlin was saying anything utterly revolutionary, but what she did say was stretching the limits of Catholic conversation back then and makes good sense still. Explaining the difference between a Christian and a Communist she made this comment: "Normally when people speak of Christians and Communists they presuppose two opposing sects. If you are a Christian, you follow Christ and think everyone else is wrong. You then have the Communists, who also allow the term to cover a multitude of sins and base their lives on Marx, who wrote a different book to Christ. Never the two can meet. I find myself with these two stereotypes, rejected by both, because I am a Christian who insists on talking Marxism, and a Marxist who insists on the relevance of Christianity."

At the time she hadn't read much theology or indeed papal encyclicals but she was adamant: "The Gospels must be relevant to our times, otherwise we do them a disservice. There is no point talking to this generation about vineyards. We are concerned with factories. Parables should be related to how we live on earth as well as in heaven.

"If there were no Christians in the world it would be a very different place," she said. "I believe Christianity will always be alive while I'm alive. And if there is one Christian in the world that is enough, provided that one is a real Christian. He will spread the faith and be a witness to the existence of Christianity. I believe the failure of Christianity in the world today is because there are so many Christians outside the Christian Churches and so few Christians within them.

"We must, as intelligent people today, work out what it means to be a

Catholic," she added. "I say I'm a Catholic and I'll be damned if I'll be pushed out of it by a load of people who aren't even Christian."

And of course she was adamant that the struggle in Northern Ireland should not be between Protestants and Catholics, but between the moneyed classes and the working classes. "The only way you can do it is to take their common interests outside their prejudices and replace sectarianism with their common class interests. Then the job of ensuring that their common class interests don't make them all atheists is the work of the clerics."

The paragraph that caused most of the problems was the one where she commented on a quote from her book. In *The Price of My Soul* she had said, "Among the best traitors Ireland ever had, Mother Church ranks at the top. A massive obstacle in the path of equality and freedom." She went on to admit that she got into trouble for saying that but still stood over it. "Irish history proves it," she said. "If you look at the Fenian movement, the Land League and in more recent times, Sinn Féin, you will see it. I think it was a papal delegate who was sent to hear confession in former times of political division because priests wouldn't do it, and he said he didn't find any bishops here, but the place was coming down with popes. That is still true today. Many young priests are slowly being squeezed out of the Church."

"It is here too that we see the balance of society taking effect. It was bound to happen that if all the radical Irish priests were sent to South America, sooner or later they would start a revolution there. That seems to be happening . . ."

Not only does the interview give significant insights into what was happening in the Church at the time, it was pre-emptive of what would happen. The episode also shows the kind of control John Charles McQuaid had at the time, how very tightly guarded it was and how difficult it was for anybody to step outside of that.

The interview was eventually translated and quoted around the world as being innovative and challenging. Much of it is now dated, but there are still many basic points that we never dealt with, to our cost. The most prophetic of all was her insight that we sent the radical priests abroad to start revolutions in Third World countries and kept the safe ones at home to keep the institution going.

The editorial in *The Cross* that got me into most trouble was a 100-word piece welcoming the appointment of a spokesman for the Catholic bishops. It was truly an innovation in the early 1970s. In welcoming the new post, I added, "I hope he gets more co-operation than the religious press does from the present Catholic hierarchy." That caused a storm and more complaints were lodged from the archbishop's office. The language was the tired old language of authority: "A Catholic magazine shouldn't be critical of the bishops of Ireland."

Yet the facts were that the only people who refused to write for *The Cross* in all my time as editor were two bishops from the Catholic Church and two bishops from the Church of Ireland. All four used exactly the same language when refusing the invitation: "At the present moment it might not be appropriate for me to put my thoughts on paper for *The Cross*."

Looking back now it shows why the leaders of the Catholic Church have a lot to answer for. So much of their communication was negative and defensive. And that's a pity.

Erskine Childers was not a Catholic but he invited me to Áras an Uachtaráin to do an interview with him and then to discuss a number of issues. He was one of the most calculated interviewees I've ever met professionally. He had asked that the questions be submitted in advance. That was not unusual for a President and is perfectly understandable. It didn't mean that he couldn't be asked supplementary questions. But it did mean that he could prepare himself in a proper way to answer the main body of questions.

When I asked him a question, he invariably stopped for what seemed like an eternity but was probably 20 seconds. Then he delivered his answers onto a tape. The answers came in perfectly formed sentences with beautifully chosen phrases and succinct points made logically and attractively. I don't think I had to insert even a comma in his answers, they were so perfect.

Later still he asked me for my advice. He knew I was an expert on the pop music of the day, or at least he considered me to be an expert on the popular songs. He was conscious that, as he was apt to visit schools and youth clubs, he wanted to be abreast of some of the more meaningful songs of the era.

Off the top of my head I thought that he should listen to such artists as Bob Dylan and Kris Kristofferson. Of course I had already mentioned the Beatles, Gordon Lightfoot and Rod McEwan, all of whom wrote lyrics with a strong message.

He had a beautiful fountain pen in his hand. He carefully removed the top and began to take notes as I spoke. I sat across the table and I knew I had lost the President when I saw him writing down Robert Dillon instead of Bob Dylan. I let that one go, but when I saw him writing Kris Kristofferson as Chris, I knew I had to correct the President of Ireland. As gently as I could I explained to him that Bob Dylan took his name from the poet Dylan Thomas and that Kris Kristofferson was Kris. He took it in good humour and continued to take copious notes.

A short time afterwards we had community television in Harold's Cross and President Childers was our guest. I was amazed to find him referring not only to authors of songs but lines from songs. And he did it as if he were the expert. It was one of the few times when I barely recognised my own thoughts coming back at me.

During all this time, I was going out to the dancehalls seven nights a week and all the guys in the bands got to know me and expected me to be there. If I didn't go, they'd contact me and say, "I missed you last night, where were you?" If they had a problem, I'd chat to them about it. The people from the floor came to me asking for confessions. In those days I heard more confessions in the dancehalls than in the confession box. I never started out to become a chaplain. It happened because I was there as a fan. I liked the music on the scene so it wasn't really a duty. I liked the guys in the bands. I liked the people. I liked their honesty. Funnily enough, there was more honesty among showbusiness people than there was in the priesthood.

I learned many positive things from showbusiness – like hard work, professionalism, never to leave anything to chance and when to leave the glamour of showbusiness behind. You can't be on the stage all of the time.

You have to be comfortable within your own skin. Showbusiness recognises that the person who is in danger is the person who never gets off the stage. I needed to be able to recognise that temptation in myself. I needed to be grounded. That was important for me. The best gift they offered me was the ability to listen to the ordinary people, which is the exact opposite of what we, in the Church, often do.

There's a whole generation of older people who know me from dancehalls, not the church. For 12 years I spent my nights in Dublin dancehalls. I learned an amazing amount from the showbands and their followers.

The showbands had to deal with real people. They were itinerants on the road and had an overall picture of life in Ireland. They weren't confined to a corner of a parish and they weren't imprisoned in a ghetto mentality. They grew with their experience and struggled to keep their marriages together. They experienced the glamour of the stage and the trials of real life and tried to cope with both.

By 1975 my name was well known throughout Ireland. That was the year the Miami Showband was blown up and I was able to minister to the families. It was also the year when Tom Dunphy, a leading member of the Royal Showband and the Big 8, died and it was the real turning point in the history of the showbands. Having to cope with so much tragedy made me think about my own future. I didn't want to stay on *The Cross* and be a journalist all my life. I wanted to develop my vocation as a priest.

I explained my position to the provincial and, as luck would have it, Fr Joe Dunn requested me to work at the Catholic Communication Institute. That innovative pioneer in broadcasting Fr Joe Dunn was suffering under the repressive system himself but valiantly fought on. Because of my work on *The Cross*, it was he who asked me to join the staff at the Catholic Communications Institute in Booterstown. I spent two very happy years working full time there, from 1975 until 1977.

My association with Liam Nolan lasted right through my days at *The Cross* and beyond. He helped me editorially and also wrote some powerful pieces for the magazine. Later when he became the features editor for the *Irish Press* and I had moved on to the Communications Institute, he wrote the following paragraph about my time on *The Cross*.

"His success as editor of *The Cross* can most impressively be gauged from the quite extraordinary fact that for 44 consecutive issues, at least one, and frequently as many as four, articles were quoted from, lifted or reprinted in toto in Ireland's national daily press. You can add to that fact that frequently radio used material from *The Cross* as the basis for programme topics."

In the same article it was recorded that frequent writers for *The Cross* were Jack Lynch and Liam Cosgrave (both Taoisigh), Erskine Childers and Cearbhall Ó Dálaigh, both Presidents of Ireland, Brian Faulkner, Paddy Devlin MP, Austin Curry MP, Mary Robinson (later President of Ireland), Ben Briscoe TD and William Deedes MP. At the time William Deedes was a leader writer for the *Daily Telegraph* and subsequently the editor of that organ, and also the Conservative Party spokesman for Northern Ireland.

Henry Cooper is one of the most famous and best-loved British boxers of all time. He was the first boxer to receive a knighthood and according to Henry it was the, "cream on top of the cake. You get knights in other sports but I was the first one in boxing. So it wasn't just for me, it was for boxing, too. I'm sorry me old mum and dad weren't alive to know that their South London boy had done good."

Despite being raised in poverty in South London, Henry used boxing as a way to get to the top. He flattened Muhammad Ali in 1963 when he was still called Cassius Clay.

Liam Nolan was a personal friend of Henry's, and arranged an interview for me.

I interviewed Henry in his home in London. It was just after he retired and I found him to be a perfect gentleman. He brought me to meet his wife, Albina, who treated me royally. He gave the interview and all he asked in return was that I would bless his brand new Mercedes parked outside his front door. I gave it a thorough blessing, which delighted Henry and Albina. He left me back to the tube station and I flew back to Dublin.

Next day Liam Nolan phoned inquiring how Henry was. Henry, I assured him, was in the best of good health. Liam was delighted to hear it and wondered how he was after his crash.

"What crash?" I asked.

"Yesterday evening he crashed his new Mercedes car and it was a write-off according to the *Daily Mirror* today."

It was the first I heard of it.

I wrote a note of apology to Henry wondering how I got my blessings mixed up. He sent me back a letter saying that there was no need to apologise. He and Albina agreed that had the car not been blessed he probably would have been killed. Henry's faith was greater than mine. I take car blessings seriously ever since.

Chapter 5

Boxed in by Julie

When I was a young priest, I had a steep learning curve on all areas of parish and pastoral life. When you're newly ordained, you're really enthusiastic. You're going to be the best confessor that ever lived. You're going to be the most sincere man at saying a Mass that ever lived. You'll always help people in trouble. You'll never be hard when people come to you with a problem. You've all these lovely ideas. At least those were the ideas I had. And I wasn't alone. Many others in the class had the same vision.

But then, life teaches you that ideals are one thing and you must have them, but prudence in the application of the ideals is part of the learning process. Unusual people can teach you about life.

In Mount Argus, in the early 1970s, there was a wonderful lady who used to visit our church and I want to be respectful to her. I don't want in any sense to demean her. She was a lady who perhaps wasn't mentally secure. I'm not sure that she was mentally deranged, either. In fact, I'm sure she wasn't mentally deranged. But she had her moments, shall we say. I think she lived in a hostel in Dublin. We knew her as Julie. That was not her real name but that was how we referred to her affectionately. She was legendary around Mount Argus.

First of all, she was no respecter of persons. She always knew when a vulnerable priest was around. She could pick us out and pick on us. Often as I sat in the box for confessions I'd open the slide to find Julie there. And she'd land a list of curses on me and a list of sins and then she'd burst out laughing. "I got ya there, didn't I?"

So who was the wise one?

For the first dozen times, I tried to be patient. "All right, Julie, one Hail Mary." And then I'd pull the slide on the other side, with great relief, only to find Julie on the other side as well. She'd say, "I'm here again." I never understood how she managed to get to the other side so quickly. She had this great laugh and everybody would hear it ringing all over the church. In those days everything was silent and sombre, almost somnolent, in churches.

Julie would just break the rules with that freedom that I, only now looking back, see as cutting through all the arrogant nonsense we used to go on with. Back then though she was a nuisance. Did she not know her place?

Occasionally she came to funerals in Mount Argus. When everybody was sitting mournfully at the beginning of Mass, with the Mass cards standing decked on top of the coffin, Julie would come running up with her handbag and, as Mass was just about to start, swipe every Mass card off the top. It was not an easy action to explain. I'd whisper "duine le Dia" or some such phrase to get over it.

If there was a wedding in the church, she'd meet the bride at the church with her handbag and green coat and headscarf tied tightly underneath her jaws. You could never see her face. All you saw was a protruding nose and mischievous eyes dancing out of her headscarf, which she wore like blinkers. Then she'd go to the bride and say, "Are you preggers or what?" The look of shock on a bride dressed in white was wonderful to behold.

Julie had this unfailing way of bringing us all down to earth. Another inexplicable compulsion she had was receiving Holy Communion. Back then you could go to one Mass; you were allowed to receive Communion only once a day. This was a big leap forward from once a month, or maybe once a year, which was the custom in the past.

Julie decided that she would, first of all, go to the Franciscan Church in Merchants Quay and get as many Masses as she could. At each Mass she would go to the far side of the rail, receive Communion, go to the middle section of the rail, receive Communion, go to the next rail, receive Communion, and do the same all along the rail. It was a big, wide church and she'd receive Communion five or six times at each Mass. This of course was a huge moral problem for everybody except Julie and Jesus.

She would then come up to Mount Argus, go to the 10 o'clock Mass and do the same thing all over again. At 6.15 in the evening, Julie was back to receive numerous Communions again. Only priests gave out Communion and we had long discussions about whether we should give her Communion. If we didn't we knew she would create a scene.

I learned about her tricks early on. I went out to say Mass very nervously one Sunday when Julie planted herself underneath the pulpit and shouted, "Would you look at D'Arcy. Look at him laughing. What's he laughing at?" in the middle of the sermon. "Look at the smile on him," she says. "Look at him, can you see him?" Try to keep your composure in the middle of that!

So you always knew that, despite the power you thought you had, Julie had all the authority. I dodged round her as best I could. Anything for a quiet life.

Move on to Ash Wednesday. I think it was Ash Wednesday, 1972. I was a young priest in Mount Argus and editor of *The Cross* at the time. There was another young priest in the community now, Fr Aidan Troy, who was a year behind me. The church was packed for Ash Wednesday Mass. Lent was taken seriously then.

I was giving Communion at the 10 o'clock Mass that morning and knew Julie had already received Communion from me twice. She had enough Communions to break her Lenten fast by now. I knew she'd also been to Merchants Quay. I was saying the 6.15 Mass and I said to Aidan Troy beforehand, "Julie was here this morning for Mass and she'll be looking for Communion from us again. We'll make a bargain – you give it to her once and I'll give it to her once and that's it."

Picture the scene. The church was full. I see six nuns in the front row. I can see green-uniformed children from the Loreto behind them and I can see St Clare's in the brown uniform. There were nearly a thousand people in Mount Argus church for the 6.15 Mass that Ash Wednesday evening.

We were doing well; I'd given out the ashes and given the sermon. I came to Communion now. Aidan Troy went to the far side and Julie went over to him. I was keeping a half eye on what was happening. She got Communion. Then she jumped up and came over to me.

I moved across and she was in front of me again. I didn't make a scene. I just passed over her. I gave Communion to the person each side of her, but didn't give it to Julie. This happened three times and she was plainly annoyed.

Communion ended and everybody was sitting with their heads bowed, reverently praying. Aidan Troy was back at the tabernacle replacing the Blessed Sacrament and the ciboria. I was purifying the chalice. Julie came up with her handbag, put one hand on the right hand side of the altar gates and the other on the left hand side. She looked me straight in the eyes and shouted at the top of her voice, "D'Arcy!" I kept my head down. "D'Arcy!"

Eyes were raised gently from the back of the church.

"Are you going to give it to me?"

I shook my head.

"Are you going to give it to me? Well, f*** you, D'Arcy, stick it up your arse!"

I collapsed with laughter. Aidan Troy was holding on to the tabernacle trying to keep himself from falling. The nuns' mouths opened in horror that their lovely little darlings were hearing such language in the church.

And Julie danced down the aisle, swinging her handbag over her head triumphantly and still shouting, "F*** you, D'Arcy, shove it up your arse!" She disappeared out the main door with a shriek of laughter. I laughed so much I cried. I couldn't say a prayer. I couldn't open my mouth. All I could do was give a silent blessing and we all went into the sacristy.

Very shortly after that, Julie disappeared and none of us knew where she went. We never saw her again. We heard rumours that she was in various mental hospitals, but I didn't know her name, and didn't know anything about her. As we grew older we began to appreciate her more and to see that maybe she was correct and we were arrogant little clerics trying to impose a regime. Maybe she had understood the essentials a little better than any of us. The next time I met Julie was a happier occasion altogether and I'll explain later.

CHAPTER 6

RINGING THE CHANGES

My first five years of priesthood were spent editing *The Cross* but I also did confessional duty in Mount Argus and said public Masses every week. One of my extra duties was to head off on my Honda 50 to say Mass for the nuns in an enclosed Carmelite convent in Roebuck in Dublin, when the chaplain was away. The first morning I went provides another good example of how people get locked into another world. I left Mount Argus at a quarter past six in the morning on my motorbike. I rang the bell at an imposing entrance when I got there. I knew nothing about enclosed orders, or that some of the nuns had never been outside the convent since they entered. It was like stepping into a time machine and landing back in 1575.

The door opened and it scared the daylights out of me because I could see nobody. I walked into the hallway and heard a disembodied voice from somewhere. I couldn't actually understand where the voice was coming from; it just seemed to come from thin air. "Good morning, Father." And I answered, "Good morning," to no one in particular. "Take three steps down the corridor, Father, and open the door on the right." I took three steps down the corridor. It felt like when I was a little child; I believed God could see you everywhere but you couldn't see God.

I opened the door and the voice was in front of me again. How she did it I really don't know. She said, "Father, that's the sacristy over there and the vestments are out and everything's there and when you have your vestments on I'll come back."

I put on the vestments nervously because I knew she was watching me. Just as I finished, she said, "Now, Father, you can go to the altar. You'll see no nuns, just say Mass and the nuns will be to the side. At Communion time you'll give them Communion through the iron grille."

I said Mass to what to me was an empty church, but over to the side was a large grille with a cloth over it. They could see through the cloth but I couldn't see them. When I went over to give Communion, all I could see was a tongue. I could have been giving Communion to the same person over and over again for all I knew, because all the nuns' tongues looked exactly the same. There were about 30 of them and I put hosts on 30 tongues. It was most unnerving.

When I finished Mass I took off the vestments. "Would you like breakfast, Father?" The disembodied voice was still haunting me. I was in my 20s at the time, frozen and underfed, and breakfast was a rare treat. She said, "Now Father, go out the door you came in." I went out. "Turn right now, Father." I turned right. "Turn left now, Father." I turned left into the room to see a perfectly laid-out breakfast table. She said, "Go over to the press and lift up the hatch and you'll find breakfast." I lifted it up and had the loveliest breakfast of scrambled eggs and buttery toast and tea. I lifted the tray to serve myself. I was eating away on my own and the voice interrupted me again. "Is everything all right, Father? It's not too hot for you, Father?" I was careful to eat properly after that.

Morning after morning the same ritual was repeated. I had lovely conversations with a nun I never saw. At the end of two weeks, the voice spoke to me: "Father, one of the nuns is sick. Can you bring her Communion?" Only a priest was allowed to touch Communion then; nuns couldn't touch the host.

She opened the door and there she was as large as life, in a long white habit. She led me up the corridor to the sick nun's room. There I saw not only a nun, but a nun with no headdress in a nightgown, which was something I had never seen before in my life. All this secrecy and invisibility, what was the point of it? It seemed so unreal, so other-worldly.

One of the interesting facts the voice told me was that they were allowed to see Pope Paul VI on television when he visited the Holy Land. He also spoke at the United Nations. They were given special permission to get a television. One of the older nuns had never been outside the convent and when she saw the Pope in a car, she was fascinated. She didn't know what a car was. There were probably none around when she entered. She'd never been outside the convent since and the car was a new experience for her. Even in the early 1970s, I thought it was a cruel life.

We often forget that there were 300 years in the Church during which time nothing much changed. I was brought up in that era when things didn't change and we were convinced they would never change. It was one of our boasts that you could go into a church anywhere in the world and attend the exact same Mass, in Latin, that you attended in your local parish. It was a mark of the Catholic Church that there would be no change because we claimed to have the fullness of truth.

We shouldn't accept too easily that this was a golden era, because it wasn't. Much of what went on was unenlightened, to say the least. As a young priest in Dublin, I had to deal with young people who joined the cult group The Children of God. I had to learn about the methods used by cults to attract and trap young people as members. Funnily enough, the psychologists said that the essence of cultic behaviour is to take an idealistic young person who really wants to achieve something. There's no point in targeting those who aren't idealistic. You have to get somebody who wants to be better and different. Hence, the cults went to universities to find their people in the same way as the Church brought their elite to junior and senior seminaries. Once the cult got them, they starved them of three very essential needs at a young age: food, affection and sleep. That's how to effect brainwashing.

It suddenly dawned on me for the first time, the kind of system I was being processed through. That was the beginning of debriefing myself and learning to think outside the loop again.

The men who upheld the system did their best, because they themselves had been brainwashed even more at a previous time. They were a part of a Pius XII Church in which anybody who stepped out of line was summarily excommunicated and mortal sins were imposed at will.

There was a superior in my order who said that anybody who took a book out of the community library without signing for it committed a mortal sin. People made themselves into gods.

And there were several gods in people's life. Priests were one of them, certainly the parish priest. And according to the parish priest the bishop was God. As far as the bishop was concerned the Pope was God. It was a hierarchy of control, not a hierarchy of choice. That is a crucial attitude to acknowledge. That's what we emerged from.

Society was little better back then. Society worked because people were compliant. When I got a slap at school, it was the last thing I told my parents, because their next question would be why. Then I got another slap from them for doing wrong. If I met an RUC man, I'd walk to the opposite side of the street to make sure I had no contact with this bogeyman in black. A boss was a boss. There was a discernible hierarchy in every walk of life and nobody stepped out of line.

The spirituality I was initiated into made me and my lack of perfection the centre of everything. All of our theology revolved around sexual behaviour. We were formed in a spiritual wasteland from which we have not yet recovered.

In effect, people at the time thought God made a mistake when he made sex. His second mistake was to make women. You're laughing. But there's a truth in it. It's amazing the number of times in confession I've heard old men say, "I wish that God would take away my sexual desires from me." Can you imagine anything more blasphemous than that? Wanting to be rid of God's greatest gift to humanity after life itself.

Really the Church doesn't have a workable theology of sexuality. Much of it is based on St Augustine's belief that women are a source of evil, and sex, at best, is for making babies. You can interpret it any way you like but the basic principle behind all our teaching on sex is flawed. As long as it remains that way the Church will continue to struggle for credibility.

For a long time even dancing was perceived as an evil. Ireland was cursed by our small, parochial mentality. In the 1950s people travelled by bicycle, which determined how far you could go to a dance – as far as your bicycle would carry you. So you rarely socialised or met with anyone outside of your own small area. Your parish priest controlled dancing, and everything else, in your area.

Emigration was a plague on our country. In the early 1950s, the custom in many places was to hold a "living wake" before a person left for America.

It even had a name in folklore. It was called the American wake. Once a person went to America the chances of returning home were minimal. Nobody could foresee air travel developing so rapidly.

Education was limited and not available to the whole community. It's hard to believe that we're talking about an Ireland of less than 50 years ago. It was an Ireland of Brylcreem, nylon shirts and elastic ties. Many of you will recall how a young girl who refused to dance was scorned.

Most dances were run in the parish hall. The person in charge was inevitably the parish priest. He had the power.

There is a true story about a parish in the North of Ireland where the priest did not like or did not want dancing of any kind in his town. He had a lovely hall which nobody could use. There were a number of popular bands in this particular town and they asked him if it would be possible to hold a dance in the hall. People wanted them to play in their own home town and they argued it would be a source of income for the parish.

"Absolutely not," was his answer. Furthermore, the bishop of that particular diocese ordered that all dancing must finish by midnight and if it didn't it was a mortal sin to attend. Even people from his diocese who went to other dioceses to a dance that didn't end at midnight committed a mortal sin. The big debate then became, "What about summertime and wintertime? Is it 12 o'clock summertime or wintertime?"

You can imagine the surprise when the priest announced at Mass: "On next Sunday night, there will be a dance in the hall." He had never mentioned this to any of the bands. "There will be a dance in the hall. It will begin at 8.30 and it will end at 11.30. Admission will be two shillings and sixpence and the band will be . . ." The congregation were in shock! And then he added: "On the following Sunday night, we'll have a dance for the women."

Showbands were part of the changing history of Ireland. Many factors converged. Electricity arrived, Seán Lemass, travel, prosperity, communication, freedom, education and showbands. Then there was Elvis Presley and pop music. Communications opened up whole new worlds for people.

The wireless went from being run on wet batteries to dry batteries and then to transistor radios. Wind-up gramophones became record players. Television edged its way into the country. Papers became more widespread. Schools were built. It was possible to go to America and not have a wake. England was much more accessible as well. Radio Luxembourg played pop music non-stop.

The late 50s and 60s saw Seán Lemass change the country. A new social structure developed. People were much better off than previous generations. This was due in no small measure to the vision of economists like Ken Whittaker and politicians with enthusiasm and initiative, of whom Seán Lemass was undoubtedly the greatest. Even those who didn't emigrate had more money in their pockets and could afford to go to dances frequently. The demand was there and the supply was about to hit the road, literally.

By way of transition from traditional céilí bands to showbands, dance bands were formed around the country. Mick Delahunty, Maurice Mulcahy, Gay McIntyre and Johnny Quigley were some of the pioneers. They used brass instruments with top-class arrangements. Showbands developed from the era of dance bands.

With the arrival of showbands, businessmen began to build huge ballrooms, and with the availability of cars people travelled 40 miles or more to dance in them. They got away from their own people, their world got bigger and they freed themselves from the clutches of the Church and social customs. The showbands were part of that.

People never got to see Cliff Richard or Elvis Presley in person, but every band had an Elvis or a Cliff on stage. You could see two or even three-thousand people in a hall at special times. There were over 600 full-time bands playing up and down the country night after night. They were playing six nights a week as fully professional bands. There was a lot of dancing, a lot of socialising, a lot of fun, a lot of experimenting going on every night of the week. It was a whole new scene and I was part of it. It was exciting and educational.

I was the only priest who worked with the bands on a nightly basis. The bands often experienced priests as promoters who wanted them to work for peanuts when they played in the parish hall, and would condemn them in sermons the next Sunday about the evils of going to dances. For example, every Lent the dancehalls were closed and the musicians were out of work for six weeks. They headed off to England or America to get a living.

Many of the bands remember parish priests who carried a walking stick to slip between couples making sure they didn't get too close. "Leave room for the Holy Spirit between you," they'd say.

The commercial ballrooms took over from the Church-run halls. That too was a significant change of power and control.

Now people began to think for themselves. People went to live in cities and nobody knew whether they went to Mass or not. The sexual revolution began. That's when the Church should have changed but didn't. It still maintained the structures and strictures that existed before this age of communication.

The international scene was changing too. Travel became necessary and accessible. Elvis arrived and so did the Beatles. John F Kennedy became the president of America. John XXIII became Pope and The Vatican Council opened in Rome.

Pope John XXIII was Pope when I was a teenager. Popes were mystical figures then. The model was the ascetic-looking Pius XII, who was certainly a walking saint if we believed what we were told. We would not be so easily convinced now.

Then Pope John came with his larger-than-life, grandfatherly, smiling face. A Pope with a smile? Couldn't be right.

What I liked most about him was that he was a stop-gap Pope. They put him in when he was 79 years of age to make sure he'd do nothing. Yet he was the one, the most unlikely one, that the Holy Spirit chose to do the most revolutionary things.

He famously convened the Second Vatican Council. The phrase was double Dutch to me as a novice in The Graan in Enniskillen when we were allowed to watch one session on TV. It was such a special occasion that every rule in the book about training novices was broken. We were allowed to join the rest of the community – unheard of then – and there was a television brought in to show the events live from Rome.

I was sitting quietly at the back of the room, mystified by the excitement of the older priests. Then in the midst of the snowy black-and-white picture there was a long shot of some of the bishops from around the world.

One of the priests shouted excitedly, "There's John Charles." I was totally confused. I knew that John Charles was a Welsh footballer who had gone to play in Italy, a real superstar. But what was a footballer doing in the Vatican? No one explained just then, but later I was told that John Charles was *not* the footballer, but was in fact the Archbishop of Dublin – a man I got to know better a few years later, as you already know.

It shows how right my father was when he told me I would not be good material for the priesthood because I was more interested in football than religion. He was right of course, but what he didn't know was that I learned more that helped my priesthood from football and music than I did from theology.

Unquestionably John XXIII has been the only truly great Pope in the last 100 years or more: a man who remained human and reachable right to the end.

He called himself an ugly Pope. He was a big, fat man. One day when a woman was looking at him as he was blessing people in the Vatican he heard her say, "Isn't he very ugly?" He stopped to address her, "Madam, isn't it lucky the papacy is not a beauty contest."

Khrushchev's daughter, Rada, and her husband were received in the Vatican by John XXIII. He asked her to name her children. "I know the names of your children already, but there's nothing as beautiful as hearing a mother saying the names of her own children. Give them all a hug from me, especially Ivan," (which is the Russian for John).

When they were leaving he gave her Rosary beads. "I know you don't believe in the Rosary, but I want to give you a peaceful memory. And the most peaceful memory I have is of my mother kneeling by the fireside saying the Rosary. And that's the peaceful feeling I want to give to you as a mother."

Finally he wanted to give his blessing to her. And his blessing was given not as the blessing of a Pope because they wouldn't accept that, "but I know you will accept the blessing of an old, peasant man." And they did.

One of the most magnificent things he did when he became Pope was to visit a jail in Rome two days after Christmas. It was called Regina Coeli, which means Queen of Heaven, a terrible name for a prison. When he arrived at the prison, to the shock of everybody he spoke to the inmates. "Since you could not come to see me, I have come to see you." That's what it means to descend into other people's hells to help them.

He told them he came from a poor farming background. In Italy he said, there are three ways to lose money: gambling, women and drink, and farming. And he added, "Unfortunately my father chose the least interesting way to be poor." He also said that his brother had done time in prison for poaching fish. So he said, "We are all children of God and I am your brother." That's what he said to the prisoners.

On the same day a murderer in the prison came to him and asked, "Can even I be forgiven?" John said nothing to him but hugged him and that picture went around the world. The hug said everything. The hug took the prisoner out of his hell of guilt.

That was the pastoral and compassionate Pope who recognised that the Church needed a more acceptable human approach to educating people in this new age. The gentle, human Pope's spirit infused the Vatican Council. The documents from the Council see the Church as a community: the "People of God" rather than a legal hierarchical institution. We must dialogue with the world and learn from it, because the world is redeemed now. The Passion of Jesus leads to Resurrection. New life. New hope.

Vatican II was a wonderful opportunity for the Church to really renew itself but, sadly, it was also one of the great lost opportunities. People remember the Second Vatican Council for turning the altar around and for translating the Mass into English, but they don't remember why that happened. That's like shifting the chairs on the Titanic. Look at churches today. They've turned the altar round, but left the reredos in place. It signifies, really, that we look backwards and forwards at the same time. So it is literally rearranging furniture. We've ditched some of the old stuff, but didn't embrace the new or the reason for it. One of the key principles of Vatican II was that the Church is the people of God. That logically implies a rethinking of priesthood – which hasn't even begun to be considered 40 years later.

The changing of the altar was to be a symbol of a community of people gathered round it, of equal standing with the presider, who is the priest. And after Vatican II the priest's function changed from being the only authority in the parish to being part of the community, listening to them and leading them. That's why a community around an altar is important. That's why the altar was turned around, but we didn't rethink priesthood or community or the role of the laity. We kept to the old way and neglected God's Spirit inspiring us to change.

One of the reasons why the Second Vatican Council never translated itself into radical change in the Church in Ireland was because there were too many priests who were trained into a particular model of priesthood and Church. We have multiple churches and parishes, built when people walked to Mass. Now everybody has cars and there's no need for the number of churches we have. The system was maintained largely as occupational therapy for the many priests that we had then. Worse still, instead of becoming involved, the laity were expected to be passive and compliant.

The countries where the Church works best are those places where old models didn't get a chance to suffocate the spirit.

John Charles McQuaid came back from the Second Vatican Council and said to the people of Dublin, "There's nothing at all to worry about, since nothing has changed." Nothing much did change and, as far as he was concerned, nothing would. What kind of leadership in the spirit of Vatican II was that? It just never took root in Ireland.

We never really addressed the question of what Christ's resurrection meant, which was a huge part of the Second Vatican Council. What does the resurrection actually mean in my life, that Jesus is alive? Despite the Second Vatican Council it was 1981 before I felt free to study a radical Christology. Who is Jesus? What was Jesus like? What did He know? What did He not know? How human was He? Yet, how can I possibly have a relationship with Jesus unless I know Him? We built our structures of pious devotions on foundations of sand.

Pope John died before the Council ended, and Paul VI succeeded him. He continued to write insightful encyclicals but never had the same credibility after he went against the advice of his advisory group and published *Humanae Vitae* condemning artificial contraception as "intrinsically evil".

As I grow old now, I despair to see our Church slide back to the defensive fundamentalism of post-Reformation days. The Church, for anyone who reflects, is a much more suffocating place now than it was 25 years ago. There was at least some hope back then.

CHAPTER 7

POP GOES THE CHAPLAIN

The Clipper Carlton Showband were the first showband ever. And they came about, as most good things do, by accident. They were from Strabane in County Tyrone. There was a man called Hughie Toorish who had a band in that area. They were a typical band of their time. They dressed in dickie-bows, black suits and white shirts and they sat behind music stands playing everything in strict tempo. Toorish was the leader of the band and the piano player. In an interview, he described them well: "We were like undertakers arriving for a dance."

But as usually happens in showbusiness, a row broke out in the band about money and who was getting more of the limelight. The whole band walked out, leaving Hughie in a predicament because he had a big dance booked that Saturday night in the local hall in Strabane. He went around on his bicycle and gathered young musicians that he had heard of, and asked them to play. They told me they knew only about 10 tunes to keep them going all night! In those days it was a five-hour gig. They got through the night mainly because Toorish himself kept it going. But it couldn't last. Because they were young and inexperienced they tried something different. A couple of them had been in amateur dramatics and knew funny sketches. In local halls the big play was preceded by a funny sketch. They began to do their routines in the middle of the dance and were suprised that people stopped dancing to look at them.

The band knew they'd hit on a good idea. Because they didn't have enough tunes, necessity became the mother of invention and so they built a show around their music. They were not yet called a showband. One night they were in Fintona in County Tyrone, in the early 1950s. The local priest, Father Carty, was raising money for the parish, and said, "Why don't you get a proper name for yourselves?" They agreed to organise a competition in the hall that night to find a name for the band, with the winner getting half a crown. Various people wrote suggestions on the back of cigarette packets. One of them was, "The Sweet Afton Band – because there's not a Player among you." However, somebody else had written "The Clipper Carlton Band". Clipper was the name given to American planes during the war that landed on Lough Erne. It created an image of flying across the Atlantic: it was daring, different and glamorous. That man won the half-crown.

Hugo Quinn was a member of the band and a signwriter. On the way home he doodled with a sign. He thought the double C would work well so they called themselves the Clipper Carlton Band. They travelled one night to Dundalk and an enterprising proprietor recognised an opportunity. He advertised on a wall: "Playing tonight: The Clipper Carlton Showband." The name stuck. That's how an industry began.

The Clipper Carlton Showband brought joy and enthusiasm to everything they did. Their five-hour show included not just music, but miming, Laurel and Hardy sketches, King Kong and Al Jolson, plus everything that was popular on the music scene.

They were the first band to bring glamour to the business. They deliberately chose brightly coloured suits. The only place they could get material for such suits was in drapery shops that sold curtain material. I'm letting their secrets out, but that's what their gaudy uniforms were made from.

As a band, the Clipper Carlton were out on their own. They had their instruments highly polished and well presented. They worked out a show which entertained people even when they weren't dancing. They were the first to throw away music stands and to stand up for the entire night. They brought excitement and a whole new world to the people of Ireland. Others followed and surpassed them but they were the pioneers.

Elvis was the up-and-coming star at the time. Music changed and bands were travelling juke boxes introducing the pop stars of the world to the most rural parts of Ireland. The clergy, however, were slow to change.

The Clippers told me they once travelled from Strabane to Kerry for a dance. Of course people hadn't got used to that sort of band in the different regions of the country. In Kerry Mickey O'Hanlon was drumming. All he could see from his position on stage were bicycles going by him. He couldn't figure it out. There was a room at the back of the stage where the people could park their bicycles for safety. They came into the hall, paid their money, rode their bicycles up the hall and parked them at the back of the stage.

There was a priest in the area who had this idea that music raised the passions too easily at dances. He instructed bands that, after every three songs, they were to stop for precisely two minutes. He stood at the edge of the stage all night with his stopwatch in hand. At the end of the set, he'd say, "Wait for two minutes," and at the end of the two minutes he'd shout, "Go now." That was his way of keeping his parishioners' passions under control.

The showband era made a huge contribution to the opening out of Ireland. It brought fresh ideas; North and South became one. People followed the bands so travelling was important. The Dixies from Cork played in Belfast. The Freshmen from Ballymena played in Cork. It was a cross-fertilisation which had never taken place on the same scale before. There were lots of people in bands whose religion I never knew or wanted to know.

The Freshmen were largely a Protestant band because they were from Ballymena, but there were Catholics in the band too – all were accepted as brilliant musicians all over Ireland. I did a series of 16 programmes for BBC and RTÉ on the history of the showbands and I interviewed all the major bands of the era. I did a 45-minute radio documentary on each one of the bands. I spoke with the late Billy Brown, who was a musical genius in the Freshmen. He was a Protestant from Ballymena and had a stutter. I said to him one time, "It must be very difficult when you have a stutter, doing all these interviews. What's the most difficult part of it?" He replied, "My name, B-Billy B-Brown." That was the kind of black humour the bands loved. He went on, "In the Freshmen, we thought we knew everything. We were Prods and used to being in charge of everything. But we realised very quickly that the Republic was an entirely different sort of place. Protestants from the North of Ireland were innocents abroad when we went down there. So we got a Corkman, Oliver Barry, to manage us and that was a shrewd move. He told us we needed a good lead singer that people in cities and rural areas could identify with. At first, we took great exception to this. But because we wanted to make money and because we wanted to be part of the bigger scene, we decided to follow his advice. We tried to work out what sort of lead singer would be acceptable; what a lead singer of a showband ought to be and what he ought to look like. We came to the conclusion that the perfect lead singer for a showband would be a fellow who looked like a clerical student, but with sex appeal."

Who needs market research with genius like that?

They picked a young man from Strabane who was a trainee teacher in a Catholic training college. He looked like a clerical student – tall, black-haired, good-looking. They had to pick a name that was neutral from a religious point of view. They called him Derek Dean. Dean of the Freshmen, as it were. People in showbands worked out what people needed. They paid attention to the "punters", as they called them.

There was a time when the transition from local bands playing in local halls to showbands who travelled the length and breadth of the country overlapped. Members of the Mighty Avons showband remember country halls where people threw paraffin oil on the floor to make it slippy. Can you imagine what a fire hazard that was? In those days people smoked non-stop in the dancehalls. You could see a blue haze of smoke rising from the hall as the night went on.

The country was economically poor back then. The main form of transport was the bicycle. There were no radios or TVs and very few phones. In most parts of the country there was no electricity, either, which meant there could be no amplification. The early showbands all remember having to improvise. They ran their amplification off a bank of car batteries.

They brought glamour, excitement and travel. Any self-respecting showband had a luxury van in which they travelled six nights a week around the country. The late Gene Pitney once said that a definition of hell for him would be travelling for an eternity with the same musicians in the same van. I can understand what he meant.

One of the most famous men involved in showbusiness was Albert Reynolds, who subsequently became Taoiseach (Prime Minister) of Ireland. Albert left school at 17 and earned four pounds a week in his first job. In 1955 he worked for CIE in Roosky, where the priest formed a carnival committee. As well as entertaining the nation, showbands were a golden goose for churches and committees. The carnival committee in Roosky was highly successful and after a couple of years they paid off whatever debts had accrued. On one occasion, the parish priest, unusually, wanted no more money and so asked Albert to cancel the bands. It was too late to do so and Albert said he'd run the dances himself. The priest was delighted to get rid of the headache and handed everything over willingly to Albert. Out of that, he and his brother Jim eventually built an empire of 14 halls at the height of showband mania. Names like Cloudland, Jetland, and Roseland still revive dancing memories for those who frequented them. Albert admits that the skills he learned as a promoter for showbands stood him in good stead when he had to deal with the IRA, Sinn Féin and many Unionist politicians in later life. Striking a deal is still essential to progress.

Monsignor Horan, who built Knock airport, first made his money running the famous hall in Tooreen. It was alleged that the devil appeared in that ballroom. Nobody's too sure whether it actually happened or whether somebody put out a rumour to damage his business. A rival promoter was suspected of being behind it. Of course we can prove nothing and it was a good story anyway.

The Royal Showband were another band who pioneered new markets. The first showband record was released in 1963. Since there were no studios here, the Royal Showband had to go to England and record in the Abbey Road studios, where the Beatles recorded some of their greatest songs.

Mentioning the Beatles and showbands reminds me of a story Brendan Bowyer recalls clearly. The Royal Showband had just received the Carl Allen Award for being the best band in Britain and Ireland. As a result of that, they were touring England. When they came to play in Liverpool there was a young band keeping the audience entertained until the Royal came on stage. That young band was the early Beatles. Brendan Bowyer remembers how Lennon and McCartney came to look at their luxury wagon. They wondered aloud if they'd ever make enough money to buy a bus like that. Brendan advised them to keep writing their own songs and they might.

And so it was that the Royal Showband released their first record, a skiffle version of Eamonn O'Shea's *Come Down the Mountain Katie Daly*. The flip side was *I Heard the Bluebird Sing*, a duet featuring Tom Dunphy and Jim Conlon

When the showbands began to record, it highlighted the need for a recording studio here at home. Bill O'Donovan, who went on to become head of 2FM, cut his teeth in the Eamonn Andrews Studios. It was Bill who produced almost all the great records of the era.

Eurovision also gave an impetus to the band business. In 1965 Ireland entered for the first time, with Butch Moore singing *Walking the Streets in the Rain*. Dickie Rock with *Come back to Stay* and Seán Dunphy with *If I Could Choose*, all did well in successive years. Dana of course won the Eurovision in 1970 with *All Kinds of Everything*. That was the first time Ireland won it, but they went on to win it more times than any other country in Europe. We have a proud record there.

The Mighty Avons were the first showband to have a record in the top 10 in the British charts. Jim Reeves was a famous country singer who was adored in Ireland. When he died in a plane crash in 1964, the famous Eddie Masterson had a song written within five minutes on the inside of a Sweet Afton packet. He persuaded the Avons to record it and they eventually did. The *Tribute to Jim Reeves* went into the top 10 of the British pop charts.

Eddie Masterson, the man who got me involved in journalism, was at the centre of the entertainment industry in Dublin and was legendary among showband people and sporting people. He was in a position to help striving musicians. A young fellow would come up from the country looking for a job in a band and Eddie would say, "Paddy Cole's looking for a drummer. Go and tell him I sent you."

There was another occasion when a young journalist who was working for *New Spotlight* magazine was looking to get into mainstream journalism. Eddie wanted to help him. So he rang me and said, "You know Michael Hand in the *Independent*. Both of us do. I'm trying to get this man a job. They've given him a week to write for the *Evening Herald*. We have to get him good stories. I'll meet you tonight and we'll come up with some stories and give them to him so that he'll get the job." After a dance one night, we sat down, the two of us, and earmarked a few good stories. This young journalist wrote the stories and the stories made the front page of the *Evening Herald* on successive days. He was hired immediately. He went on to become an editor with the *Independent*. That's how Eddie helped people.

Eddie was also well known for playing tricks on people. There was a great drummer called Mickey O'Neill who used to play with the Capitol Showband. Mickey was up from Castleblayney. It was a wonderful, glamorous opportunity for him – being a drummer in the top showband in Ireland. The band had been off down in Killarney and had come back up to Dublin and were staying overnight in Barry's Hotel.

Eddie was sitting in the foyer of the hotel at about six o'clock in the morning. He called Mickey over and spoke to him sharply: "Listen, don't you ever use me like this again. There's a photo call for you in the Garden of Remembrance tomorrow morning at nine o'clock. I'll do it for you this time but if they ever want to send you messages like this again, get them to do it some other way. Be in your band suit at nine tomorrow morning outside the Garden of Remembrance."

Mickey was delighted. At that time, the Capitol Showband wore fluorescent green suits; they were always red or pale green – anything but what a normal man would be seen in. So Mickey got dressed in his pale, lime-green suit and walked to the Garden of Remembrance. The whole of Dublin was passing by looking at this eejit standing in a pale-green suit during rush hour at the gates of the Garden of Remembrance and everybody laughing at him.

Mickey was getting more embarrassed by the minute. And then Eddie walked past and said, "Did they not arrive yet?" And Mickey knew he'd been set up. That was Eddie, full of harmless genius.

There are many hilarious stories too about bands who bought their own records. They certainly weren't beyond doing it. The bottom of many a river was polluted by the vinyl records dumped in them by over enthusiastic showband managers wanting to make the elusive number one spot. It paid them to do it because a number one filled halls and coffers – in that order.

I don't know when it was that I realised how important showbands were to the people of Ireland. Like most things in life, I didn't appreciate them when they were in their hey-day. At least I didn't appreciate the significant contribution they were making.

By 1972 the showband era had peaked. That year I was in Nashville, Tennessee, in the company of Brian Coll, Ray Lynam and Larry Cunningham, Mick Clerkin, Pat Campbell from the BBC, Jimmy Magee, Seán Reilly and a few others who were fascinated by the connection between showbands and international country music.

Back then we loved our local heroes, but the international heroes were something special. People like Buck Owens, Merle Haggard, Charley Pride and George Jones were the heroes every self-respecting showband paid tribute to night after night on the stages around Ireland.

But in Nashville I discovered that the country stars admired Irish singers and saw Celtic music as the basis of their country-music industry.

For example, George Jones thought Ray Lynam's voice was one of the best he'd ever heard. Charley Pride wanted Brian Coll to go to America. He saw him as a natural successor to Slim Whitman. Pride's manager tried his best to encourage Brian to leave Ireland and work in Nashville.

Brian was doing so well at home that he couldn't take the risk. Nobody will ever know whether he would have made it in Nashville or not, but the country-music industry head-hunted him openly. It proved to me that our singers were as good as any in the world. That was one of the great contributions showbands made to the Irish music industry. It gave everybody confidence.

When the Royal Showband went to Las Vegas, it seemed it would be the end of them as an attraction at home. Yet to this day Brendan Bowyer can still draw crowds 30 years later when he returns from Las Vegas to tour Ireland.

Elvis Presley also admired the talents of the Royal Showband. Late at night he often went to see them perform after his own show. One of the highlights of the show was Brendan Bowyer doing an imitation of Elvis Presley. Elvis loved that part of the show.

There were, at one time, 600 full-time professional bands playing up and down the country. And a whole business built up around them, because it meant work for hairdressers, for people who provided minerals, and for fast-food people who catered for these big dances. There were more people employed in it than in the beef industry, which was supposed to be our number one industry at the time. And out of it came recording studios, radio stations and the infrastructure on which today's music industry is built.

Showbands gave a break and sometimes encouragement to musicians who later became famous in other forms of music. Van Morrison played in a showband and so did Rory Gallagher. Terry Wogan remembers that he was hooked on the glamour of showbusiness after he watched the Clipper Carlton play in Cobh. Phil Coulter got his early education working with the Capitol Showband. The Corrs' parents were part of a showband in Dundalk. Even Louis Walsh, the mogul of pop today, cut his teeth working with showbands. Daniel O'Donnell is one of the biggest attractions in America. His early days were spent with his sister Margo, pretending to play guitar in her band around the country. He himself went solo and is now one of the most respected artists in popular music anywhere. He'd be the first to admit it, that without showbands he would never have got a start. His manager, Seán Reilly, so important to his success, served his apprenticeship in the halcyon days of the showbands.

Showbands reflected the Ireland of the time. They were mainly Irish. They were mainly men, the exceptions being Margo, Eileen Reid, Eileen Kelly and Susan McCann, as well as Philomena Begley years afterwards. Their aim was to entertain. They're often denigrated now, because of their copycat style. Yet in the space of one decade they made over 2,000 records. Not all of them were original, but many of them stand up better than their pop counterparts in England do to this day.

The real gifts showbands left to the people who followed them were happy memories and self-confidence. Dickie Rock, Joe Dolan, Seán Dunphy and all the others were role models for young stars. They brought a sense of freedom and joy to the country. They showed the people of Ireland that another world of entertainment and glamour did exist.

The Church had its say though. Every Lent, dancing in Ireland stopped and showbands crossed to England and America to find work. Bands had to go away from home and leave their families for six weeks. It was unfair in many ways but that's how Irish society was in the 50s, 60s and indeed 70s.

As I've said, their main vocation in life was to entertain people. That they did night after night in a professional and wonderful way. It took talent, initiative, enthusiasm and stamina. The old motto for showbands was that people should go home happy and looking for more. It was summed up brilliantly in a phrase that has gone down in showband lore: "Whatever you do, send them home sweatin'."

Many of a certain generation will identify with the last dance of the night. The band working up to a musical frenzy, the men and the women charging across from their respective sides of the hall and hoping for one last dance and perhaps one new date. There's many a family that owes its existence to the showbands sending them home sweating. There's not a night goes by that I don't say a prayer for all those good people who taught me so much. It struck me recently that maybe it was their constant journeying with which I identified.

For those who lived through it, it was the best of all possible times. I know that it was the people in the showband industry that made it so. I'm thinking in particular of friends like Seán McGrade, Séamus McCusker, Peter Smith, Gene Stuart, Seán Reilly, Big Tom, Tony Loughman, Henry McMahon, Christy Gunn, Jim Aiken, Chris Roche, Matt Carroll, Con O'Mahony, Dermot O'Brien, Paddy Kennedy, Mick Nolan, Noel Carty, Donie Cassidy and Frank McCloon in Dublin. All of them accepted me and welcomed me into their ballrooms seven nights a week. I learned everything that was useful from those friends who were supposed to be "phoney" showbusiness people. Far from it, they were generous, open, charitable and very loyal.

Looking back, there is a solid connection to the showbands at every stage of my life. In return I hope I helped their careers. I had an expert ear for picking hit records throughout the 70s and 80s. I was also useful when called upon to write sleeve notes for their albums. I still help them and am occasionally asked to write sleeve notes for CDs. Joe Dolan said to me recently that if I knew as much about religion as I did about music, I'd have been Pope years ago.

The golden age of showbands began with the Clipper Carlton and who knows where it ended. It gave employment to thousands of people. The industry they founded grew in an entirely different direction and led to Thin Lizzie, Boomtown Rats, U2, Westlife, the Corrs, Boyzone, and all the other fantastically successful Irish artists around the world today. Many of the people who made the biggest contribution are forgotten. Rarely are they given the credit they deserve. It would be ungrateful of me not to remember the friends who made me what I am today.

Recently, Larry Cunningham summed it up to me brilliantly: "In the old days we used to play to 2,000 people with a wee, small amplifier of barely 200 watts. Everybody heard every word we said and sang and they remember the tunes to this day. Now we play to 200 people and use 2,000 watts. The sound is no better but the fun goes on."

If I was asked to say when the Golden Age declined, I would have to say it was when the Miami Showband were murdered. That's when the fun ended. The Miami massacre was tragic for a number of reasons, the main one being the death of three lovely, talented musicians – Fran O'Toole, Tony Geraghty and Brian McCoy. In the beginning, it was Dickie Rock and the Miami. Things moved on and we were coming to the end of the halcyon days of the showband era. Pop groups, ballad groups and folk groups took over. Pubs were replacing the ballrooms and the country was experiencing some prosperity. The world was a smaller place.

People went abroad on holidays. English newspapers were on sale. The BBC was available on televisions all over the country. Communication broadened minds. In Church, State, sport and entertainment the old order was passing. The 70s is thus important as a period of transition.

The Miami incident was a reminder to us that things were changing in politics, too, and that nothing was sacred. Showbands in the North brought all communities together. They crossed the sectarian divide.

Depending on the area, the bands played *God Save the Queen* or *The Soldier's Song*. They had both anthems in their repertoire. It was always a running joke in the bands. One of them on one occasion didn't know where they were. Half the band played *God Save the Queen* and, simultaneously, the other half played *The Soldier's Song* and both sides turned on them. That was the worst of all possible worlds.

The Miami was truly a mixed band. There were Catholics and Protestants in the band. There were Northerners and Southerners in the band. There was one from Cork and one from Ballymena. It was just about the most perfect mix you could get. If you were going to attack a band for sectarian reasons, the Miami was the worst choice you could make. They were young and fresh with no history behind them. Fran O'Toole was an up-and-coming young star, one of the new breed. He was writing his own material, performing his own songs. They were a perfect example of where music and Ireland were going. Furthermore, up until then, showbands were untouchable. In the worst days in the early 70s, when tit-for-tat murders paralysed the North, the bands never stopped going there because the Northerners always supported the bands. Bands loved going there. They always said the Northern audiences were special because they really appreciated the chance to enjoy themselves.

The Miami were travelling home from Banbridge the night they were killed, July 31, 1975. The full story has never been told. But briefly, they were stopped on the road outside Banbridge, by what seemed to be a legitimate UDR road check. They were taken out of the van because somebody with an evil mind decided to set up the Miami as bomb carriers. The plan was that this bogus road check would put a bomb in the Miami van which would explode somewhere down the road. It would then be said that showbands from the Republic were smuggling explosives across the Border. That was the evil plan. In fact, the bomb went off while the bogus UDR group was planting it in the van. One of the band members who survived, Stephen Travers, to this day insists that the leader was not a bogus UDR man, but a soldier with an upper-class English accent. In other words, it wasn't just a group of terrorists who did it. Some of them were terrorists, but they were helped by members of the security forces.

The bomb went off and three of the band were blown to pieces. Others were badly injured but survived. Some of those planting the bomb were also blown up. There's an amazing sequel to the night of terror. One of the people tried for their murders was identified by his spectacles. The force of the blast blew his glasses off and a small fragment of the lens was found at the scene. Even in those days, forensics proved that it was a very rare prescription. There were only a few of them in Northern Ireland, all of them easily identifiable. They were thus able to convict him from that fragment of his spectacles.

For me, the Miami massacre was the day the music died. It was the day innocence died. The showband scene never recovered. Many of the big bands stopped going north. The entertainment scene changed completely. The innocence of the whole showband era, which had been thriving since 1955, was now sullied. Everything changed and moved on. It was a sad time which brought home to me that life changes us whether we know it or not.

Part of my job then was to help with the funerals of both Tony Geraghty and Fran O'Toole. Fran O'Toole's wife and their two little children were devastated and emigrated shortly afterwards. I remember going to their house in Bray in the weeks that followed and finding a family utterly paralysed by grief. I wondered then, as I do now, whether those who commit murder ever think of the grief-stricken relatives. Fran's parents and brother also suffered greatly and all of them died too young.

It was devastating for the McCoy and Geraghty families, too. Their lives changed forever on that fateful July night. Maybe the 30th anniversary commemoration ceremony we had in 2005 brought some healing and a little closure to the whole sad tragedy. With the Miami massacre the last untouchable group fell victim to the terrorists' evil. There were no more boundaries after that and so many died needlessly. That's what war does. It destroys the most artistic, the most innocent. It destroys even those whose only ambition in life is to make other people happy.

The showband age is over and gone forever. It's nothing but a memory. When I was a young priest I went to dances seven nights a week in Dublin. I thought it would never end. But it did end. Life moves on and there's nothing we can do about it.

The showband era brought Ireland from dancing at the crossroads to taking their place proudly on the stage of Carnegie Hall in New York. There's so much more to be said about the showband era but my purpose is to show that these were brilliant, intuitive businessmen and entertainers who did much to brighten dark days. These were the people with whom I was lucky enough to mix from an early age. They taught me so many skills that I can never thank them enough. It's impossible to name names, but my closest and best friends in life are still the people who travel the roads as many nights as they can making a living simply by making people happy.

CHAPTER 8

MAN OF THE WORLD

In 1974 the *Sunday World* came on the scene as a loud, brash, Irish tabloid. By today's standards those back issues are as dull as ditchwater, but they were gaudy and controversial back then. The late Hugh McLoughlin and Gerry McGuinness did everything they could to grab headlines. One of their most famous ploys was to publish deliberately provocative articles which would be sent round the country in time to be condemned by priests on Sunday. Saturday evening Masses are not favoured by Sunday newspaper editors. Occasionally they hit the jackpot if someone of the stature of Bishop Lucey of Cork ranted about "the filth" in the *Sunday World*. It was the best publicity possible and went a long way to saving the *World* in its early, shaky days.

A few weeks after it started I was visited in Mount Argus by Joe Kennedy, the first editor of the *Sunday World*, and Kevin Marron, who was one of the shrewdest and best journalists I ever knew. He had a genius for recognising an angle to hang a story on.

They asked me to write for the paper every week. I declined, mainly because I was too busy making *The Cross* a success but also because I was afraid to risk writing for a hard-nosed red-top. The only way I could get out of it was to promise I would consider the offer if I ever left *The Cross*.

Two years later, I had moved on from *The Cross*, had left Mount Argus to live in Wicklow, and was lecturing, editing and producing in The Catholic Communications Institute, Booterstown. I was still going to dances every night and was writing a regular pop music feature for the *Sunday Independent* as well as working on radio and television.

The phone call came. "Kevin Marron here. Now that you're not doing *The Cross*, you have no excuse. When can you start writing for us?"

I thought of every excuse in the book but two stood out. I really didn't feel comfortable writing as a priest for the *Sunday World*, given the kind of stories they did and pictures they highlighted. The joke at the time was that in most papers you had to read between the lines to find the truth, but in the *Sunday World* you had to read between the legs!

Secondly, I didn't think I would be able to turn out an article every week.

Kevin was devastatingly simple in his reply: "I am offering you a pulpit every week to nearly one million readers, most of whom don't go to Church, and you say you won't talk to them. What sort of priest do you call yourself? And anyway, try it for a month and if it doesn't work we can both walk away from it."

I had no answer. I knew he was right.

The *Sunday World* has been part of my life now for exactly 30 years. Every Sunday since July 1976, there I am with a frozen, paper smile: *Father Brian's Little Bit of Religion*. That's well over 1,600 articles (I've often had more than one piece per issue) and nearly two-million words. It has mothered 10 books, endless interviews, triggered heart attacks in over-anxious bishops and, I hope, has been a lifeline for those on the margins.

It was Kevin Marron who thought of the title. He didn't waste time on long briefings. He kept it all in his brain.

Once, when he was a feature writer on the *Sunday Press*, he did an in-depth article about my work around the dancehalls of Dublin. He came to Mount Argus to interview me. He drank cup after cup of home-brewed coffee, talked to me, listened to me, argued with me, but never once took a note. He sent a photographer to take pictures of me working the halls, but I dreaded what he would write. It was serious stuff and a body could end up with a single ticket to Africa for stepping too far out of line.

I needn't have worried; he wrote one of the fairest and most accurate articles any one ever did. And it was littered with quotes – every single one of them accurate.

So I knew how he operated. When I went to him to discuss what sort of column he wanted, his instructions were so precise that I think of them every time I sit down to write for the *World*.

"You can write about anything except religion. Write about human beings and the struggles they have, and that's all there is to religion. A little bit of religion is all we need," he said. He stopped for breath. His eyes lit up and his dishevelled hair seemed to stand on end. "That's what we'll call it: *A Little Bit of Religion.*" That was the end of the discussion. 30 years and four editors later, the philosophy and the title remain the same.

Gerry McGuinness wondered what I should be paid. I didn't want money. I have a vow of poverty as a member of a religious order and personal money doesn't worry me. Like all Religious, if I left in the morning, I wouldn't have a penny to my name. I'm not putting on the poor mouth. I am well cared for now – though for years we lived in dirty, demeaning surroundings. As Fr Edmund Burke – what an appropriate name for a man who was an expert journalist as well – an elderly Passionist renowned for being tight, once explained to me: "In our day, they taught us to be mean and called it poverty."

Gerry and I settled on £30 a week to be used on petrol, post and secretarial expenses. That's what I still get today. Later the *Sunday World* gave me the use of a car, which was the best payment possible – I could now get rid of my little Honda 50 motorcycle.

In 30 years I've had only one serious disagreement with the *Sunday World* and it certainly wasn't about money. They treat me well in other ways and when I was raising funds for Mount Argus Restoration Fund throughout the 80s, I couldn't have done it without the *Sunday World*. I have no complaints at all.

Yet when I began writing for the *Sunday World*, not many of my Passionist family were in agreement. That was understandable since I had reservations myself. The provincial gave his permission, reluctantly, but it is to his credit that he allowed me to write at all.

Initially I used the letters CP, which represent Congregation of the Passion or Passionist after my name; I thought it might be good PR for the order. How wrong can you be? After a few weeks a group of priests based in Mount Argus told me that I was disgracing the name of

Passionist by writing for the *Sunday World*. They did not want to be associated with such a scandalous paper. Some told me to stop writing for it and others insisted that I not use the letters CP after my name so that they would not be part of such a "scandalous rag in any way". That's why I've never used CP in *A Little Bit of Religion* since.

What I say in the *Sunday World* is what Brian D'Arcy thinks. I don't speak on behalf of the Church, or on behalf of the Passionists, or on behalf of the *Sunday World*. I write for those who read the paper, in a way they'll identify with, and about topics they are interested in.

Catholic Church authorities did, at one stage, go to my provincial arguing that since I am not a recognised theologian, all my articles for the *Sunday World* should be vetted by selected theologians before publication.

The provincial asked me what we should do. I told him I wasn't writing for a Catholic paper or indeed a Catholic audience. I write for all readers of the *Sunday World*. Some of them are Catholics, some are not, some of them have no religion at all. If the archbishop wants a Catholic article, for Catholic readers only, he should have his own publication. I'm a priest but I'm also a journalist hired specifically to share my opinions.

I suggested that my provincial ask him to write to me personally, if he had any further difficulties about it. I never heard any more about it.

It is up to others to assess the impact of my presence in the *Sunday World*. For the first 10 years, every time I was interviewed, the same old question was put to me: "Why do you write for that rag?"

I write for the *Sunday World* simply because it is the place a priest should be. It is a special skill writing for a tabloid paper. The language has to be simple and direct. Sentences must be short. The story has to flow. The theory was brilliantly summed up by our rival *News of the World* in its slogan: All human life is there.

Any priest should be able to write an occasional article for a broadsheet, where there is time and space to develop a line of thought. That's not a luxury we have in tabloids.

A priest should write for the *Sunday World* for another reason. There are people who read that paper who never darken the door of a church. Furthermore many younger people get it and selectively read it for sport, fashion or pop. I don't claim they all read my column. But it's there and they have a chance to read it. As a priest I have to be comfortable in the market place.

Every week I get letters from people who are reading my article for the first time. They say it was a godsend to them. God can use people like me to be a voice of compassion and encouragement.

More and more I find complete strangers approaching me to thank me for being there and for what I say. They invariably tell me they read it now because their parents used to read it when they were young. More and more say it's the only contact they have with a God they can identify with. They feel I am someone like themselves struggling to find a place in an often unfriendly Church.

The late Cardinal Ó Fiaich was the only member of the hierarchy who understood why I wrote the way I did. I never once met him without taking away some sense that I was doing a good thing for the Church. It was never better exemplified than when the Pope came to Ireland in 1979.

Whenever I met the cardinal at football matches, which was where I met him most often, he'd discuss the article in that day's paper. He used to confide that he couldn't be seen buying the *Sunday World*, but his housekeeper or driver always bought one for him. He often told me I was saying the very things he'd like to say but couldn't. His favourite encouragement was, "For God's sake, keep writing for your people. You have a whole diocese of your own out there. Keep telling them they don't have to be perfect to be loved by God."

When I was well established in the *World*, he invited me for lunch one day. Cardinal Ó Fiaich was sounding me out, or maybe filling me in. I can't reveal details but the gist was that I should think about grooming myself for consideration as a bishop. He said, "The *Sunday World* isn't the best place to be noticed by the nuncio. Do you not think it might be better to stop writing for them?"

He saw the look of horror on my face.

As a final parting shot I added, "Anyway, to be a bishop now you have to agree that artificial contraception is intrinsically evil, be against married priests and not even speak about women priests. And you have to be passed by Opus Dei. On that score I'll be lucky to get a Christian burial, never mind be a bishop."

The two of us laughed our heads off and went back to the serious stuff – who'd win the Ulster Championship. We agreed it wouldn't be Fermanagh anyway.

Shortly afterwards I was invited for tea with the Papal Nuncio in his Cabra residence in Dublin. It was interesting, but as I left, the nuncio firmly told me that what we had discussed was to remain confidential or, as he put it, "in perpetuum" forever. Obviously I have to respect that confidence but what I can say is that he and the cardinal had been talking and I can safely say that I will never be a bishop – thank God.

Not every cleric had the grace or the vision of Cardinal Ó Fiaich.

During the 80s, in particular, I seem to have been public enemy number one in the mind of many clerics, because I was writing for the *Sunday World*. One priest in the North of Ireland was prepared to take his anger at me out on my family, which is always difficult. I was to do a relative's wedding. Everything had been arranged but when I drove up from Dublin it must have dawned on him who I was. He asked to make sure.

"Are you the renegade who writes for the *Sunday World*?" That's a difficult one to answer. Say yes and you allow yourself to be called a renegade. Say no and it's a lie. So I agreed that I was the journalist who wrote for the paper as well as being the parish priest and rector of Mount Argus.

"Well, you'll never stand on my altar," he huffed. Remember this was the day of the wedding and the groom was out in the church waiting on me to officiate. At the time I was timid enough to back down. And as a matter of canonical fact, a parish priest has to give his express permission to the priest who does the wedding for it to be valid in the eyes of the Church.

I asked if I could concelebrate the Mass. "Did you not hear me?" he barked. "You'll never stand on my altar. If I had my way you wouldn't even sit in my church." That's the kind of thuggish behaviour that has destroyed the Catholic Church in Ireland. The heresy of *my* altar, *my* church wasn't lost on the guests.

I sat in the church. My family were at first worried that I must be leaving the priesthood or be in some kind of trouble, and then furious that he got away with it. They were even more disgusted when he came to do the wedding. He kept asking the groom his name. That's the extent of the interest he had. Three times he shouted at the groom to speak up. He was more concerned about getting at me than he was with the couple's welfare. It is a classic example of how we priests abuse power and use sacraments as weapons. People today would recognise the ignorant bully for what he was and wouldn't put up with it.

I was regularly refused permission to do funerals of friends or even to concelebrate, but I survived and, to be fair, those priests were in the minority. Most priests tolerated me with courtesy and a few were kind and encouraging.

The point I'm making is that writing for the *Sunday World* has defined the kind of priest I have become. The fact that I resolutely wrote for the marginalised meant that I myself became marginalised. It caused me more suffering than anything else in life because I'm not a natural rebel. But I know the kind of priest I have to be and the kind of apostolate I have to work at.

When I was working in the Dublin archdiocese in the 70s and 80s, I was a representative on both the National and Diocesan Council of Priests. That's where I encountered the career clerics. They had a prudent solution to everything but rarely thought of the pastoral needs of their people.

There were outstanding exceptions, many of whom are now married and referred to as "ex-priests". There is no such thing as an ex-priest: once a priest always a priest. They are good men who were forced to resign from the active ministry, usually because they fell in love with a woman.

I usually found myself on the pastoral side of the argument and because I wrote for the paper was never really trusted by my fellow priests, even though I never, ever broke a confidence.

Ironically, when I started going to meetings of the National Union of Journalists I was treated with great suspicion by fellow journalists who regarded me as a spy for the bishops. They wrote about me as the acceptable face of the Catholic Church. Little did they realise that I wasn't accepted by most of them, either.

The best gift I got from the column was the letters from readers. That's what kept me going for 30 years. For most of that time I have continued to get an average of 100 letters per week. Many are serious, difficult and urgent pastoral problems. Others just want to complain. A few want to share thoughts on where Ireland and the Catholic Church are heading.

I've been educated by the people of the nation and no university can compare. I know I'm privileged because no other cleric has had such an opportunity to know exactly what the people of Ireland think. What I get is a broad spectrum of advice and opinion. I get people who share their secrets and their real opinions with me. If I went to their houses I'd most likely be told what they thought I wanted to hear. There is a huge difference.

Through the column I was able to predict that the sex-abuse scandal would be seismic here. After Brendan Smyth, many sat back content that the bulk of the bad news had passed. From my letters I knew it was only the tip of the iceberg. When I warned senior members of the hierarchy of the problem, I was accused of being sensationalist

During the 30 years in which I've been working for the *Sunday World*, one of the most unheralded yet one of the most useful parts of the apostolate was being able to help the poor. I did it through the Helping Hand Fund and it was part of the column for most of its existence.

It began in December 1977 in tragic circumstances. I wrote an article, based on a true story, outlining what happened to a young mother and her children. I began by saying, "There are times as a priest when my faith in God is put to its limits. This is especially true when little babies have to suffer." And then I took the readers through, from memory, a few meetings I'd had with a girl I called Marie, which wasn't her real name.

As is often the case, Marie's life story seemed to go from bad to worse. As I remember it, she was one of 10 children whose mother died giving birth to the youngest of those children. Her father did a good job with the children, but it meant that money was scarce and there wasn't much time for normal family love and attention.

Marie had to leave school as soon as the law would allow and go to work.

It often happens that those who missed out on personal affection will get overly attached to the first person who shows them kindness, real or imagined. So, at 18 she met a boy who was six years older and gave her the special attention she craved. In the early days he was the perfect boyfriend with charm, good looks, and, as far as Marie was concerned, a deep love for her. She was not from Dublin but he came down to visit her town almost every weekend.

Travelling didn't suit either of them so Marie moved to Dublin. She fell for his charm and wit and powers of persuasion and after she came to Dublin, he soon persuaded her that in the big city two could live as cheaply as one. In those days it was not the norm for couples to live together so soon.

Marie got pregnant, which didn't go down well with her family either. He was good to her during that pregnancy, but soon the bachelor life was more attractive than life with Marie. Marie made all the excuses that women usually do, blaming bad company, her own inability to be an attractive person, the arrival of the child, everything except her husband.

By the time they were two years married he had lost all interest in her and, as she put it, it was "just the time when I needed him most because I was pregnant again." She pleaded with him to stay in with her, even one night a week. But he wouldn't. He went out every night drinking with the boys and furthermore, drank every penny he earned.

There were many nights when Marie sat at home, sick and pregnant and without a slice of bread in the house.

She admitted that when the baby was born she was weak and sick and had no money. "We had rows every night because he'd come home footless drunk at four or five in the morning." He frequently brought all his drinking pals with him and then would drag Marie and the baby out of bed so that he and his drunken pals could sleep off their drunkenness before heading out again. Obviously she had no family of her own to turn to, but his mother took her in. He inveigled her away from there with the usual promise that he would mend his ways.

It was then that Marie really suffered. I quoted her words. "One night he and two of his mates came home at three in the morning. He ordered me out of bed but because I was pregnant I was slow getting up. He dragged me out of the bed and after he had given me a few punches in the back, he made me cook food for him and his friends. There was very little

My father and mother, Hugh and Ellie D'Arcy, and baby Marie

The original
homestead in
Bellanaleck.
Mammy and Joan
in the doorway.
Daddy's bike
taking pride of
place!

My First Communion
Day, 1952. That's me
on the right. Gaby
Maguire (left) and
Matt Snow are
alongside. Peter
Nolan, Bridie Maguire
and Eugene McHugh
are at the back

The D'Arcy family in 1963: (from left) my brother, Gaby, myself, my mother, Ellie, my sister Marie, my father, Hugh, and my sister Joan

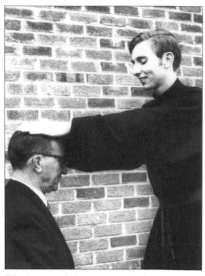

Blessing my father on my Ordination Day, 1969

The D'Arcy siblings: myself, Marie, Joan and Gaby – with a photo of Mammy and Daddy on the wall

Daddy, shortly before he died, cutting the cake on his 70th birthday

With the nephews and nieces (from left) Gerard D'Arcy, Eileen Brogan, Adrian, Margaret, Carmel and Sinéad Lunney and Desmond D'Arcy

The prison like corridor – my introduction
to Passionist life at The Graan

Profession Day, 1963,
with my mother and
father

The Godfather! – 1964

The fight to save Mount Argus

Devenish Island in Fermanagh

Preaching at the Grotto in Lourdes, 1978

Studying at the Franciscan School of Theology in San Francisco with Dr Kenan Osborne, 1981

Light at the end of the corridor – Mount Argus, Dublin

The men behind the wire! Watching an Ulster football final in Clones, Co Monaghan, with Cardinal Tomás Ó Fiaich, Bishop Edward Daly and Liam Mulvihill (centre rear)

Cardinal Tomás Ó Fiaich and myself blessing the shrine of Blessed Charles of Mount Argus, October 1988, and (facing page) on my way out of Mount Argus

Showbiz from an early age – backstage with (from left) Fr Michael Cleary, my friend Michael Carroll and Butch Moore (Capitol Showband) in 1966

On my Ordination Day, 20th December 1969, with Eddie Masterson (left) and Brian Coll

November 1970, with Fr Edmund Burke CP – admiring my first edition as editor of *The Cross*, with the Beatles on the cover

Still friends after *that* "memorable" *Late Late Show*. Bishop Cathal Daly and myself at the launch of his autobiography

Man of peace: with Bill Clinton at the Clinton Centre, Enniskillen

During the visit of Bill and Hillary Clinton to the Clinton Centre

Face to face with the Duke (not John Wayne!)

President Mary McAleese, Dr Martin McAleese, Jimmy Magee and myself at the special tribute to the showband generation hosted by Áras an Uachtaráin

Blessing the big top for Fossett's Circus

in the house but I gave them everything that was there. As soon as I gave him the coffee, he lifted the mug and poured it over my head and face.

"He said I had brought him bad luck because he had lost £20 on a horse that day. There I was, pregnant and trying to look after a young child without a penny in the flat, and he was gambling £20 on a horse.

"Then he said to his mates that he was going to show them what he thought of his wife and child. He pulled me across the room by my hair and tied me to a chair and began beating me. He took the stockings from the little baby's foot and lit a cigarette and after every drag of the cigarette, he and his mates thought it was funny to touch the little baby's feet with the lit cigarette. He kept beating me and asked a few of his friends to do the same."

Marie's screams were piercing, and luckily for her, disturbed three men who lived in nearby flats. They came in and rescued her and held the husband and his friends until the guards arrived and arrested them. By now the little child was screaming in agony from the burns on her foot. That little baby was in hospital for 15 weeks because of the abuse her father and his friends had inflicted on her. Mercifully, the husband was sent to prison.

At that time Marie had come to me in Mount Argus looking for help. She knew me from the *Sunday World* and had travelled quite a distance. I gave her whatever money I had, which wasn't a lot, to keep her going through her pregnancy and asked the St Vincent de Paul to help her.

She came back to me again when she was eight months pregnant. On that occasion she had been put out of her flat by the landlord because she couldn't pay the rent. Again I was able to help her in a small way and she got another flat. But sometimes the hand of fate is indefensibly cruel. Her flat was broken into and she was attacked again, this time by three robbers, even though she had nothing in the house to give them. That wasn't unusual in the Dublin of the time. There were flat complexes in my parish and the poverty there was awful. Gangs ruled these flats. The Corporation abandoned them to the criminal element who took over the flats and rented them to tenants they thought should get them. They demanded a weekly rent for the Corporation flats. There were so many of them at the time that the Corporation seemed to do nothing about it.

These were the kind of people who assaulted Marie. They beat her, kicked her, and left her hysterical. One of them even stabbed her in the back and she had to get 19 stitches in the wound.

That night she was taken to hospital and the baby was induced. And this was the bit that broke my heart. The little baby's legs were damaged because of the beatings Marie had received.

That was the story I wrote at the end of November. My main task was to find a place for Marie and her two babies to live where she would be safe and where she and her children could have time to heal from the attacks.

I wrote about it in the *Sunday World*, not because I was looking for money, which I wasn't, but merely to expose the kind of scandal which was going on but rarely reported.

The reaction was amazing. The following week so much post came to the *Sunday World* that two of the staff in the offices in Terenure, where the *Sunday World* was based at that time, had to work full-time opening and trying to acknowledge the letters. I can still remember Sophie Hunt and myself opening sacks of mail in her office. Sophie was highly organised and was secretary to the managing director of the paper. On many an occasion during that week, she spent all of her lunch time voluntarily opening and helping me with the mail.

Thousands of letters came in. People from all over Ireland and England sent money. There were children who sent 10-pence coins. Most people actually sent £10. And two anonymous letters had £500 in each of them. When all the money was counted there was over £7,000 received; that was the beginning of the Helping Hand.

At that point Micheline McCormack, who was the star writer for the *Sunday World* then, came on board. She had wonderful contacts and took it as her personal task every Christmas to raise thousands of pounds. Those were poor days in Ireland and people wrote in asking for help to put food on their tables at Christmas. Hampers of food were sent out to many of them.

Later still when Bryan Kelly joined the staff and worked full-time on the Helping Hand, he did Trojan work helping to furnish flats, pay rent for people and work with voluntary agencies to make sure that the poor we worked with were looked after. Many of them wrote to me confidentially and there was then and still is a number of people who will write their stories only to me because they know they will remain confidential.

The *Sunday World* set up a trust fund for Marie and she was able to get a regular income for as long as the money lasted. Marie still lived in fear. She dreaded the return of the people who beat her up, but because of the fund she settled and went off into life.

When she reached some level of comfort and safety, naturally enough, I never heard from her again. But her story was the reason the Helping Hand was founded.

The readers of the *Sunday World* were all extremely generous. I have no idea how much we handed out but at one stage it was in the region of £60,000 a year. It was largely unheralded but is something I am very proud of.

I know for certain that Micheline McCormack and Bryan Kelly deserve all the credit in later years. They were wonderful people while they were at the *Sunday World* and I could never thank them enough for their generosity and for their Christian spirit in helping so many people. Not too many people ever saw the *Sunday World* in that light and it wasn't a part of our work we highlighted.

Many of the showband people appreciated the work we did and were extremely supportive. The Memories ran a gig for at least 10 years and raised thousands of pounds. They did it on their own initiative and all I had to do was appear at the gig and give it a little mention in my column.

There was so much goodness harnessed by the Helping Hand Fund. Marie's sufferings were unbelievably cruel but I hope that she got some consolation from the fact that not only was she helped, but because she was brave enough to share her story, thousands of people had a Christmas dinner for two decades afterwards. It's just a little corner of good work that was done and harnessed through *A Little Bit of Religion* and the *Sunday World*.

One humorous little footnote to it all was that the late Hugh McLoughlin, who was the initial managing director of the *Sunday World*, really hadn't much time for anything in the paper that didn't produce money. Initially, he was of the opinion that *A Little Bit of Religion* was a useless column in his paper. He could never see how it would sell papers.

His attitude changed completely the day he came in and saw 1,000 letters bulging with money scattered across the floor of his office with Sophie Hunt and myself down on our knees opening them and counting the notes. His eyes came out like gobstoppers and as I looked up at him he said, "I'll admit I was wrong. I didn't think there was that much money in religion."

It was then the paper discovered that *A Little Bit of Religion* certainly pulled its weight in the sales department as well. And that's the only reason my column has appeared for over 30 years in the *Sunday World*. I am there because what I write attracts people to buy the paper. There is no greater satisfaction for a journalist than that.

Many people still ask me what happened to Marie. The truthful answer is that I don't know and there's no need for me to know. As long as she was able to find her way in life, I was quite happy to have helped her put her foot on the first rung.

CHAPTER 9

THE GREAT AND THE GOOD

When I became parish priest of Mount Argus, my district in the parish had lovely, solid, working-class people. The parish was split by Lower Kimmage Road and the people on either side were different in so many essential ways. I couldn't believe how effective a border a busy road could be. Mount Argus became a parish only in 1974 when they took bits from other, existing parishes. As a result it was hard work building a community. Initially, we opened a new community centre in the heart of the parish, well away from the church, which wasn't the natural centre anyway. I also tried to visit their homes as much as I could. Every Lent, on Ash Wednesday, I began knocking on the doors of every home in my district. Every September I did it again.

I brought Communion to the sick every Friday morning. This meant that I was on every street, every week. People saw me regularly and I became as familiar as a bad habit. I wanted to attend the sick every week rather than every month because I've always believed the prayers of the sick are extremely powerful. It meant the rest of the people waited for me and made arrangements for all their needs and appointments. I was flying around the country at that time too and they needed to be convinced I really was their priest. Or maybe it was just guilt on my part. It also meant I got to know the people well. And that they got to know me well. That was crucial.

As in any parish, I had the usual selection of family problems and domestic rows to deal with. Before I went there I had no experience of parish life and never thought I would work in a parish. It was a whole new life which I had to learn. Even the civil service of running a parish – marriage papers, baptisms and finances – was a new experience for me. Naturally I talked to other priests who worked in the parishes all their lives because it would take me a lifetime to learn what they knew instinctively.

One of them offered an unusual piece of advice. "If there's a row in a house, the one who shouts loudest is the one most listened to." He explained, "Go into a house. If there's a row going on, you shout louder than anybody else and they'll listen, but if you go in nice and quietly, they will shout you down." I thought he was mad.

There was one house I went to which was notorious for family rows. When I saw windows broken when I was passing, I knew there had been a row and I'd have to call.

I got a call from the woman of the house one Sunday evening. There were cups flying and children crying. The couple had a big family and it was really a pathetic scene. Children whimpered in the corners, the older ones ran out and the couple fired abuse at each other. I decided to follow my priest friend's advice and started to shout at the top of my voice: "Sit down you. Take your chair over there. I'm going to listen to her story and then I'll listen to your story. And if either of you interferes or butts in, I'll thump yez, right?" Not my usual style, I admit, and I wasn't sure what the reaction would be.

Extraordinary quietness came to the house, if not to the priest.

I said to the wife, "What's the problem?"

And she said, "He's the effing problem, Father."

"Why is he the problem?"

"You know he hasn't been here for the last six months and you've been giving me money to keep me going, so nobody knows it better. Now he's arrived back yesterday. His sister brought him back. I call her Elizabeth Taylor. She has three husbands and married to none of them. And she's trying to tell me how to run my life. She brought him back to me and do you know what she said to me? She said to me, I should be damn glad to have him, he's a good-looking man. And anybody would be happy with him."

The children were relaxing a little at this stage. She ended the attack with real style.

"Him, good-lookin'? Sure, if me arse had a nose, it would be better lookin' than him!"

At which stage, I collapsed laughing, I couldn't stop. Then she started to laugh. Then he started to laugh. And the row ended and I suggested to him that peace had reigned for six months when he wasn't at home and maybe he'd do better to go someplace else and let peace reign again.

He packed his bag and went away and that was the end of the row. In fairness the family did well afterwards. So that's one way to settle domestic rows. You won't find it in any book. And you won't find that sort of practical psychology either. It might not always work, but on a frustrating Sunday evening it was all I had to offer. The shouting worked and listening also worked. You have to have a sense of humour and you learn to accept people where they are at, rather than where you'd want them to be.

Humour got me through many a sticky parish situation and humour is always a great leveller. In showbusiness circles the humour was wicked. Eddie Masterson was known as the master, and so he was. He had friends everywhere but was very close to the Reynolds family. He often went to the Reynolds house for weekends. Kathleen and Albert would tell you to this day that he taught their youngest son how to back horses and gamble. That young man is now one of the major players in the stock market on Wall Street, which in its own way is the ultimate in gambling.

Eddie knew Albert from showband days. Albert left showbusiness and entered politics in the 1970s. Quite quickly he became Minister for Posts and Telegraphs at a time when a phone couldn't be got in Ireland.

The first morning Albert was Minister, the postman arrived at his home outside Longford with a huge, brown envelope. The postman was really embarrassed because he would have called at the Reynolds home for years. He apologised to Albert before he even entered the kitchen.

"I'm sorry, I know you're my boss now, but there's no stamp on this big envelope. I have to ask you for it because I don't know whether it's you or me is being watched. I hope you don't mind."

Albert said, "It's no problem. How much is it?"

"Fifty pence."

"No problem. You're doing your job right. That's what you have to do.

If there's no stamp on it, I have to pay the same as everybody else."

In his head he was wondering who the hell was sending such an important-looking envelope without a stamp.

Kathleen and himself sat down together and opened this big envelope. They fished out a note written on a Sweet Afton cigarette packet and discovered a message scrawled across it. "Congratulations. This is the last one you'll have to pay for. Eddie."

Albert went on to do a good job as Minister. He became known as the Minister for phones. It's hard to believe now but there was a two-year waiting list for phones in the 1970s. Albert did one of his famous deals with the unions and got a system that was effective and acceptable. By the time the Pope came to Ireland, phones were readily available.

Maeve Binchy remembers in a humorous way how getting telephones to Ireland was the greatest miracle the Pope performed while he was here. In fact Albert Reynolds had much more to do with it than the Pope.

The visit of Pope John Paul II to Ireland was a wonderful occasion for the ordinary people of Ireland at that time. It is probably the most exciting memory of my entire life and yet now it's sadness which predominates. In a way these pages are a reflection on the legitimate reasons for sadness. How did it happen that the greatest occasion in the Church's history in this country dissipated so quickly and with such bitterness?

In my mind's eye I can still see the million-plus people stretched across the plains of the Phoenix Park, all neatly fenced into manageable squares on a beautiful day when the atmosphere was as close to heavenly as you can get on this earth. Out of the sky an Aer Lingus jumbo seemed to be within touching distance of the congregation. We knew then that the Pope had arrived. It was the first time in our long history that a Pope had visited our little island. Feelings of genuine pride and gratitude welled up. It seemed as if the Church in Ireland would forever be the bastion of everything good and moral.

I was around the high altar for all of the Pope's Mass and had my own jobs to do.

Afterwards one of the most embarrassing moments of my life took place. When I thought the Pope had left, I went underneath the high altar where there was supposed to be a toilet. A young guard showed me where to go and I burst in with great relief, if you'll pardon the pun.

What I didn't realise was that it wasn't a toilet at all. I had instead gatecrashed the Pope's lunch. Sitting at the table with the Pope were my very good friends the late Jack and Maureen Lynch, President Hillery and his wife, Cardinal Ó Fiaich and Archbishop Ryan. The latter was none too pleased to see me.

At that moment the Pope's minder, Archbishop Marcinkus, came in and almost forcibly took the Pope away to put him on a helicopter. In those days helicopters couldn't fly at night, so timing was crucial. The Pope gave me one of those wincing looks as he brushed passed me in the doorway. He looked furious.

Cardinal Ó Fiaich, being the gentleman he was, invited me in and made me sit down in the Pope's chair. "It's the nearest you'll ever get to being a Pope, Brian, so you might as well enjoy it," he laughed.

The Pope hadn't been able to finish his lunch. Jack Lynch said it would be a waste of good food not to eat it, so that's what I did. I ate the remains of the Pope's dinner and enjoyed every mouthful of it. It's not everyone can say he stole the Pope's dinner – literally took the bit out of his mouth.

Cardinal Ó Fiaich was always most appreciative of my efforts in helping to persuade the young to come out for the Pope, even if I failed to impress the other archbishop or even the Pope.

As it happened, I was also on duty in Galway the next day and in Maynooth on Monday morning. At the Galway Youth Mass the Pope uttered the phrase, "Young people of Ireland, I love you." I could never understand the incredible reaction it got that morning in Galway and to this day I don't understand why it became the central phrase of the Papal visit. What sort of a Pope would he be not to love young people? Yet it proved to me that John Paul II was a masterly showman who knew exactly how to enthral an audience. It's a rare and precious gift.

The Pope went from Ireland straight to America. Those of you who were around at that time will surely remember the sight of the Aer Lingus jumbo leaving Shannon and heading into the great west for another first, the Pope on tour in America.

I went to America myself not long after the Pope's visit. Being Irish we were able to bask in the glory of a successful Papal visit. The Irish visit was even the talk of America.

This time I was on my way to Nashville but on the way back I called into Washington just to see how Capitol Hill worked. I had an ulterior motive. I was a great fan of the Kennedy family. By now Ted Kennedy, the last of the three brothers, was everybody's hot tip to be the next Democratic president of the United States.

Getting through to Senator Kennedy was much more difficult than getting through to the Pope. I know because I got through to both of them. Before I arrived in Washington I made plans to get an interview with Ted Kennedy. Seán Donlon was the ambassador at the time and a few people in Government here made arrangements for me to meet the ambassador in America. I was assured he would look after me and if anybody could get an interview with Kennedy, it would be Seán Donlon.

The Washington office, in typical Irish fashion, told me to come over and they'd see what they could do. I took that to mean the deal was done.

Once in Washington I tried the highest diplomatic avenue that I could, without much success. Instead I got to talk to Tip O'Neill. He was leader of the house at the time and, apart from the president, was the most influential man in Washington.

He took me to lunch. It was fascinating to see how he operated. By the end of the meal I realised that he had found out more about Ireland, particularly the North of Ireland, than I had found out about how to interview Kennedy. There's no such thing as a free lunch – especially on Capitol Hill.

Eventually I decided to go to Kennedy's office and see if I could breach this wall of security myself. Most of the people in the office were very helpful but two of his advisors said that he would give no interviews. Period.

Waiting around outside, I was surrounded by TV crews from all over the world. They were allowed to follow him anywhere the CIA would permit, but they got no interviews either. They could film speeches if they wanted but nothing personal.

One of his aides told me that I could get a close-up picture next morning during a special Senate sub-committee hearing. She showed me to the room and showed me the best place to sit. I was there at 9am. Kennedy arrived at 10am and as he passed by he stopped and asked me where I was from. I told him I was from Ireland and that I was looking for a few words with him but I was finding it impossible to get through his advisors.

"Would you like a picture here?" he asked, in friendly, helpful way. The photographer lined up the picture and Kennedy spent a long time making sure the photographer got it right. What he was actually doing was taking time to speak to me. He said that he wouldn't be able to spare time for a long interview today but that if I waited until the end of the sub-committee hearing, he would take me to his room and give me five minutes. He was as good as his word and I was most grateful for his patience.

When the sub-committee hearing was over we finally got to meet. He wouldn't be quoted directly at all on Northern Ireland. But he was pleasant and genuinely concerned about Ireland. He was well-informed too. Once the interview was over he spent another five or 10 minutes asking about life in general in Ireland, particularly the North. Of all the Irish American politicians I met up until the time of Bill Clinton, Edward Kennedy was the one who had the best feel for the political situation in Ireland. He was the one who seemed to me to be genuinely interested in Ireland rather than using it for his own career.

At that time the split between Ted and his wife, Joan, was becoming public knowledge. When the Pope landed in America, the one everyone watched for lining up to meet him was Senator Edward Kennedy. Joan was with him for the first time in months. Throughout the rest of the Pope's visit, the political commentators noticed that Kennedy was conspicuous by his absence. In America that was taken as a sure sign that Kennedy would run for the presidency and, like his brother John F beforehand, wanted to play down the Rome influence. It didn't get many votes in America, at least, not until George W Bush arrived and discovered how to manipulate the fundamentalist right in all religions.

I always loved the story about John F Kennedy and the fundamentalists. There was serious opposition to JFK because he was a Catholic. One of his powerful advisors at that time was Adlai Stevenson. The evangelical groups in America got together to object to Kennedy becoming president. They threw their weight behind Nixon, who was much closer to them anyway. This included people like Billy Graham and a famous writer and motivator at the time, Norman Vincent Peale.

Norman Vincent Peale was both a writer and an evangelical preacher. On television he proclaimed that the Scriptures forbade Catholics holding political office because they couldn't make decisions free from Vatican interference. Norman Vincent Peale quoted chapter and verse from St Paul backing up his argument.

Later on Adlai Stevenson was confronted with the accusation on a news bulletin. His answer was brilliant. He began by saying that there was nothing in the Scriptures or anywhere else that said a Catholic couldn't become president of America. Furthermore there was nothing in the constitution which forbade it. He made an unanswerable case that Kennedy's religion shouldn't be part of the debate. And he ended by dismissing Norman Vincent Peale's plea to St Paul in these words: "In this matter I find Paul appealing but Peale appalling."

Wouldn't you die to have thought up that line?

The people around Ted Kennedy weren't concerned about his Catholic image but being Irish was important. When I went to his office, naturally enough there was strict security. The security guard did his job but added, "Anything for the Irish."

The papers in America were saying that Kennedy was willing to do interviews at all times as he prepared to make his bid for the Democratic nomination. They even detailed how he continually wore blue shirts and a well-pressed suit to make him look his best. Actually, when I met Kennedy on his way into the hearing, he had an off-white shirt which was in need of ironing. His hair was unruly and unkempt and what I noticed most about him was that he had a hole in the seat of his pants. No wonder he never made president.

Surprisingly for me, he was a hesitant speaker. At the hearing, he left many sentences unfinished and thoughts vanished into a stream of ems and aahs, never to be recovered again. As chair of the hearing he seemed to fall asleep on several occasions. As he subsequently proved, he was just impatient to get on with it. One professor of economics meandered on and on reading from his paper. Kennedy whispered to one of his aides, got agitated, and then lit himself a cigar. He finally interrupted, "Sir, kindly move the microphone nearer you because I can't hear you and please just hit the high spots of your paper – we can read the rest later." Abrasive but effective.

In later life I met his sister Jean when she was ambassador to Ireland and found the same insightful but courteous attributes in her. Ted Kennedy told me that in both America and Ireland the expectations from the Kennedy clan were unrealistically demanding.

At the time his wife, Joan, was recovering from alcoholism. Many in America blamed Kennedy's womanising and lifestyle. But Kennedy in the short talk I had with him spoke well of Joan, as one would expect him to do. He said, "I regard alcoholism as an illness. It should be treated as such. She's making great progress in her struggle and she's doing a fine job."

Before I met him I had a jaundiced view of him. But when I met him I came away convinced that he was an intelligent man but ruthless enough to be a successful operator in American politics. He was more helpful to me than he needed to be. He did it because I was Irish, a priest and a journalist. Being Irish was the key.

CHAPTER 10

ALTERED STATES

My father was born on the 12th of July, which meant he could never celebrate his birthday in the North. The one birthday we did celebrate for him was his 70th birthday, his last. It fell on a Sunday, which meant that there was no 12th of July parade. We had a surprise party for him and our neighbours and friends had a great time. Because of his 70th birthday, we have happy pictures of my father which we wouldn't have otherwise. It was a family gathering. We had Mass in our home in Bellanaleck. The only time I've ever said Mass in the family home was that Mass for my father.

On Sunday August 9th I was in Croke Park, attending the 1981 All-Ireland semi-final between Mayo and Kerry. I was enjoying the match when Seán Ó Síocháin, who was then the director of the GAA, whispered to me, "Father Brian, there's a phone call for you. Here's the key of the office to use the phone. It's Store Street Garda station. I hope your car hasn't been stolen."

I made the phone call, expecting news of a stolen car. At the other end of the line a pleasant garda said, "Ah, Father Brian, there's no point beating round the bush with you, you're a man of the world yourself. I might as well tell you straight, your father was found dead this morning. They've been looking for you in Mount Argus and they knew you were in Croke Park so they phoned here to get the message to you. If you phone Mount Argus they'll fill you in on the details."

I phoned Mount Argus and they confirmed the news.

My father, Hugh D'Arcy, lived with my brother, Gaby, and his wife, Maura, and their two young children, in the family home in Bellanaleck –

remember, my mother had died in 1965. Gaby and Maura had gone to Knock for the weekend. My father was on his own, which was most unusual for him. A neighbour, Jimmy Timoney, watched television with him on Saturday night and found him in his usual good spirits.

Next morning it was noticed that Hugh D'Arcy wasn't at Mass. Some of the congregation speculated that he must be away. Jimmy was able to tell them he wasn't away and that he was still at home because the door was open as he cycled past the house on his way to Mass.

They found him dead, sitting in the chair with the television still on. It was a real shock as he was a healthy man. He'd been to work as usual that day. I found his funeral almost impossible to do, but I still remember the support I got from the people who attended from all over Ireland. Ever since, I try to attend as many funerals as I can because I know what it means to those grieving.

A few weeks later I was due to go on sabbatical for a few months to Berkeley College in San Francisco. It was 1981 and time to get myself sorted out. I knew the theology I had learned and studied wasn't enough to carry me through a changing world. I spoke to Brendan Comiskey, who was not then a bishop, and he advised, "The only place to go is America. Don't go near Rome; that will only destroy you. Go to America where the future is."

It was great advice and I took it. I had arranged all this before my father's death.

Through all of this, trying to preach at my father's funeral and coming to terms with his death, it really bugged me that I had been with hundreds of people dying but missed my own father's death. I like to think my presence might have helped so many to cross to the Land of the Living, yet my father died in a chair alone. In time I realised that was how he wanted to die, but at that time I felt a bit cheated. We had to bring his month's mind Mass forward so that I could go to America. And when I went there, I realised that I really was shattered by his death, even though I fooled myself that I had taken it in my stride.

Mostly as a priest you get used to death, with the exception of a child's death. I never sleep the night before a child's funeral. I had to do my own nephew's funeral. Brian was five years of age when he died. I've done up to 30 children's funerals in my life as a priest. I never got used to it, because there's nothing you can possibly say that's helpful.

When I was in Dublin, Mount Jerome cemetery was in our parish, and I often had to do burials that were not from our parish.

I remember three occasions when I did funerals for travelling people and their children. Not even the hardened gravediggers in Mount Jerome wanted to be present at a child's funeral. The graves were deep in Mount Jerome and, because it was a child's coffin, one of the gravediggers would climb into the grave and gently lay the remains on the floor. On a couple of occasions, there was no gravedigger to do that service. I understood their fears and got into the graves myself to receive the little coffin, place it on the bottom and climb up the ladder again to say the prayers. When you've done that a few times, you just don't want to do it again.

By then I'd been through the lot – the Miami funerals, road-accident victims, old people, young people and celebrities. I'd done paupers' and millionaires' funerals. But your own flesh and blood is different and I learned that I had to deal with my own emotions as a grieving son.

When I went to America I lived in a presbytery in Oakland, California, working for my keep. It was the only way I could afford to take a sabbatical. Brendan Comiskey put me in contact with a monsignor who gave me free board in exchange for me saying Mass each day for him, as well as having all the additional duties at the weekend. It was too much work considering I was studying and producing projects for class. But then it's possible to learn more in a parish than in a classroom. Each morning I went to the Franciscan School of Theology on the Berkeley College campus in San Francisco.

The lectures were wonderful. Kenan Osborne, a Franciscan priest, was a brilliant and challenging teacher who confirmed that the doubts which had begun to cripple me were in fact part of any normal thinking person's development. The attitudes I was taught and freely accepted as a student no longer worked. Not only had the world moved on, but so had I. Advances in psychology and theology demanded change.

Through Kenan Osborne's lectures, for the first time in my life, I encountered Christ as really human: truly divine but really human at the same time. Jesus became accessible to me and I realised that it was possible for me to have a real relationship with Him. For me, it was like growing up spiritually. You have no idea how I was affirmed and helped through his commonsense approach. This was what the Vatican Council really intended to be available to every Christian.

Kenan gave us a background against which to ask searching questions. Questions about what Christ knew and didn't know; questions about the sacraments – how many are there, what are the essential ones and how did Christ expect us to use the sacraments? I also got, for the first time in my life, an understanding of and a love for God's Word in Scripture. It was only a four-month sabbatical – not nearly long enough at that point in my life – but I learned more in that period than in the six years I spent as a student. I knew what I wanted to study. I knew what I wanted to get out of it. It set me off on a journey of reading, reflecting and praying. It gave me confidence to trust God's Spirit.

There is a providence guiding everything in life. Opportunities come when we need them most. The way God continues to care for me is something I don't fully understand, but I suspect my mother didn't leave this world early for nothing.

In the summer of 1981, I was open to a fresh start in life because of my father's death. I wouldn't have chosen it this way, but I knew I was struggling to find answers. The tank had run dry. When both your parents die, it has a huge impact for all the family but even more so for a single person. It had for me anyway.

Whilst one parent is alive, we are still somebody's child. But when both are gone we have to become adults. The theory works in reverse when parents, particularly mothers, live to a ripe old age. It's hard for a "child" of 60 to suddenly grow up. I was full of grief when my mother died young, but with hindsight, I can thank God for the gift.

In 1981, at 36, an ideal age, both my parents were dead. I had 12 years of priesthood behind me. I was young enough to change and I was old enough to understand the necessity for it. It was a wonderful opportunity but sad too because I had to get used to life without my father, and at the same time deal with doubts about my priesthood – one of which was: did

—

I stay only to keep my father happy?

I was on my own, in a foreboding presbytery on the west coast of America. The desert experience doesn't always need a desert.

The old monsignor I went to live with was of German extraction and a former navy chaplain. "We have to run a tight ship here," was his mantra. His parish was 90 percent Black. He detested most Blacks – thereby excluding most of his own people.

I was allowed to join him for meals. He had an elongated dining table, which meant we sat at least eight feet apart, shouting at each other. The kitchen was three feet away to his left and there was a friendly old lady, also German, and in the early stages of senility, who was his housekeeper. He had a large, loud bell at his right hand. She brought out the soup, he shouted at me about the events of the day. I nodded agreement and enjoyed the thick broth. Then he rang the bell with great swings and deafening peals. From all of three feet she appeared smiling to lift the soup plates. More bells, more food. This went on at every meal every day. He'd shout at her to bring the next course. She'd serve him. Then she'd walk the eight feet to serve me. And there was nothing I could do about it. It just was a madhouse but I adored both of them.

After supper he went to his plush room to have his nightcap and watch TV. I went up to a bedroom without a television and studied all night and that was it. That's what I was there for.

I said Masses for the people, heard confessions for him, and preached at all the weekend services, for which he was grateful, as were the people, who were solidly loyal. He didn't really bother me or even acknowledge me very much. I was just a young nobody from Ireland who was easy to live with and gave him no trouble. Since no other associate pastor (curate) would stay with him, this was as good as it got.

The old lady liked me a little too much. Every morning at 3am, she would ring the intercom to my room – an old, black phone beside the bed, with no dial so I couldn't make calls. She said exactly the same thing every morning: "Father D'Arcy, you'll never leave me, so you won't?" The first night, I argued with her and said, "I have to go back in a couple of months." She wouldn't accept any excuse and repeated, "You won't leave me . . ." over and over again. We argued for an hour until I got exhausted and said I'd never leave her.

The next night at 3am the phone rang again. "Father D'Arcy, you will never leave me, so you won't?" It was a short conversation. "Betty, no, I'll never leave you." Now she was happy. Every night I was there, we had the same early-morning, meaningless, five-second conversation. It was a wonderful, mad, other-worldly place. She was lovely and lonely.

The people of the parish were great to work with. I appreciated the American Church back then. There was a pride in being Catholic. They gave their time and their talents enthusiastically, unlike the Ireland of the 1980s. The parish set-up was well organised and professional – maybe too professional at times. There was less expected from the priests and more involvement of parishioners. There were many initiatives in liturgy which I really enjoyed. Sadly, most of those initiatives were stifled by Big Brother in Rome.

All in all it was a good learning experience for me in the college, in the parish, and most of all in the city of San Francisco.

One evening when I came home from college the monsignor was unusually excited. For a start he met me at the door. His opening words were, "What kind of guy are you?" It's a question I have spent some considerable time pondering since, without much enlightenment.

"What do you mean, Monsignor?"

"Two cardinals phoned for you today. Are you a spy from the Vatican, or what are you?"

"Who was on the phone?"

"Some guy, O'Fuck or something like that. That's what it sounded like to me."

"Would it have been Cardinal O'Fee?" He was the only cardinal I thought might ring me.

"That wasn't it."

So I used the Irish Ó Fiaich.

His eyes lit up. "That's it!"

I couldn't think what Tomás Ó Fiaich would want with me over in America.

"He's ringing back at five o'clock."

Then he dropped the bombshell: "Worse still, Cody wants to talk to you."

"Cardinal Cody?"

"Yeah."

John Cardinal Cody was the first cardinal in the modern era to hit the front pages because of scandal. The Cardinal Archbishop of Chicago was of Irish extraction and was a senior churchman in America. He was of the old school, the only school there was back then.

In the summer of 1981 the *Chicago Sun Times* published a series of allegations against Cardinal Cody of Chicago. The paper implied, to say the least, that the Cardinal's lifestyle owed more to the example of the Borgia Popes than that of Jesus Christ. They made a series of specific allegations:

That the Cardinal kept a woman friend, Helen Dolan Wilson, in a life of luxury by misappropriating diocesan funds.

That Mrs Wilson, a widow, amassed a personal fortune worth over a million dollars from those funds and that the cardinal was a frequent visitor to her luxury homes in Chicago and Florida.

That Mrs Wilson's son, David, who called his mother's powerful friend "Uncle Jack", owed his lucrative insurance career to the amount of business he did with the Catholic Church in Chicago; business which earned him almost 100,000 dollars in commission.

These were all allegations which were repeated. They had not been proven to be true, but neither had they been defended or explained by the diocesan office or Cardinal Cody in any meaningful way. The strategy seemed to be "say nothing, suffer in silence and it will eventually go away."

Mrs Wilson, it was claimed, was a cousin of the cardinal's and had taken out a million-dollar policy on his life, in which she was the sole beneficiary, on the grounds that she was his cousin. The Chicago paper claimed their only link was that an aunt of the cardinal had become Mrs Wilson's stepmother when her father remarried.

It was complicated stuff.

As it happened, when I was leaving for America, Kevin Marron, God be good to him, the then editor of the *Sunday World*, had said to me, "I'll believe you're a real journalist if you get me an interview with Cody while you're there." It was a total joke between us, because Cody would talk to nobody, absolutely nobody. The world's press was looking for an interview or even a statement. There was none.

I could see why the monsignor was excited. As it turned out, Cardinal Ó Fiaich was easy to deal with. He was in Sacramento on a visit and would be in San Francisco next evening. He was taking me out for a meal and a chat.

At six o'clock, I was sitting by the phone in the monsignor's room. The phone rang. The monsignor didn't even speak; he handed the phone to me.

"This is Cardinal Cody."

What happened was that I had an aunt in Kerry, a Mrs Mangan, who was my father's sister. Her husband, John, had a brother, Fr Frank, who knew Cardinal Cody. Cody's father came from Thurles and his mother from Charleville in Cork. When the Cardinal was a young priest, he studied in Rome but, because of travelling problems, spent his holidays in Kerry with Fr Frank's family. Ever since then he had kept in touch with many of the people there. My aunt and he exchanged Christmas cards every year.

She had written to him when I went to America to study. She told the cardinal about my father's recent death and gave him my phone number. Now in the midst of his own trouble, he took time to ring me to see how I was settling in America. I thought it was a lovely, generous thing to do and told him so.

"I don't know what you are doing for Christmas, but if you want to spend it here with me, you'll be most welcome," he said.

While I was still speaking to him, the evening news came on the monsignor's television. I had to turn the volume down because the headline on the news was a press conference held by some of the cardinal's priests and lay people in Chicago, calling on him to make a statement clarifying whether he was guilty or not.

I was afraid he'd hear what they were saying. Meantime he was telling me what a wonderful place Ireland was, how he had such fond memories of it, assuring me that the most beautiful place in the world was the Kerry coast and saying his one wish was to go back there. He wanted me to send greetings to his friends and relatives in Ireland.

I knew that he was in fact ill at this time, so I was reluctant to mention the alleged scandals. But it wasn't easy to ignore the elephant in the kitchen either. Then I thought of Kevin Marron's challenge. I approached the subject with all the diplomacy I could muster.

"I see, Your Eminence, you have your own troubles just now."

He took off. It was all lies, a plot to get him to resign, organised by priests in his archdiocese with their own agenda and led by a well-known novelist. It was another case of anti-Catholic newspapers wanting to destroy the work of Christ. He was clearly surprised and annoyed to hear that the stories were being carried by Irish newspapers. That shocked him.

I then revealed that I had a weekly column in the most-read Sunday newspaper in Ireland and I would only be too happy to let the people of Ireland know his side of the story, but only if he wished me to do it, otherwise our conversation would remain confidential.

He was so relieved to hear that I could put his side of the story that he gave me permission to write what I wanted. I came up with another suggestion, to protect himself and to give him time to rethink whether he wanted to make a statement or not. Remember everyone, including his own priests and people, was calling for such a statement, but his advisors had effectively muzzled the cardinal.

What I suggested was bad practice for a journalist looking for a scoop, but the only decent way to treat a man good enough to ring me in my grief. I suggested that I would type up what I thought he had just said, ring him back in half an hour, read it to him and then he could decide whether he wanted me to use it or not. He said there was no need to, but he agreed to my suggestion anyway.

The monsignor was like a lunatic wanting to know the news. I ran up to my room to the typewriter. It was Friday evening and I could see the front page of the *Sunday World* in my mind's eye. I typed everything I could remember and rang him back. To my surprise and relief, he answered the phone himself. I read my piece.

"I think I'll hire you as my press officer. That's the perfect answer to their allegations in a few paragraphs. I wish my people here would let me say that."

He was thrilled and so was I. He asked me to phone nearer Christmas to make arrangements to go to Chicago if I was free and asked me to ring him any time for a chat. "I know how lonely it can be away from home," he added as he said goodbye.

By now the monsignor had phoned all his friends to tell them that Cardinal Cody was talking to *his* priest. All I could think of was how I would get it to the paper before the cardinal's advisors realised what he'd done and maybe stop its publication.

I told the monsignor I needed to use the phone and would pay him for the call later – and would tell him the hot news. No problem.

I phoned the office in Dublin and asked Sophie Hunt, the MD's secretary, to take my "copy", ask no questions, and get Kevin to ring me later. I couldn't get rid of the story quickly enough.

The following Sunday, November 8th 1981, the *Sunday World* had a world exclusive. "Cardinal Cody talks to the *Sunday World*" screamed the front page. It was all there spilling over to page two. "Cody breaks his silence to tell the wonderful people of Ireland, 'I am in high spirits. Tell them that the strong Irish character given to me by both my parents is standing me in good stead in the face of this latest attack'." It was all there.

"This is an organised campaign against me. It is only one of many in my life. I am used to being attacked. In my lifetime I worked in New Orleans for the rights of the Black people, when it was neither popular nor successful. I was attacked then too. When I came here they said I never did anything for the Blacks. But the people know and that's all that counts."

Then came the real punchline.

"People say I misused diocesan money over a period of 16 years. Do you know that the diocesan budget for this year alone was 285 million dollars? A friend told me jokingly that if I could only siphon off one million dollars over a 16-year period, I must be a poor thief. That about sums it up."

The Diocesan accounts for 16 years were subpoenaed. The Cardinal revealed they had taken "truck loads" of paperwork away.

Finally he said, "I want the Irish people to know the truth. I did not steal the money and I have no intention of letting this attack prevent me from continuing the work God wants me to do."

We had the whole story on Sunday but, when I came back in from college on the Monday evening, there were television cameras all around the presbytery door waiting for me. The monsignor was in his element. He now had a man of influence staying in his house, he thought.

I had to explain to the crews that I had nothing to add to what was in the interview. They even used that. The story was lifted and reported on all over the US. "American papers please copy" was never more honoured.

Afterwards, I did try to contact Cardinal Cody but by then they'd got to him and he wasn't allowed to take calls. I never spoke to him again and he died a short time afterwards.

Every Wednesday night, the monsignor invited all his monsignor friends in for dinner and drinks. That was the only night I didn't eat with him. Afterwards they went to his room to play cards. The following Wednesday night it was all so different.

"Brian, I want you to join us for dinner and I want you to tell Cody's story to my friends." After dinner he brought them for drinks and at the appropriate time he invited me to stand in the middle of the room.

"Now, Brian, stand up there and tell the story."

I did as I was told and the five monsignors sat very respectfully with their whiskeys and listened. One or two asked questions: "Did I think he was guilty?" "Would I visit?" At the end, a chuffed monsignor said, "There's the man who told the truth about Cardinal Cody. Now, Brian, go back to your room." My 15 minutes of fame were over in less than five.

I noticed a specific difference between the Irish and American cultures as a result of the Cody story. The Americans worried about money and where it went; the Irish worried about sex and the cardinal's relationship with his cousin. That was before the Celtic Tiger.

I was due to go home in January. It was a lonely-enough old Christmas. Three people rang me. Gerry McGuinness and Kevin Marron from the *Sunday World* were two of the callers. And Gerry McGuinness has rung me every Christmas day since no matter where either of us is in the world.

The monsignor spoke to me two days after Christmas: "Brian, I'm going to phone your provincial today. I want you to have a six-month extension here."

I explained I couldn't because I had my own parish in Dublin to look after.

He said, "You can't go, the collection has gone up 500 dollars a week since you came, and if you stay another six months we'll have the water rates for the year."

I had found my vocation at last.

I loved my time in San Francisco. I promised myself I would go back but now, 25 years later, I've never had the time. Life is what happens whilst we are making other plans.

It was while I was there that I heard of AIDS for the first time. San Francisco was where many of the gay community lived. It was the first time I saw two men kissing each other on the street. Talk about a culture shock. They used to tell me that if I lived in San Francisco long enough I'd see everything there was to see in the world.

At the college there was a strong movement to help women find their voice in the Church. Down in a basement there was a group of women, nuns and others, who assembled to rewrite prayers in non-sexist language. In 1981, that was a pretty radical thing to do. They began with the Sign of the Cross which, when you think about it, is a male prayer: "In the name of the Father and of the Son and of the Holy Spirit." After a week they came up with "In the name of the Parent, the Sibling and the Holy It." I thought if that's it, I'll stick to the ould way.

When I eventually came back to Dublin, I arrived just in time to experience the worst snow for 20 years. I got another shock and learned another lesson. Some people who were close friends had got used to life without me. When you leave your surroundings for a considerable time, you're not the only one who changes. Those at home also take the opportunity to review their life.

The principle is that you can never put your foot in the same river twice. It might be the same bank, but it's not the same river. Things change.

After San Francisco, there were relationships which were never the same again.

As a result of the material I sent back to the *Sunday World*, Gay Byrne asked me on the *Late Late Show* for the first of many appearances. The programme was on Saturdays back then. But the snow meant only a few guests were able to make it. They sent a truck over to Mount Argus to collect me.

After the show, I was expecting the truck to leave me home. There was none. It's a long way to slide from Donnybrook to Mount Argus on a bitterly frosty night, especially after four months on the west coast of America.

There was another lesson to learn. Gay was much more interested in the kissing gays than he was in the cardinal's money. Guess who knew his audience best.

Chapter 11

The Clones Cyclone

There's a story that has become legendary in the music business. Dave Pennefeather is MD of Universal Music in Ireland. Initially he worked for RCA, which was then a major label in world music, mainly because it was the label for which Elvis Presley recorded.

In the 1980s RCA had their wholesale store and offices in Cork Street in Dublin. Once a week I called to pick up the latest releases for review. You need to know at this point that Dave is a member of the Church of Ireland. He played for the Jimmy Magee Allstars and we always had a gentle way of ribbing each other. He called himself "The Token Prod". If there was a picture taken he always stood between Fr Michael Cleary and myself. "Crucified between two thieves," he'd tease.

One day when I called to see him in Cork Street, I didn't realise his sales manager from the UK, Dave Harmer, was visiting him. As soon as I walked into his office Dave Pennefeather winked at me, a signal to be careful. Mr Harmer was a little nonplussed that a "reverend" should be in the offices of a record company.

I could see Pennefeather was up to his tricks. He said, "You've come to pray as usual, haven't you, Fr Brian?" I caught the ball and ran with it. I explained how once a week I came into the offices of RCA to pray for the success of the new releases for that week. Mr Harmer swallowed it hook, line and sinker. I got down on my knees, followed quickly by Dave Pennefeather, and then this senior executive from the UK fell to his knees too. There was a moment of silent reflection and I began to name all the records I knew were being released that week, including a new single from

Clannad. But before long both Pennefeather and myself burst out laughing.

Until that moment the executive from London, perplexed as he was, believed that this was a feature of Irish business and that I, as chaplain to the entertainment industry, called in regularly to hold prayer meetings. Before he realised it, he found himself bowing his head for the continued success of RCA's sales, but when he heard the splutters of laughter, he knew he'd been had.

The incident spread around the music business within hours. It was in all the Sunday papers that weekend.

On Sunday afternoon I went to a match and was sitting beside Cardinal Ó Fiaich. At half time he told me how delighted he was to hear I was able to pray for RCA's success. I thought he'd got the joke until he quite seriously asked me, "Does RCA mean Roman Catholic Association? What sort of religious records do they sell?" I had to explain to him that it was all a joke. He enjoyed it even more then. It must have been the first time Cardinal Ó Fiaich had anything in common with a British executive.

The clincher came a week later when I went to London and dropped in to see Tommy Loftus, who also worked with RCA in London. By now all the staff in England had heard of the incident in Dublin. It was the talk of the London office too. As soon as I called at the reception everybody knew me and willingly directed me to Dave Harmer's office. They even followed me up to the office. "Come in," I heard Dave say, slightly agitated.

I put my head round the door: "Hello, Dave, your prayers were answered. I see Clannad have made the top 10."

"Fr Brian, you are nothing but an Irish b*****ks." It got me a free lunch that day anyway.

But it had one more sequel. Dolly Parton also recorded for RCA. And as everybody knows I am an incurable fan of everything Dolly does. One of my aims in life was to interview her. It still is – any time, anywhere.

She came to London to headline a concert in the Dominion Theatre. Through the good offices of Pennefeather and Harmer, I got an exclusive interview and pictures for the *Sunday World*.

Tom McElroy came with me to take special pictures of Dolly and her priest "friend". Actually, I wasn't a friend at all; I was just a fan. After the interview Dolly was about to go on stage and posed very patiently while Tom lined up his pictures in the precise way he was wont to do. It must have taken two or three minutes.

Dolly looked at me and uttered the immortal line: "Father Brian, I think you should be looking at the camera." I had been caught. But I will ask you an honest question. If you met Dolly Parton, where would you be looking?

In my role as chaplain I often encountered others in sport who prayed for success in more serious ways. One of those was Barry McGuigan. I knew his father before I knew Barry. Pat McGuigan, or Pat McGeegan as he called himself, was lead singer with a number of big showbands including the Victors and the Big Four. He represented Ireland in the *Eurovision Song Contest* and came fourth with *Chance of a Lifetime*.

He had a beautiful voice and a good sense of humour. When he was being interviewed before the *Eurovision Song Contest*, Peter Murphy, who presented a programme on farming on radio, suggested to Pat, "Many people say that you have the best voice in Ireland at present." Pat, with typical Clones modesty, quipped, "As Bob Hope says, 'it's only a rumour, but keep spreading it.'"

I knew Pat well and he kept telling me that he had, in Monaghan and Fermanagh parlance, "a great cub". This meant a son who was good with his fists. Barry McGuigan was equally good at soccer and singing, but he chose boxing. I went to see him boxing as an amateur in the National Stadium and he was magic. Even as a teenager his talent was awesome. I have a great love of amateur boxing and when I was in Dublin loved going to the Stadium. I am not as keen on professional boxing because there are so many side issues and scandals. The boxing's fine but the sideshows are appalling.

In the Stadium it was great to see young men learn the art of self-defence. Amateur boxing should be a sport of discipline and managing aggression in a positive way.

For young Barry McGuigan it was the perfect sport. He trained hard, always wanting to better himself. I got to know Barry during those early days. Barry then became a professional boxer, but the path to success had many a hiccup.

Early in his professional career, a Nigerian boxer, Young Ali, died after a fight with Barry. Barry was devastated and for a time I thought he'd pack it in.

In fact, Young Ali had a brain injury before he came into boxing at all. It should have been picked up, one would have thought, but it wasn't. I don't think Barry ever got over the shock of that sad event in his life.

At the time I had quite a few chats with Pat and some with Barry about how to handle something so serious, and something outside his control. Barry had to make his own decisions whether he wanted to be involved in the sport after that. He came through the crisis a stronger man.

He changed his style completely as a result. He was reluctant to strike his opponent's head and developed his unique skill of body punching, which could be as devastating but not as dangerous.

Whenever I went to a fight with him he always asked for a blessing before going into the ring. I was amazed that a boxer so ruthless in the ring was so nervous before the fight. He really suffered, looked as white as the wall, and sat there shivering in the dressing-room.

After the fight he came back to the dressing-room, calm, clinical and analytic. To be successful you have to use all your gifts. But he rarely went into a fight without a blessing.

I remember him asking me what he should pray for. A good question. We settled on a formula: that he wouldn't be injured and that he wouldn't seriously injure his opponent. That was always first on the agenda. Then he would pray to do himself justice in the ring. If that meant winning, so be it. But he never actually prayed to win a boxing match. He knew that if he did his best, he would win. We settled on that formula and we used it all the time.

I was there in Las Vegas on the night he lost his world title. I always felt sad about that because he was a better boxer than the man who beat him.

I will never forget that day in the open car-park of Caesar's Palace in Las Vegas. The heat was over 100 degrees. I was at the ringside using a clear-perspex plastic pen. After each round all the journalists ducked in under the ring to get out of the heat and to top up fluids with 7-Up. At the start of the third round, I tried to write with the pen, but it simply melted into a plastic heap. The heat was unbearable.

Barry was still ahead at the beginning of the 15th round but, through sheer exhaustion, he was knocked down in the last round and lost the fight. If it were now he would have won the fight easily, because fights today last only 12 rounds. I still maintain that was the bravest fight of Barry's life even though he didn't win it.

Afterwards he was taken to hospital and I gave him a blessing in the ambulance before he left. While I was blessing him the ambulance crew were checking that Barry had his credit card with him.

I was with him the night in Manchester when he retired. He was fighting a boxer called McDonnell, whom he could have beaten with one hand tied behind his back when he was in his prime. But in every sport the time comes to move on. The fight was stopped on a cut-eye decision. Barry knew he hadn't the hunger any more. So he called a press conference there and then and announced his retirement. He got out with his brain intact. Thankfully. That too was a brave decision and the right one.

He has done phenomenally well since. He works hard at everything he does. Barry thought his vocabulary was too limited for his roles in commentating and after-dinner speaking. Off his own bat he bought a dictionary and took to learning 10 new words every day. He's done that for 20 years. Now he picks his words and uses them precisely and accurately. He brought the discipline of boxing into the rest of his life.

Barry was always a hero of mine as well as a friend. And he still is a hero because he has done so much with his life. He also crossed the religious divide at a time when it wasn't easy. He married Sandra, who is Church of Ireland. Even though he was from south of the Border, to further his career, he had to fight for the British championship. That didn't go down well in some parts of Monaghan. But he was brave enough to know what he had to do to get to the top of his profession. I admire people who aren't imprisoned by foolish prejudices.

CHAPTER 12

THE PASSION OF FR CHARLES

The Passionists, an Italian order, came to Ireland 150 years ago. We came to Mount Argus on the 15th of August 1856. Our most famous member was a Dutchman called Father Charles Houben. He's a perfect example of God writing straight on crooked lines. Traditionally Passionists are supposed to conduct missions and retreats and, through preaching, spread devotion to the Passion of Christ. Too often our preaching has emphasised that it was our sins which caused Christ's suffering. That meant scrupulous people were left with a crippling sense of guilt. It is more encouraging and accurate to see Christ's Passion as the ultimate proof of God's love for us.

Father Charles was born in the quiet village of Munstergeleen and his life could be seen as a series of failures. He was a slow learner in his youth, one of 11 children in a poor family. It was only after his mother died that he could think about entering the priesthood.

First though he was conscripted into the army and he was a failure there too. But out of that failure he discovered a Passionist monastery and felt the call to become a Passionist. And he did. Before his ordination, however, his father died and the family were so poor they couldn't afford to go to his ordination, because of the expense of the funeral. After ordination he was sent to England to help establish the Passionists there.

The priest the Passionists sent to found Mount Argus was a member of the aristocracy, Lord Longford's great-uncle, Paul Mary Packenham. He was a young man in his early 30s, a former officer in the British army, highly intellectual and competent. A born leader, he was the ideal man to be the first rector of Mount Argus. However, six months after he came to

Ireland, he died unexpectedly.

They had no one else to send in his place except this Dutchman who knew little English and was so pedantic they couldn't allow him say a public Mass. He never conducted a mission and his only suitable tasks were blessing the sick and hearing confessions. Yet Mount Argus monastery was built on the reputation of this apparent failure, while the one the Passionists considered the ideal man was taken by God.

Despite his failures, Father Charles had something people identified with and they came in their thousands to him for healing.

Every day, hundreds of people came to him in Mount Argus. It didn't impress his community in Mount Argus, many of whom didn't understand him. He became so popular with the people that the diocesan authorities, not to mention the medical profession, grew suspicious of him. They got their opening when a couple of Dublin rogues came to Father Charles and asked him to bless a barrel of holy water for them. They then sold it at a shilling a bottle as being "blessed by the holy man of Mount Argus". It's hard to beat the Dubs.

Poor old Father Charles was banished to England. Before he left, there were elaborate plans to build a new church and retreat house at Mount Argus. The foundation stone was laid before Charles was sent away, but during his eight years away, Mount Argus went downhill and nearly closed.

Eventually it was decided to bring him back to Dublin. When he came back, Mount Argus took off. People returned and Charles took up his healing ministry again. Mount Argus once more became so popular that they decided to resume building the church. The problem was nobody could remember where the foundation stone was laid, it was so overgrown. Nevertheless, because of Fr Charles's ministry, Mount Argus was saved and the buildings we know today were completed.

When I entered the Passionists I had never heard of Fr Charles of Mount Argus. But as a student I soon understood his appeal. Compassion for the sick and dying were the hallmarks of his life.

In time I got to know the real Father Charles from Mrs Cranny. Her father brought him in a pony and trap to bless the sick around Dublin in the latter part of the 19th century. She herself was blessed and cured by him when she was a child. It was an effective blessing because she lived to be 107.

She remembered him clearly and insisted Fr Charles wasn't a severe old man, with dead eyes looking down at the ground, as he is often portrayed. On the contrary he was a smiling, friendly man and good fun. When her father brought him around Dublin to heal the sick, Charles always encouraged people to trust God to walk with them in their suffering, whether they were cured or not.

For Charles, God isn't the cause of suffering but neither is suffering a curse. If we accept God's will strength will come. He preached the Passion by telling simple stories about Christ's suffering and by reassuring the sick that their pain was linked to Christ's, and therefore never wasted. Mrs Cranny's father memorised his stories and repeated them to the family when he came home.

Unusually for a healer, Charles sometimes told those who came for a blessing that they wouldn't get better. There is a documented case where he said to a sick man, "It is not God's will that you should get better. This is God's gift to you so that you should go home and prepare for your death." The man, to his credit, accepted his advice and died a month later.

I experienced Charles's unusual way of answering prayers in my own life when as a young student my mother got sick. As I have already explained, we prayed to Fr Charles for guidance and healing, but Mammy died despite all our prayers.

I was devastated that my prayers weren't answered then; later in life I realised that all prayers are answered, but not necessarily in the way we want. As the song says, "Some of God's greatest gifts are unanswered prayers." I keep insisting, if my mother hadn't died, I might not have been a priest and I certainly would not be the kind of priest I am.

My father worked on the railway but in 1962 he was told the railway was closing and he'd have to train to be a bus conductor. A short time afterwards, conductors were done away with and he had to learn to drive a bus. My father was over 50 years of age without a job and he asked me to send him a relic of Fr Charles. He trained as a bus driver even though the only thing he had ever driven before that was a tractor. He passed the test and for the rest of his working life drove safely. But he'd never leave home without the plastic relic of Fr Charles in his coat pocket, which was his way of showing his appreciation of Charles's intervention.

When I was rector and parish priest of Mount Argus from 1983 to 1989, my biggest problem was the restoration of the monastery and church. In 1983 we discovered that the timbers and walls of the monastery and church were in an advanced state of dry rot. We had to take every slate off the roof, every rafter, every inch of plaster off the walls of both buildings. We had to lift all the floors in the monastery and restore the complete fabric from foundation to roof.

When Mount Argus Monastery was first built in 1863, the leading newspaper of the day said, "Mount Argus Monastery is the noblest religious house built in these countries since the Reformation." Later, when the church was completed, it became a famous and majestic landmark. Now in 1983 the entire complex was in danger of collapsing.

At first we thought about demolishing it, but because it was such an historic building, that was not possible and anyway the most economical solution by far was to restore it. There is a fascinating and varied meeting of cultures in the history of Mount Argus. James Joyce mentioned it as a centre of spiritual comfort in *Ulysses*. Both Brendan Behan and Christy Browne came regularly to Mount Argus, and mentioned it with affection. The leader of the 1916 Rising, Pádraig Pearse, came to Mount Argus to make his peace with God and brought many of his comrades with him on Good Friday 1916. James Pearse, Pádraig's father, was received into the Church in Mount Argus in 1877, and his firm made and installed the pulpit that's in use in the church to this day. On the other hand, the first rector was Fr Paul Packenham, who hailed from the British aristocracy. Before the founding of An Garda Síochána, the Dublin Metropolitan Police took Mount Argus as their church. After 1922, An Garda Síochána continued the association with Mount Argus.

Of course the reason it survived at all was Blessed Charles. In his lifetime 300 people every day came to be blessed by him and 20,000 attended his funeral. Mount Argus had such an important heritage that it had to be saved.

It's difficult for somebody who wasn't there to understand what an impossible task it was at the time. There were over 80 priests, brothers and students in the community.

In the 1980s Ireland was an economic mess. Unemployment was high; the best of our young, educated people emigrated to find work and a future. A Government Minister actually said that the island was too small for the number of people living on it and that it was a good experience for our talented graduates to emigrate. It was the worst possible time to ask people for money to restore a church and monastery.

Father Charles was the man that I put my trust in. I lived in a wee room next to the room where he died. I discovered then what a friend I had in Father Charles. I had to raise two-and-a-half million pounds to save the buildings. It was as part of that fundraising process that I appeared on the *Late Late Show*.

Pictures of the decaying monastery appeared in the *Sunday World* and Gay Byrne couldn't believe the conditions we lived in. He sent his researcher Brigid Ruane over to Mount Argus to check it out and she reported that it was even worse than the pictures. As a result of the *Late Late Show* appearance, hundreds of thousands of pounds were donated from all over the country. The showbands came on board and raised thousands more. So did the gardaí. Every county in Ireland contributed to the fund. To me it was a miracle it was ever completed and Charles was the miracle man.

Towards the mid-1980s, we had to begin a major project in the church. We decided to split the church in half and keep services going in one half whilst the other half was being restored. It was nerve-wrecking for me because there was no money to finish it and I wasn't even sure if we'd ever reopen the church.

The work began at the end of September, the Monday after an All-Ireland final. When I finished 8am Mass I went to introduce myself to the workers arriving on site. Kerry had beaten Dublin in the All-Ireland football final the day before.

We decided there had to be Dubliners employed on the building, otherwise security would have been impossible.

Three or four "real" Dubs appeared on the first morning. One of them was a tough little bearded man. He had bloodshot eyes and black hair and he'd obviously been on the tear the night before, drowning his sorrows after Dublin's defeat. He wasn't interested in a sermon from anybody.

I was on the steps of the church and I spoke a little nervously about the ground rules. "Listen, lads, I know it's a building site, and I know that I can't expect you to behave as if you were in a church all the time. I know that. Can you do a few things for me? While you're working here, Masses will be going in the church. At least during the Masses, mind the language, keep the noise down. Weddings will be going on. Remember that it's their biggest day, so don't spoil it for them. Funerals will be going on (this was my big line). Funerals will be going on and it's a sensitive time. If your own mother was being buried, you wouldn't want to hear effing and blinding and shouting and roaring during the Mass, would you?"

The wee Dublin man with the squinty eyes looked up at me and says: "Ah, you needn't worry about us, Father. You'll hear no f*****' cursin' from us." The rest just laughed.

There were moving statues all over the country at the time and finally as a joke I said, "By the way, if you see any of the statues moving, for God's sake don't mention it to anyone."

And the ever-ready Dubs were up to it: "Jaysus, Father, if we see any of the statues movin', we'll hand him a bleedin' shovel."

We got on the best after that.

By 1987, goodwill towards Mount Argus was exhausted. We had been going for over four years and we simply succumbed to charity fatigue.

We ran one last draw, the fifth in all. Some 3,000 participants paid £100 each into what was supposed to be a massive draw. It turned out to be a disaster. The committee was afraid to tell me how bad it was. The leader, Joe Morris, called me into the office one morning and told me we were going to lose thousands.

I had always said that if Fr Charles wanted Mount Argus to be restored, it would happen. All we had to do was the same as he had done: trust in God. But I was in no humour for pious thoughts that morning and in an offhanded way I said to Joe, "Wouldn't you think, if Charlie wanted

Mount Argus restored, he would get off his backside and help us."

Poor Joe was shocked at my disrespectful attitude to such a saintly figure.

I went on to RTÉ to do an interview with Mike Murphy, but when I came back two hours later I was told that Rome had phoned in my absence to inform us that Fr Charles would be beatified in a few months' time. That was his way of telling me that he was still in charge.

Needless to say the draw was filled, the Church was completed and we were even able to build a shrine to Blessed Charles as well.

In 1988, Father Charles was beatified. Most people wanted to go to Rome for the beatification. I made a conscious decision that the last place I wanted to be was Rome. Father Charles's remains were in Mount Argus. We would have a big service in Dublin that day for the people he loved, which we had, on the 18th of October 1988.

Cardinal Ó Fiaich came to Mount Argus as did the papal nuncio and other dignitaries. There were so many people that they couldn't all fit into the church.

At my suggestion, Cardinal Ó Fiaich and I went outside to bless the people in the porch. Amazingly we found thousands upon thousands of people standing out in the cold on a dark October evening. Cardinal Ó Fiaich was blessing the sick in wheelchairs, parked at the hall door, which really annoyed me. Had I known they were outside I would have brought them into the sanctuary.

There was one frail little plump lady sitting in a wheelchair at the church door. She said to me, "Do you not know me, D'Arcy?" And I suddenly recognised the voice. I went over and I said, "Julie!"

She said, "That's not me name, but that's me."

"Where are you?"

"St Loman's."

"God, Julie, I'm so glad to see you. How did you know about this big day?"

"Ah sure, poor old Charlie kept me going for years. I'm delighted to see this day. I saw it in the paper and I wouldn't miss it. They brought me over."

I have to say, I cried like a baby. Nearly 20 years before, I regarded Julie as a nuisance always looking for more and more Communion. But now, wiser and older, I knew how wrong I was. She was the one with real faith.

Now that Mount Argus is in crisis again because of a lack of vocations, Charles will be made a saint, 150 years after he first came to Ireland.

Fr Charles had three simple rules about suffering: he told the sick to thank God in the midst of their suffering, to offer their suffering up to God, and to expect God's help and sometimes healing.

Fr Charles believed that Jesus walks with us during our suffering. It is a Way of the Cross. On the Way of the Cross Jesus fell three times but got up each time. He needed help. He needed Simon. He needed people. He needed a mother to touch him. He needed a towel from Veronica. He needed compassion from the women of Jerusalem. After his resurrection he proudly displayed his wounds to Thomas.

Thomas is often referred to as "Doubting Thomas" as if doubting were a sin. Doubt is not the opposite of faith; certainty is. Thomas wanted to see the wounds of Jesus. And when he did, he believed totally: "My Lord and my God," he said, before going on to give his life to spreading the Gospel. Because of Thomas's doubts, we know for certain that Jesus carried the wounds of his Passion after his resurrection, showing that the new life of the risen Jesus was won by the wounds he still bore. St Peter later summed it up: "By His wounds we are healed." That's what Charles believed and furthermore he was convinced that our own woundedness as well as His wounds save us. He knew that we don't need to be able to make sense of suffering, as long as we remember that "Nothing is impossible with God".

Charles is not a remote saint with nothing to offer our generation. As a Passionist, I should learn to look at his life and discover that our greatest gift is to be people of compassion; to be willing to walk with people along their Way of the Cross, in search of meaning rather then handing out futile answers.

The Dutch artist Van Gogh also said that God always sends works of art so that we might recognise ourselves in the works of art. "Christ is the greatest artist of all. He works not in canvas but with human flesh," he concluded. Blessed Charles, for me, is a wonderful example of a human canvas that God made into a work of art. He was a poor preacher, ridiculed by those who lived with him. At the end of his life he suffered pain but remained human enough to have a sing-song and a glass of whiskey when he needed it. He's my kind of saint.

He called himself "poor old Charlie" as he walked along the corridors. One lasting memory that Fr Eugene Nevin (a contemporary in Mount Argus) had of Charles, was his fear of death as he hobbled down the 59 steps from his cell on the top floor, to bless the sick in the parlours. All the while he would be repeating the second half of the Hail Mary: "Holy Mary, Mother of God, pray for us sinners, now and at the hour of our death, Amen."

In theory, Charles was not the ideal model of the perfect Passionist. Yet of all the Passionists who've lived and worked here for over 150 years, he's the only one to be canonised a saint.

Through the bad times, Charles still keeps me going. There have been many times, and I'm sure there will be many more, when I wondered why I remained a priest or a Passionist. And I still do to this day. These days as I look back and reflect on my life honestly, there isn't much to enthuse over. But then I think of Charlie. An old man full of pain praying for a happy death, recognised by the people as a holy man but not really by those in his own house. And now he's a canonised saint in Heaven. That's what keeps me going. Even broken failures like me can be a work of art when I allow God to work through me.

Chapter 13

Don't Shoot the Messenger

I have a surefire best-selling book that can never be published. Conscience demands that it be forever locked within me. Confidentiality is the basis of trust. People's personal secrets and failures must be treated with respect. In fact they are sacred. Because I'm a priest, confidentiality is even more important.

I am not just referring to confessional secrets. As most people know, I must be prepared to die rather than to reveal a person's confession. But I also have to be scrupulous about confidential information taken on outside the confessional. The personal lives of showbiz friends, the crippling doubts of prominent politicians, as well as the mistakes of the famous and influential, will go to the grave with me.

Even in everyday life a priest who gossips will never be trusted. One of the invaluable contributions priests and religious make to the community is our availability to listen to family and personal traumas, in the sure and certain knowledge that they will never be talked about inappropriately.

It's the main reason why I don't drink alcohol. I could never live with myself if I thought I might have even inadvertently revealed a single secret a person trusted me with. I like to be in control of my senses at all times.

That sense of confidentiality was one of the reasons I was often asked to mediate in business disputes and, on at least four occasions, kidnappings.

As far as the general public are concerned people vaguely remember two of those cases. Those are the only two I can talk about here; the other two never became public and, as far as I am concerned, never will.

The first time my role became public was when a gravedigger in Mount Jerome cemetery was kidnapped. Even in the late 1970s and early 1980s it was obvious that particular areas of Dublin were training grounds for future criminals.

The area of the parish I looked after had some of the best people I ever worked with. But in one small corner of the district there were a couple of families who did their best to hold the entire area to ransom. I had a constant battle with them because their tactic was to move into the flatland area, take over the flats and drive all the good families out of them. That's precisely what was happening when I came to the parish. Day after day I would make contact with good families and day after day they would ask me to write letters to the Corporation to try to get them new houses in a better area. They didn't want their children contaminated by the criminal element.

Part of my job was to make friends with the criminals. They had their own code of honour and if I was to influence them at all, I had to at least get to know them.

Almost instantly I realised that many of them were serving an apprenticeship to crime. Starting at the very bottom rung, young boys and girls of 11 and upwards began by robbing old ladies' handbags and breaking into their houses when they were out to steal whatever cash they could find, as well as stealing from the shops and pubs in the district. I began by arranging a meeting with the politicians and gardaí of the area. I needed their help to break this cycle of crime.

When the youngsters had served their apprenticeship of petty crime, they moved up to more serious activities like robbing milkmen and shop owners. Right at the top were their older brothers, who used guns for the big stuff.

Within a six-month period I noticed that as the older criminals were caught and sent to jail, everyone moved up a rung on the ladder and took their place. When those young men went to jail, it was like completing their university degree in crime. They came out skilled in all the tricks of the trade, which meant they moved up in the criminal world to become involved in the growing, citywide drug trade.

Subsequently some of the leading criminals in Dublin came from that area and a few of them were well connected with Martin Cahill, The General.

Those were the circumstances in which we had to try to build a community. The politicians understood the problem but it was difficult to get overworked gardaí interested. Security and the North were their priority.

But by the time I was asked to intervene in a kidnapping I knew the local scene pretty thoroughly.

The events surrounding the kidnapping have been well documented elsewhere because it was connected to the famous robbery of O'Connor's jewellery factory in Harold's Cross.

At the time I was not privy to all the details, and didn't want to know them either. On that occasion a number of criminals and illegal groups came together to carry out the robbery. Millions of pounds worth of jewellery were stolen. For its time it was a daring escapade. The problem was that nobody knew where the loot went afterwards and to this day much of it remains unaccounted for.

On the day of the robbery I was as usual visiting the sick in my parish. And when I came across a van burning on one of the streets, I thought very little of it. It was probably another stolen van that somebody wanted to destroy before the gardaí came around. I went about my work of visiting the sick and let the fire brigade deal with the van. A few hours later I realised that the van was one of the vehicles used in the robbery and was a vital clue in the investigation.

Later still when the various groups who carried out the robbery fell out among themselves, one of the families alleged to have been involved in the robbery had a brother who was a gravedigger in Mount Jerome cemetery. Mount Jerome is an ancient burial place with many mysterious and ornamental vaults. The rumour went around that the goods taken in the O'Connor robbery were buried in one of the vaults. But which one? That was the question. They decided to kidnap the gravedigger that they falsely suspected of hiding the gold.

The poor man was missing for days when his family called a press conference to ask people to help them find him. This particular family lived outside our parish but were well known to me. Usually I was the one they loved to hate. But they also knew that I could be trusted. So they asked me to allow my name go forward as the person the kidnappers would contact if they knew where their son was. I gave my word that I would do my best as long as it was within the law. They accepted that too.

Over the next few days there were many phone calls to me claiming sightings of the missing man. I diligently passed each one of them on to the authorities. Most of them were nothing more than deliberate decoys. The gangs went on with their own peculiar form of civil war, including a shoot-out in the Phoenix Park. Each night, some of them would ring me to brief me where they thought the missing man might be.

Then towards the end of the week, I was at the front door of Mount Argus about to go on a sick call. The receptionist called me back to say there was an urgent message for me on the phone. On the other end of the phone was an anxious and distorted voice which shouted a brief message at me: "Your f***** friend is on the side of the road at the ballroom outside Limerick."

The phone was slammed down before I could ask a question. I knew from my showband experience that he must have been near the Jetland ballroom so I phoned the gardaí to tell them, not knowing whether he was dead or alive.

I went straight to the family to tell them to expect some news about their brother soon. While I was there news came through that indeed he had been found on the side of the road outside Limerick, alive but very distressed. The family gave me more credit than I deserved and their associates made a solemn promise to me that they would never rob cars in Mount Argus again, out of gratitude. And they even kept their promise for two weeks.

The next kidnapping that I was publicly involved in was much more high-profile and right to this day captures the imagination. By the mid-1980s kidnapping the newly rich was providing an instant income for criminal and illegal groups. One of the most notorious was Dessie O'Hare from Armagh. By this time he had passed through the ranks of the Provisionals and the INLA and was a maverick criminal with a reputation for great cruelty.

He was released from jail in 2006 having served a mere 19 years of a 40-year jail sentence handed down to him for kidnapping and mutilating the Dublin dentist John O'Grady in 1987.

It's only appropriate to say now that I agreed with John O'Grady and with the Darragh family never to be too precise about the details of the kidnapping negotiations or the extraordinarily lucky release of John O'Grady. This is for two reasons. Firstly, if the full story is ever to be told, John O'Grady is the only one who has the right to tell it. Secondly, the less detail given, the more difficult it will be for criminal gangs to carry out the "perfect" kidnapping in the future.

In fact John O'Grady should not have been kidnapped at all. The man O'Hare and his gang was looking for was Professor Austin Darragh. At the time he was a high-profile businessman and medical doctor. He had bought Sir Patrick Dun's hospital and, quite frequently, estimates of his personal wealth in many millions appeared in the papers. That's the first lesson to learn. The higher the estimates of your wealth the more vulnerable to kidnapping you become. Austin Darragh was well known in sporting circles too. He was a commentator and rugby analyst in the early days of Radio Éireann. His son Paul, who died tragically young in 2005, was hugely successful and a famous member of the Irish showjumping team. So the family were constantly in the news.

The Darraghs had once lived in a beautiful house in Foxrock, a wealthy suburb of Dublin, but in 1985 they moved from Foxrock to a new location on the Hill of Tara. Their daughter and son-in-law, the O'Gradys, moved into their old house in Foxrock. So when O'Hare plotted to kidnap Austin he got the most basic fact of all wrong. He kidnapped the wrong man.

I was friendly with Austin Darragh through broadcasting, and when his son-in-law, John O'Grady, was kidnapped in the most horrific circumstances, I contacted the family to tell them I would help in any way possible. Little did I know how that promise would be fulfilled.

As the days went by, the police were closing in on the gang with their kidnap victim. O'Hare and his men became more and more volatile. They sent notes demanding a ransom of one-and-a-half million sterling for the release of John O'Grady. Unfortunately, they left the notes in churches under statues – but tragically, they didn't know the names of the saints. O'Hare was a master criminal, but religion was not his forte. In one instance his gang didn't know the difference between a statue of Our Lady and a statue of St John. It almost had tragic results. He thought the Darragh family were ignoring his notes. In fact they got them too late.

But on Wednesday the 4th of November 1987 I got a call to attend an urgent meeting in Dr Darragh's office. When I went there it was obvious that it was now a race to find John O'Grady alive.

What had happened was that in one of the notes that had been found, O'Hare enclosed two half fingers, one from each hand. Later we discovered that in his panic and with an evil desire to be listened to, he had chopped off both of John O'Grady's little fingers. He put a towel in John's mouth, put a foot on his hand and with a hammer and chisel cut each little finger at the middle knuckle. John, with his medical experience, knew that he could bleed to death. To cauterise his fingers and stop the bleeding, he himself took a knife, heated it on the bar of an electric fire, and applied the burning knife to the ends of his fingers to stop the blood. Even now, thinking about it sends shivers down my backbone.

O'Hare then enclosed the tops of the fingers in the ransom note with the threat that if the million-and-a-half was not paid over by noon on the 5th of November, he would saw O'Grady's legs off.

This was the news that greeted me at the meeting. The family wanted to pay the money to ensure they got John back alive. By now they had been able to negotiate with the Bank of Ireland to get the money in the form requested – used sterling currency in £20 and £10 denominations. The money was to be brought to the Bank of Ireland in Dublin that evening, and the family asked if I would bring the money to O'Hare and if possible negotiate the release of John O'Grady.

It was made clear to me that it could be a very dangerous operation, and indeed one garda told me to be aware that I might not come out of this alive. Austin Darragh gave me one hour to think about it.

I told him I didn't need an hour; I would do it provided the gardaí knew what I was doing and would not accompany me or come near me during the negotiations. I wanted to do everything in a trustworthy way. They could carry out their investigations afterwards, but if they wanted me to help negotiate John's freedom, then I wanted to do it on my own. I felt it was the only chance of success I had. The principles were agreed. It was to be a top-secret operation and I was sent home to rest until the next morning.

I told them I wouldn't be able to rest, as I had to go to Omagh that night. A senior garda on duty went apoplectic. Wherever I was going, I certainly was not going to the North of Ireland through Monaghan – the heart of O'Hare's territory. I told him I had to.

At the time I was going around the country practically on a nightly basis to raise money to restore Mount Argus.

People were helping me to raise the money by running little functions. I did my best to attend as many as I could throughout the country. On the 4th of November 1987, Kathy Coll, the daughter of the legendary country singer Brian Coll, was holding her 21st birthday party in the GAA Centre in Omagh. She was inviting as many of her friends as she could and charging them £4 each, with the money going to Mount Argus. I told the gardaí I had to be there. If I didn't go I would be letting the family down but also people would be wondering what I was up to. The safest thing was to go.

So at five o'clock I headed to Omagh in the company of the Coggins family, who were also friends of mine and of Brian Coll's. I couldn't tell them what was happening the next day.

As it turned out it was one of the worst nights of my life. There was a pea-soup fog. I hoped it would clear by the time we were coming home. But when the function was over and I was about to head back to Dublin, the fog was worse than ever. My sister, who lives in Omagh, wanted us to stay. Of course she was absolutely right. It was madness trying to travel back. But I had to tell them I had an urgent meeting next morning. To be honest and convincing I had to give them a clue that I was involved in some negotiations about John O'Grady, without revealing too many details. And so we started for home at midnight saying many a Rosary along the way. The fog never relented and we arrived back at Mount Argus at 4am. I was due to be collected at 5.30am to go down to the Bank of Ireland, where a specially constructed car and the money awaited me in an underground car-park.

I lay in bed for half an hour and then went to offer Mass in the little oratory that had been the bedroom of Fr Charles of Mount Argus. In that room I said what I thought would be my last Mass. But I decided not to dwell on it. And so early in the morning a Garda car brought me to the Bank of Ireland. There I had the first inkling of what £1.5 million looked like. There were seven suitcases full of money chained in the back of the estate car. I was brought out to the Naas Road and sent on my way. All the way down in the car I listened to stories about Eamonn Andrews. That was the day after his death and the two events are indelibly linked in my mind. Eamonn was a man I knew very well and in fact I had been on a plane with him a couple of weeks previously to London. A chauffeur-driven car awaited him and he brought me into London. He often came to Mount Argus and I knew him well from the entertainment industry. So I was doubly sad.

A little way down the road I realised just how impossible the whole thing was going to be. I had thought of everything except how to go to the toilet. I was dying to go to the toilet but couldn't. Can you imagine leaving £1.5 million unguarded on the side of the road to go into a toilet? Can you imagine even stopping along the road anywhere? I visualised people jumping out of the hedge to hijack me – and the money.

Eventually I arrived in Cork with an aching bladder and followed the instructions I was given regarding the kidnapping. I was told to fill the car with petrol because most likely when I arrived at the Silver Springs hotel I would be asked to drive somewhere else. The plan was to keep me driving around the country until darkness fell. Then, it was assumed, I would be stopped on a quiet road somewhere and the money would be taken from me, if I was lucky. If things went wrong something worse would befall me.

When I pulled into the petrol station I was supposed to be anonymous. But the owner of the station came out to me and greeted me with the words, "Are you on the way to meet O'Hare with the ransom?" I was stunned. Apparently somebody had leaked the story to the *Irish Independent*. They had it on its front page that I was on my way to hand over the money. I had every right to be anxious on the way to Cork.

As it so happened I couldn't get the petrol cap off the tank. By now I was panicking because I was 10 minutes late to meet O'Hare. Visions of John O'Grady being shot because I couldn't get the cap off a petrol tank were etched on my mind. I had a small relic of Fr Charles of Mount Argus with me and I blessed the cap with the relic, praying for guidance. Instantly the cap came off and I got my car filled with petrol.

Being 10 minutes late proved to be a blessing in disguise. As I turned into the Silver Springs hotel, a newsflash came on the Mike Murphy show on RTÉ that John O'Grady had been found in a house in Cabra, alive.

For a second I panicked. What was I to do with the money? In the instructions I was given, I was told not to go on a solo run. It was always best to keep to the plan. That's what I did. So when I got to the Silver Springs, two groups of gardaí were close to firing at each other. The Cork/Dublin rivalry was there in the Garda too. Eventually I shouted at them to put their guns down and they did. I went in to await a phone call, but I knew it would never come now. Instead I went to the toilet and had the sweetest pee of my life!

At this point all the gardaí left me and I was stranded in Cork with £1.5 million not knowing what to do with it. Someone advised me to drive back to Dublin. I wasn't going to do that and run the risk of it being taken from me. So I drove to a Garda station and handed them the keys of the car. Dr Darragh was on the phone to tell me to get the money to the bank as quickly as possible. Obviously with interest rates as they were in 1987, it was clocking up by the second. Eventually I got somebody to take charge of the money, went to the airport and flew up to Dublin.

This is probably the only funny incident in the whole event. Brendan Grace is a good friend of mine and always has been. His late mother, Chrissie, was also a friend of mine and I had attended her in her last weeks in Our Lady's Hospice in Harold's Cross. She had said to Brendan that she wanted me to conduct her funeral in Mount Argus. When news of the negotiation came to me I had to phone Brendan and say I wouldn't be able to do the funeral and that he would understand why not the next day. He was none too pleased. Now that I had got back to Dublin in time I wanted to receive her remains into Mount Argus as a pleasant surprise for Brendan.

It seemed that every television station in the world had cameras waiting for me to discover if I'd handed over the money. One sneaky reporter, a correspondent with one of the national dailies, thought he would get the inside track. As I was about to sprinkle holy water on the remains of the late Mrs Grace, he stepped right in front of me and said, "We know each other a long time, Brian, and I know you're busy, but tell me how much was handed over to O'Hare?"

On one of the few occasions I can ever remember being deliberately rude, I put the funeral book across my face and said to him, "Would you ever f*** off," and continued, "eternal rest grant unto her, O Lord, and may perpetual light shine upon her."

Unfortunately for me, one of the other reporters heard this and it went around town like wildfire. It was taken in the right spirit, I'm glad to say.

After the funeral I got into the car and drove to Lisnaskea, Co Fermanagh, where a local group had a function in the Ortine Hotel. I had handed over one-and-half million pounds that day and now went to Lisnaskea to collect £250 to help put the roof on Mount Argus church.

John O'Grady's rescue in Cabra was a total accident. Sadly, one of the gardaí on the case was very seriously wounded in the shootout. Thankfully, Martin O'Connor survived and for many years afterwards, on the 5th of November, John O'Grady and Martin O'Connor and I had lunch to celebrate the gift of life. But for the grace of God all three of us would have been dead.

For almost five years afterwards I was constantly reminded of my role, not only by the papers but also by the fact that some of O'Hare's gang thought I had tried to double-cross them. Nothing could have been further from the truth but mischievous statements by some politicians could have given that impression.

The result was that every couple of months, especially if I was in the Border regions, a mysterious Hiace van would pull alongside me, usually in the dark of night. It would neither pass me nor pull in behind me. It would just drive alongside me. The first few times it was absolutely scary. Usually a few days later some shoddy character would appear out of nowhere and would walk beside me in a Dublin street or outside Mount Argus to remind me I was still on their hit list.

Once outside Mount Argus my car was completely wrecked. On another occasion the two front wheels of my car had the bolts loosened on them. Luckily the Garda had warned me always to check the car. I was heading out to do an early-morning broadcast on 2FM and I still shudder at what might have happened had I not checked the wheels. Who did it? Who knows? But the local gardaí were convinced it was the O'Hare gang. Thankfully as time went by they left me alone.

At that time I was so busy I didn't stop to reflect on the events. But it had a devastating effect on me two years later when I eventually found time to think about it.

I was on my own away from all the attention and the rush. I began to have vivid dreams of what could have happened. It was of course delayed shock as well as exhaustion.

I found myself full of uncharacteristic anger. Then one night I realised why. I had been in a dangerous situation, which I know could have cost me my life. In my mind I had faced death more realistically than I imagined. In a way I was feeling almost guilty because I was alive – when I should have been grateful. But what bothered me most was that not one of my brethren asked me how I felt about it. I know none of them intended this, but in my loneliness I interpreted their silence as indifference as to whether I lived or died. I repeat it wasn't really what they thought, just how it was perceived by me. It changed my life completely and shifted the centre of my commitment radically.

CHAPTER 14

MAN ABOUT THE TOWNSHIPS

I always had this longing to go to Africa. It was one of the reasons why I was happier in a religious order rather than a diocese. I had quite poor health before I was ordained so when it came to going to Africa I wasn't even considered. They thought my place should be at home editing *The Cross* magazine.

The overseas missions were the glamorous life. That's where real priests went, as it were. That whole idea of rough living had a rugged, macho attraction for people. I discovered afterwards that whether at home or abroad each life had its own special difficulties and its own blessings.

By 1988, I'd been on the parish of Mount Argus 11 years, had worked hard at the restoration of the buildings and raised the funds to pay for it. Blessed Charles was now beatified as well.

One of our priests in South Africa took seriously ill and the provincial superior put it as gently as he could: "It would be nice for you to have a few months in Africa. The climate will be good; you'll be able to work a little bit there, but not nearly so hard as you're working here. It would be good for you, if you don't mind being away for Christmas. And it would also take us out of a big difficulty, because we have nobody to run the parish there."

Off I went to live on my own for the first time. I went to Johannesburg in November 1988, which was summertime there. I couldn't declare I was going in as a priest because I wouldn't have got a visa. So I had to use a holiday visa, which was valid for only two months. I remember having to drive from Johannesburg after the two months were up, to one of our houses in Botswana, which borders on South Africa, and then come back into South Africa to be granted another two months.

In Johannesburg I worked in a suburb called Carletonville. It was the town in which the Whites lived but I couldn't relate to apartheid at all. This was 1988, when apartheid was rampant. When I went to the parish house the priest had left an Alsatian dog to guard the place. I had to befriend her, which wasn't easy. The Alsatian was originally trained in the goldmines and could smell Black people 50 yards away. She went berserk, barking, running around in circles, creating a racket, and would rush to attack them if they rang the doorbell.

A White person could take everything in the house and the dog would lick his face. That's how deep-seated apartheid was. Even the dogs respected Whites and attacked Blacks. At that time there was a 7pm curfew for "non-Whites".

The Black people lived five miles out the road, in the township of Khutsong. They had Hiace carriers which bussed them in and out of the White town all day. There were no shops in the Black township, which meant that the Whites in Carletonville took their money and then bussed them back out to the township.

White people were allowed to have Black servants working for them. They could stay on their property but not in their houses. So house owners had huts at the bottom of their garden where the Black maid slept. That's how pernicious the system was.

No Whites could enter the township but clergymen were allowed to minister there. I was one of the few people in that whole parish who knew what the township of Khutsong looked like. The White parishioners had never been in there and knew little about it.

When the Black people came to Mass in Carletonville they always sat in the back seats in church, well away from the Whites. None of the parishioners was in favour of this practice, but that was the law and we could do nothing about it.

Initially I thought it was ridiculous to have Black servants in the house. I explained it to the cook: "I'll keep paying you, but I don't really want you here at all, because I don't want to play the apartheid game."

There was another servant who came to mow the lawns. I decided to mow them myself.

A delegation of Blacks came to me: "We understand your intentions, but you're not helping us. Unless we get jobs and are seen to work, and unless we can be of service, our dignity is gone completely."

Here was I, a White man coming in from a foreign place, trying to help but doing so in an unhelpful way. It's the White man's mentality; he thinks he knows what's good for Black people. After that I treated them with great dignity and made sure that, if they were eating, they sat down at the table with me. It wasn't much but it was a start.

I also looked after the township and the goldmines. I was on the road at a quarter past four to go to the mines to say Mass for the miners at five o'clock on Sunday mornings. There were 9,000 people working in that particular goldmine. They came from all over Africa. They worked almost 18 hours a day down in the mines for nine months of the year. They went back to their homelands to be with the families they'd left behind for the rest of the year.

Many came from other countries in Africa and were willing to put up with this awful treatment because it was better than what they had at home. That was a big shock to me too. They thought they were in heaven once they got work in this awful place.

They were housed in dormitories and had no life at all. They worked all day in seriously hot, bad conditions. Much later I discovered just how bad those conditions were.

Quite a number of the White parishioners had administrative jobs in these mines. The Whites also came from different backgrounds. Some came from an English or European background but the majority were White Afrikaners, who were the ruling class.

Afrikaners rarely spoke English. They spoke Afrikaans instead, a mixture of the German and Dutch languages. They were frightened, overly officious people by 1988.

The Portuguese were different again. Many came from other countries in Africa where they had been the ruling class but, because of freedom and independence, they'd lost their place in society.

The Portuguese were good business people, wonderful market

gardeners, strong Catholics, but never trusted Catholic clergy with their money. They suspected the Church was giving aid to the ANC, and to people already displaced by freedom fighters, supporting that cause would be like a turkey voting for Christmas.

Instead they would come to the parish council with an offer: "The church needs painting this year. The Portuguese will do it." They raised funds through their wonderful fiestas. South Africa is a great country for vegetables of every kind, especially corn on the cob and beautiful, fresh fruit. The Portuguese were particularly generous with their produce. A full basket of fresh fruit and vegetables was left at my door every other day. That's how they showed their support.

There are 11 official languages in South Africa, which is only a fraction of the number of tribes and tongues that exist.

The first day I said Mass in the Black township, all the altar servers were dressed immaculately in colourful uniforms. They absolutely loved dressing up. They came out of these awful little tin hovels but dressed beautifully and were proud of themselves.

The entrance to the township had rows of good, brick houses. There was usually only one major road in a township, so that it could be policed easily. Some of it was tarmacadam, the rest was mud. The farther in you went the worse conditions got. Roads disappeared and then you just had tin shacks that looked like henhouses. They were half houses really, not even high enough to stand up in. People had to crawl into them. They ate outside. Often there was no sanitation except for an open drain through the complex. Water generally wasn't a problem in this area, because there was plenty of water from the mines.

Out of these dusty streets and awful places came the well groomed children to church, walking barefooted. In the yard of the church there were a number of water taps. I couldn't figure out why until I saw them wash the dirt off their feet. In their plastic bags, they carried their good clothes and after washing they put on their shoes and their virgin white shirts. It was like a First Communion every Sunday.

The liturgies were incredible. Mass took two hours even without a long sermon from me. The first Sunday I made a big mistake. I worked hard on my sermon. When I said a few sentences a man in the corner stood up and translated it. Then another man in another part got up and translated it. And then a third person translated it. In that township there were three distinct tribal languages. I realised that this sermon was going to be delivered four times, so I cut it short instantly. My sermons, from then on, lasted two minutes, which, by the time they were translated into three languages, became 10-minute sermons. I kept things simple and learned quickly.

They sang their way through Mass. They couldn't afford an organ, but had this little tuning fork. They sang four-part harmony absolutely naturally. To me it was uplifting but some of our men who were there 30 years were driven insane listening to the same hymns over and over again. I could understand that too.

They genuinely appreciated the little I did for them. They really loved performing in church and were rightfully proud of their faith.

On my first day, the altar servers lined up to greet me. "Morning, Father." I thought they were great because I couldn't greet them in their language.

On Tuesday evening I was back for Mass. I went into the sacristy and again, there was a row of servers: "Morning, Father." I realised they didn't know what they were saying. They just knew this phrase to keep Father happy. That was what they had to do to survive. They learned enough Afrikaans to be able to get employment, enough Portuguese to take instructions and enough English to get the job. Even people who had never been to school knew enough to get work

Funerals were three-hour affairs. I simply said the Mass; somebody else gave the oration about the deceased person they knew.

The coffin was a status symbol. I buried one old lady in a makeshift box. The lid was made in three pieces from ill-fitting wood. She kept an eye on me out through the cracks. I was half expecting her to wink out at me.

The next funeral was entirely different. It had a super casket so valuable that they had to cement it into the grave lest it would be stolen and used again. The cemetery was at the deepest level of the township. Yet everyone at this deprived part spent at least an hour in the graveyard while they reverently danced on the grave to pack the red soil in. They had their own ritual and I was quite happy to let them get on with it.

While I was in South Africa, some people from the township approached me to offer Mass for another group of workers who lived out on the farms. I couldn't really understand what they wanted me to do but I agreed on a Sunday afternoon to join them and say Mass where the farm workers lived. They lived miles out into the country down an intricate maze of side roads and through beautiful farmlands. They were the most exploited people I met during my time in South Africa – even worse than the miners.

They had Mass once a month years previously, but for some reason this group had no access to the sacraments. When I agreed, some of the workers went round during the very few free hours they had, because they work all day every day, to other farms. The first day about 100 people turned up.

The conditions these workers lived in were deplorable. Yet the hut chosen for the Mass was totally cleaned up. They took what little furniture there was out of it and allowed the congregation to crowd in, out of the afternoon sun. Afterwards they all went home having shared whatever little refreshment they could afford.

I arranged to say Mass for them again in two weeks' time. That was when they brought all their children to be baptised and asked me to bless a number of marriages.

I asked them what they did when no priest got to them. On those days, and they had done this every Sunday for three years, they met in the afternoon, which was the only time they had off, and they prayed for about two hours. They didn't have Communion but they read the scripture and discussed it among themselves. That is what kept the faith alive.

As I drove back to the presbytery that Sunday afternoon, I couldn't help thinking that perhaps that's what kept the faith alive in Ireland in troubled times. The people took responsibility for their own faith. It's a model that shouldn't be ruled out in the future. Obviously faith can survive outside the structures we now think essential.

One Friday morning I was driving into the township when a wild horse was killed by a minibus. The people rushed out of their tin huts to cut the horse into manageable pieces. This was a real feast for them. They were cutting the horse up to bring home and have their meat for the week.

Even in 1988, I could see the influence of the wider world approaching. Outside their shacks, they'd have a stick in the air with a television aerial on top. Quite frequently they were watching soaps from America. Even then, the educated ones knew it could change South Africa. The young people could see Black people driving fast cars, dressed immaculately, in big jobs. They could see successful Black people everywhere. It was only a matter of time before they wanted the same for themselves.

I was a month there when I had a wedding in the Black township. Most everything was on a Saturday in the township because that was their day off. If somebody died on a Monday, they were kept until Saturday. Weddings were the same. This particular day, I did a wedding for a lovely couple. They were so delighted and dressed up like any bride and groom would.

We did the wedding in the township church but this young groom, by profession, was a park attendant in Carletonville. He planted the flowers, cut the lawns and pulled the weeds. They drove from the township to get photographs taken in the beautiful garden he looked after. The police arrived and put them out of the park because they weren't allowed to be there at the weekend. They never had their wedding photographs taken in that lovely garden, even though he was the guy who made it lovely. Apartheid was a malicious, evil system.

The first time I went there I had to wait until I got home to write anything for the *Sunday World*. If I'd been discovered writing from South Africa, I would have been deported. One of the tasks I gave some of the young people in the township where I worked was to explain to me what it was like to be black in South Africa in 1988. These are parts of what they gave me:

"It's very difficult to be Black in South Africa today. First of all I'm not free to choose where I want to live. I'm told from my earliest day where I am to live and that implies what conditions I have to live in."

"In townships there are middle-class Blacks, rich Blacks and very poor Blacks, the same as every other society. But they're all Blacks and they all have to live here because they have no choice. Everybody is condemned to live in a ghetto for life."

"To be Black means others will take my money in shops, in courts, in taxes, but they will not let me live alongside them. I can live with a White family provided I sleep in the servants' quarters."

"Whites want to use Blacks but not become friends with them. For example, there are beautiful parks in White areas and dirt roads in Black townships. The beautiful parks are kept spick and span by Black workers. You as a White can walk through those parks, even though you are here only a few months. I and my people have lived and worked here for centuries, yet I can never walk in the park unless I'm there to mow the grass or weed the flowerbed."

"I go down the street and I see signs which say Whites only."

"When I go to a hotel, I cannot get in, unless of course I am needed to scrub floors or clean bedrooms. As a guest, though, I am not wanted. I cannot be served the beautiful food which my Black brothers and sisters cook in the kitchen for Whites only. I cannot go to church where I wish. You as a priest cannot live in our Black parish because you are White. You can only come in and visit my area. Some day I hope we will have enough Black priests so that we can have one resident here."

That was how the Black South Africans saw themselves.

South Africa in 1988 was good for me. I learned a lot and longed to go back. In fact, if I had been given a choice then, I would have chosen to spend at least another 10 years in Africa. I could see it was an emerging society and Church. The Church was different there. We hadn't the strictures which stifled the Church at home. The future was there and I wanted to be part of it. There was a "sense of life", an enthusiasm, a hope and a freedom, that even in the 1980s was missing in Ireland.

Chapter 15

Give Up Yer Auld Sins

One of the worthwhile things I did in life was rescuing the Bible stories of children in Dublin from a wastepaper basket. I didn't record them; I just saved them from destruction.

There was a wonderful Donegal lady called Peg Cunningham who taught children from the inner city in Dublin. It was difficult for her to teach them, because they were large classes and pupils came to school only when they were well enough and had food and clothes to do so. She tried to give them something to help them in life. Being a seanchaí from Donegal, she composed little Bible stories in a Dublinese way and then got the children to learn them off by heart.

She brought in a tape recorder with a plastic microphone and told them that the best children at telling the stories "would be on the wireless". Being little show-offs, as all kids are, they wanted to be on the wireless. She built up, over years, 30 or 40 fantastic stories spoken hypnotically by the children. I had heard one story when I was a student learning to broadcast on a programme called *Network*, produced by the Catholic Communications Institute in Booterstown.

Occasionally, because I was writing for a pop magazine at the time, they asked me to review significant new pop records. That's how I began in broadcasting 40 years ago.

The story I remembered was about the Visitation – the angel coming to greet Mary – and it was fantastic, but I could never find out who did it or where it came from.

Fast-forward another 10 years to 1976 when I was teaching in the Communications Institute as well as producing tapes for the new catechetical course.

I was tidying up late one night when I saw a spool of open reel tape lying in the wastepaper box. It was nearly a sin to throw away a spool. You might throw out the tape, but you kept the spool. I lifted it out and put it on the machine. As good practice, I always listened to it to ensure it wasn't a valuable recording that was being thrown out.

I spooled it through and heard the voices speeded up, and then I slowed it down and eureka, wasn't it the same story of the Visitation that I'd heard 10 years beforehand. I'd looked everywhere for this and then discovered 11 classic stories in the wastepaper bin. I rewound the tape and took it home with me.

Now, move on again another seven or eight years. In the early 1980s, I'd been asked by RTÉ to do morning reflections live on 2FM on the *Ronan Collins Show*. It meant getting up at six o'clock, driving out to RTÉ, reading the papers, writing a reflection on the day's news, broadcasting it live at a quarter past seven, driving home and saying the eight o'clock Mass in Mount Argus. The reflection was repeated from a recording at a quarter past eight. I did that for nearly six years, on alternate months with Fr Jack Harris, five mornings a week for £5 a week – a pound a morning.

I explained to Bill O'Donovan, who was the head of that area of 2FM at that time: "Easter's coming up. I'd like a break away for a week to see my family." He told me to record a few pieces in advance so I told him about this tape that I'd rescued years ago.

I brought it to Bill and, being a Dubliner himself, he recognised sheer poetry when he heard it. He called in a sound engineer. When he heard the kids, he came in, in his own free time, to clean up the tape. They took out coughs and hiccups and dogs barking and doors slamming and children hitting microphones. They got five stories out of it and broadcast them in my reflection slot during my week off.

The country stopped. Everybody wanted to hear them again. A good idea had found its time.

A comment made during one of the recordings gave us a clue about their origin: "We don't know the end of this story because Miss Cunningham hasn't told us yet." But who was this Miss Cunningham? We couldn't find Miss Cunningham or couldn't be sure of the school.

I wrote about it in the *Sunday World*. No luck. Then I happened to be in Veritas bookshop in Abbey Street one day when a priest approached me. "Did I hear you were looking for Peg Cunningham?" Fr O'Keeffe was the priest who worked in the area years before and who actually brought the stories out to *Network*, for Pat Ahearne, the producer, to listen to.

Radharc films had recorded one or two of them on film as well. The lady was Peg Cunningham and he told me she used to live on Rathfarnham Road in Dublin. He didn't know whether she was alive or dead.

I checked in the phone book and there was only one Cunningham in Rathfarnham Road – 9 Rathfarnham Road. I went to the *Sunday World* offices, because that's where they were based at the time. I asked the security man where 9 Rathfarnham Road might be. "It's there across the road," he pointed.

I went to the door and this lovely little lady came out and said, "Oh, I thought you'd find me eventually." She knew exactly who I was and she knew I was looking for her. She was generous and lovely and respectful. There was another teacher with her and that turned out to be providential.

We had a lovely chat. Miss Cunningham was modest, while the other lady was insistent: "She wrote those stories and she did a great job with them. She doesn't know her own talents. Do you realise she has a box full of them upstairs?"

What?

"I'm too old to go upstairs to the attic. You're not getting them. But I did get a man to put the best ones on a cassette for me. And only it's you I wouldn't lend it to you. Make sure nothing happens it."

I went straight to RTÉ with my green cassette. Bill O'Donovan got the sound man again and we copied them to an open reel tape for safety. I gave her back her tape that evening. Now we had 17 wonderful stories.

We had another week and another week and the whole thing built up until EMI asked me to pick the best of them, write links and introductions for them, and then they would put them on sale as a cassette. The next day I recorded my links and it came out as *Give Up Yer Auld Sins*, in cassette form only. It outsold U2 that Christmas.

Poor Miss Cunningham. By the time all this had happened, she had Alzheimer's and was in a nursing home and didn't really appreciate the success of her work.

After Christmas the cassette went double platinum. I brought the double platinum award to Miss Cunningham in Ratoath in her nursing home. She was pleasant and gentle but not very aware. I remember this vignette as a beautiful insight into a life.

The nuns and the whole community of Ratoath were there as I made the presentation to Miss Cunningham. She was all done up. We got pictures taken. Then she lifted the platinum disc and said, "Ah, isn't it a lovely wee mirror?"

And wasn't that exactly what it was: a mirror of herself. Her own spirituality was mirrored in the lives and in the stories. She did more for catechetics and Bible history than all of the bishops in Ireland ever did. Or indeed, all of us journalists either.

When she died, at her removal, I was able to tell that story. The Word of God was mirrored through her, and in her innocence she had got it absolutely right.

It was because of Peg Cunningham and *Give Up Yer Auld Sins* that I got to meet Nelson Mandela. I met Nelson Mandela for about four minutes, but that's all you need with the most charismatic leader in the world. It happened to me totally by accident.

I went to South Africa for the second time in 1994. There was a famous broadcaster there called Paddy O'Byrne, from – where else? – Dublin. He heard that I was in South Africa and he loved those stories. He rang me up and asked me to go on to his show to talk about them. I talked about them as best I could, wondering if the listeners understood even the children's accents.

Nelson Mandela was coming into the studio as he had just been elected president. I met him and spoke with him and felt unbelievably honoured. That should have been enough for me, but the journalist in me got the better of me. "I write for a paper in Ireland and do you mind if I ask you one or two questions while you're waiting?" He generously agreed.

"People across the world now call you a saint. Are you really a saint?"

His answer was wonderful. "Well, I don't know what a saint is, as I am not of your religion. But as far as I know, in your religion, a saint is a sinner who tries harder. And if that's the definition of a saint, yes of course I'm one."

That little gem has kept me going through many a hard day. I'm sure Nelson Mandela has no idea he even said that. And yet it has given hope to people everywhere I've mentioned it for 12 years and it's still being quoted.

Eventually, they rereleased the tapes 10 years on, in early 2000, this time on CD format. There was the usual publicity. I was on the *Marian Finucane Show* one morning and it helped the CD to reach number one again.

There was a young man who had just qualified from art college driving to Galway that day listening to the radio. He had never heard these tapes before. They were totally new to him. He thought they were unique. He got in contact with EMI to see if he could do a cartoon feature based on one of the stories. He and his work colleague did a cartoon of the John the Baptist story. It was a delightful, four-minute masterpiece and went on to be one of five nominations in the Oscars in the animated section.

To be even nominated for an Oscar is amazing. As a result of that, EMI got him to do several stories in cartoon form. They brought out a video of the stories from *Give Up Yer Auld Sins* and it spread the Good News to a whole different generation.

It all started with Miss Cunningham trying to control a class and doing what she could to teach them something that would help them through life. The tape was literally thrown in the wastepaper bin and the only thing I can take credit for is lifting it out of the basket and for recognising it was good.

In the 1990s and in the early 2000s, no matter where I went, football matches, pop concerts, round the country – everybody knew the stories. Everybody bought it for their mothers. It was like a Daniel O'Donnell CD. Nobody admitted buying it for themselves, but everybody knew every story on it.

That's the wonderful thing about the power of God's word. There's a lovely piece, I think it's in Isaiah, where God says, "Like the rain that comes down from the heavens and moistens the seed, so my Word never returns empty-handed."

We don't know where the seed we throw out will land or how it will produce. I did my own little bit for it, as did thousands of others, but Miss Cunningham planted the first seed and God did the rest.

CHAPTER 16

THOMAS MERTON – MY HERO

I'm not really a political animal, yet I've been involved with people in politics all my life. I got to know Jack and Maureen Lynch exceptionally well during my years in Mount Argus.

Both of them came to Sunday Mass in Mount Argus. It was a privilege to be invited to their home, as I was on numerous occasions. Jack and Maureen were unusually private people for a couple that spent their lives in politics. I really enjoyed their friendship. Mostly we talked about sport and religion and only rarely about politics.

An exception was the time I was changed from Mount Argus to Enniskillen. Jack and Maureen did something that was typically generous. They called to see me one day and asked if they could take me out to dinner. They wanted to say thanks for the hard work I'd done in Mount Argus and for "being a supportive friend in a quiet sort of way for 15 years". There is nothing I like better than a meal and a chat with good friends.

It shows the kind of people they were, that they encouraged me to bring a friend in case I got bored talking to, as they called themselves, "two old fogeys". Of course there was no possibility of me being bored and I said so. Anyway, they reckoned that someone of the calibre of Mike Murphy would be a good man to come to the dinner with us. And so it happened that Mike, Maureen, Jack and myself had a most wonderful night out in the Fitzwilliam Tennis Club in the summer of 1989.

At that meeting Jack and Maureen presented me with an engraved bowl of Galway crystal. During a very short and humorous speech, Jack became serious and asked me to make one promise to him. He knew I rarely kept anything for myself. He suspected I might pass this bowl on to my family. He asked me not to do it because he was aware that my family lived in the North of Ireland. And he said, "I'm afraid I'm hated equally by both Protestants and Catholics in the North. I would ask you not to give it to your family lest it would bring trouble to their house."

He was deadly serious. He went on to tell me that as a member of the board of Bushmills whiskey he could not travel to the board meetings held in Antrim because the then RUC couldn't guarantee his safety. They told him he would be in equal danger from both sides of the community.

Both Mike and I found this shocking. Jack was a good and honest man who worked to bring peace in his own quiet but effective way.

Only once did we talk about the Arms Trial and the events of that time. It would be wrong of me to divulge any of what he said to me on that issue. But I can tell you Jack's version of events was very different from the revisionist theories emerging now. I would still back Jack's as the true version of events.

After I finished my term in Mount Argus I was appointed rector of St Gabriel's, The Graan, outside Enniskillen, Co Fermanagh. I was scared stiff of going back to the North, because I was brought up in a divided and bigoted, pre-civil rights time. Then Catholics were oppressed in a way that is hard to imagine now. I feared I still had that mindset which would be disastrous in a priest working in Northern Ireland. Secondly, Enniskillen was always home and the only place in Ireland I could escape to. It was where I went on holidays when I got them.

Now I was returning to this place to work, and the last corner of privacy was taken away when I became rector of The Graan. From now on, even at home, I was on duty round the clock. It sounds pathetic and sad, but that's how I felt.

Pride came into it too. Maybe my own people wouldn't accept me at all. Maybe they'd say, that's Hugh D'Arcy's cub, who the hell does he think he's talking to? We know his seed, breed and generation. Or his 21st cousin's marriage broke up and he's telling us about marriage? Wasn't it his great-great-uncle who was taken up for sheep stealing?

Taking a short time out between Mount Argus and my return to

The Graan, I went to America to study in a Passionist College in Chicago. There was a lot of stuff I needed to deal with in my life and this was a major shift in direction. I needed to study and to reflect. I got inspiration and encouragement there from fellow students, those who taught me, especially Paul Weller and Donald Senior, the Passionist president of the college.

Donald Senior is one of the foremost scripture scholars in the world and specialised in the study of the Passion. He was the first to point out to me that the Passion of Jesus was the inevitable result of the preaching, lifestyle and choices made by Jesus Himself. Jesus knew what He was doing. He knew it would mean death. He knew it would mean rejection. Yet He made his choices knowing where it would end. Jesus was in fact choosing life through death. For me, that is a central insight into the love of God, not only in the life of Jesus but in my life too. I should not be afraid of death, because for the Christian, there is no other gateway to life. I have to let the little deaths happen so that new shoots can live.

Providentially, another spiritual hero came back into my life at this time. I began reading Thomas Merton again. He is a hero of mine because he had so many uncharted journeys to make in life.

He came from atheism into Catholicism and from that to being a Trappist monk. From the seclusion of his monastery, his dialogue with the world made him the most influential spiritual voice of the 1950s and 1960s in America. He advised the Kennedys as well as the anti-Vietnam heroes the Berrigan brothers. Joan Baez, the singer, was another who sought his advice. His autobiography, *The Seven-Storey Mountain*, was the classic spiritual book of its time.

Thomas Merton, held the view that Catholic, or maybe even all Christian, Churches fail to live out the implications of the Incarnation; that we don't realise what it meant when God became fully human. If we did, we'd jump with joy at the goodness of our redeemed human nature rather than think of humanity as evil.

It's true that because of Adam and Eve we all are all tainted with original sin. But the same logic must acknowledge that the power of Jesus' birth, life, death, resurrection and ascension means that we're on a higher plane now, that we are children of God. We are an Easter people. We're no longer like chickens forever scratching in the earth, but rather, we are soaring eagles.

As part of human nature, we bear the scars and guilt of original sin. I don't have to be reminded of that in my own life. But sinful human nature is not the whole story. Our human nature has been redeemed through Christ so that we share in the life of God. Why don't we let God be God, without trying to box Him into our tiny human imagination?

The spirituality I was initiated into made me and my struggle with personal sin the centre of everything. It took years of unlearning to allow God's life and grace to take centre stage. If I actually let God be the centre of my life, acknowledge the power of God within me, I'll realise that my human nature can't be bad if God is willing to live in me. My human nature can't be bad if, when I say the words of consecration, God speaks through me. At the words of forgiveness in reconciliation, God speaks through me. When I go to a hospital bed and sit down, not as a priest, but as a human being, and listen to those who are dying, telling me their story, I will help them to meet a welcoming, forgiving God. At times like that I realise the more human I am, the more God-like I am. That was the essence of what Merton brought me to realise.

Merton's own life was a constant, complicated journey, inspiring and stranger than fiction.

Thomas Merton was born in southern France in 1915. His father, a New Zealander, and his mother, an American, were both artists.

Merton's early life set the stage for the confusion of his later life. Owen Merton and Ruth Jenkins had two sons, Thomas and John Paul. Owen, the father, was Church of England and his family hated Catholics, Jews and foreigners. Ruth, his mother, came from an Episcopalian background and eventually became a Quaker. She was a pacifist but always remained distant and cold. She died when Merton was a mere child.

He lived in Paris, Bermuda, England and the West Indies. He was educated in France and in an English private school.

Owen, his father, was a writer. After Ruth died he became the lover of Evelyn Scott, the writer. Young Thomas objected to the tussle for his father's affection but he always remained fond of, and extremely close to, his father. His father died when Thomas was 16.

After that young Thomas went to Cambridge. He lived a wild life there. He had many love affairs and as a result of one of them a child was born.

Merton took his responsibility seriously but lost contact with the mother and his son when he went to America. It is thought that both the mother and son were killed in an air raid on London during World War Two. However, Merton was never sure. He tried to find both of them later in life.

In his early 20s he was not religious but went to teach at a Catholic college. There he came under the influence of an influential philosopher, James Walsh, who taught him to harness his genius. He brought him for weekends to a monastery in Gethsemane, Kentucky. It was a very strict order of Trappists.

Eventually, having sown his wild oats, Thomas decided monastic life was for him. At 27 he gave up everything and joined the monks in Gethsemane, about 60 miles from Louisville, Kentucky. For the next 27 years he wrestled with his vocation. He was never absolutely sure if he had made the right decision.

From the monastery he wrote one of the literary and religious classics of the century – *The Seven-Storey Mountain* is the story of his own faith journey. From that monastery, too, he influenced the shaping of American society in the 1960s. He helped to change the world through his spiritual books, lectures, novels, poetry and essays.

And yet he was not readily accepted there. Much of it was his own fault. He was not an easy man to live with. He seemed to want the best of both worlds. He had a running battle with his abbot, an Irishman, James Fox, who incidentally was a former Passionist. Yet both had a dignified respect for each other at the end and are buried side by side in the community graveyard.

Merton is credited with being one of the thinkers who pushed the Church towards Vatican II. And yet it was the changes as a result of Vatican II that led to much tension within his own life.

In the early 1960s he was tipped to become abbot of the monastery in which he lived. He turned it down because he said his son might arrive at the gate some day. Potential scandals are nothing new. He even left some royalties from his many books to his son and the boy's mother just in case they should be found alive.

Because of his fame the vocations in Gethsemane spiralled. At one stage there were over 200 monks in the monastery. Merton thought that the spirit of the monastery had fallen apart.

Ultimately, he couldn't find peace even in the monastery because he'd become too famous. So he went to live in the wood belonging to the monastery, in a hermitage, and practised contemplation. Then he got into transcendental meditation, something that the Catholic Church didn't want.

Merton will be best remembered because of his original insights. The Church at the time was a stifling place to live in. The world was looked upon as evil.

Merton never accepted that. "Human nature is not evil," he said. "All pleasure is not wrong. All spontaneous desires are not selfish."

He was not afraid of humanity. Nor was he afraid of love. He criticised the awful sterility of those who, claiming to love God, had in reality dispensed themselves from the obligation to love anyone.

It was that willingness to risk love that caused him his greatest trauma. He had a painful back and went to hospital in Louisville. There he fell madly in love with a nurse who was half his age.

Merton realised it was the best thing that ever happened to him. His image of God changed completely. He said that he never even knew God until he fell in love with a human being. He shocked his friends by the openness of his new-found love.

His relationship led to some of his most beautiful poetry. The poetry is full of the joy and delight of being with his loved one and the sheer pain and agony of being separated. "We are two half people wandering in two lost worlds," he wrote.

God became less stern. For the first time, Merton understood what the love of God meant. And he had been introduced to it by the love of a beautiful human being.

He realised that for anyone to be remotely holy they must first be fully human. We cannot run away from the world and treat it as a mistake in God's plan. To be fully human is to be fully spiritual. The only true holiness is a true acceptance of the goodness of the humanity that God gave us and took on Himself when He became one of us.

Then he scrupulously struggled with whether he should leave the priesthood or indeed whether such a famous man could leave. As it happened, the nurse later went on to marry another man and Merton stayed in his hermitage.

Towards the end of his life Merton became interested in Zen Buddhism. He was invited to Bangkok to address others interested in the same subject. After giving an address he went to his hotel room to shower.

Later in the evening he was found lying dead on the floor of his room. The electric fan had fallen across his chest and electrocuted him. He died on the 10th of December 1968, the same year that saw the deaths of his friends Bobby Kennedy and Martin Luther King.

Back in his monastery a card arrived from Merton to Gethsemane at the precise moment that the phone call came announcing his death. The postcard was to an old brother whom most monks never noticed. He rarely got a letter from anyone. Merton remembered him on his last journey. The old monk was delighted with his letter and he went along to tell the abbot. As he spoke to the abbot the phone rang with the news that Merton had been electrocuted.

Merton himself had foretold his death. Two years before he died he wrote about a dream he had experienced. In the dream he was looking down on a wide bay as he faded out of life.

When his possessions came back to America, some of his friends found his camera. The last picture that Merton took was from the window of his room. When the picture was developed it was in every detail exactly as Merton had described the place of his death in his dream two years previously.

A certain mystery surrounds his death. Just how it happened has never been adequately explained. Some think that sinister powers were involved. Certainly his influence on the civil rights movement and his vocal and effective stand against Vietnam made him a marked man.

But perhaps the simplest answer is that his time had come. After a life of endless searching for the key to life he died still wondering and searching, still only glimpsing the incredible mystery of God. But he died knowing, however obliquely, that God is love and that we experience

God's love in human love.

Everyone in the Merton family died young and tragically. Ruth died from cancer of the stomach, his father from a brain tumour. His brother, John Paul, died in the war as a young airman. His first lover and his son died as a result of an air raid. Thomas himself died of electrocution at the height of his career. There are no children, no survivors.

The nurse who changed his life and taught him the real meaning of true love heard about his death on the car radio as she drove home alone from work. There was nobody to share her pain.

When I was studying in Chicago in 1989, I visited his monastery in Kentucky. There were some ironic coincidences in all of this. Two American Passionists came with me. We rang the bell of the guest house and when the brother answered, they told him I'd come from Ireland and would like to look around. The brother then asked me if I knew the Dolans from Belcoo in Fermanagh. I told him it was my parish and I knew them well. They were his cousins!

We were treated royally. He brought me in, sat me down, and showed me Merton's grave. He showed me his room and as a special treat, brought me to see the hermitage. To me it was like a shrine. The ordinariness of it consoled me greatly.

At the time I was in transition, moving from Dublin to Fermanagh. Somehow, what I got at the hermitage allowed me to see that some of my mad thoughts were actually from the Holy Spirit and not so mad after all. But it was looking at the life of Merton that allowed me see that God's care is in every doubt, and every choice we make. It all has a purpose. I couldn't actually see it in my own life, but I recognised it through Merton's varied journeys.

One final irony in all of this was that the first funeral I did when I came back as rector of The Graan in early 1990 was the funeral of Father Angelo Boylan, the man who'd brought me into the order in 1962. It couldn't all be by accident.

CHAPTER 17

PAIN AND FORGIVENESS

"I bear no ill-will. I bear no grudge. Dirty sort of talk is not going to bring her back to life." Those words changed Gordon Wilson from a God-fearing Methodist shopkeeper in Enniskillen into an international hero for the cause of peace. They were not cheap words because they cost him dearly, especially within his own community, something I know pained him deeply.

I heard news of the awful bomb in Enniskillen, my hometown, through a Sunday morning phone call from my brother. It was a few days after I'd been involved in the John O'Grady/Dessie O'Hare kidnapping, so I was at a low point anyway; then this.

The bomb was planted in what was formerly a school, one which I'd attended as a boy, in a yard where I kicked football, threw snowballs, played cards, sneaked a cigarette and admired the girls going to Mount Lourdes convent school on the hill. It was a deliberate attack aimed at decent people remembering their dead, dead who themselves gave their lives in the cause of peace in the First World War. Could anything be more evil?

I had a picture of Gordon Wilson in my mind. As a boy, walking through Enniskillen to and from the bus, I passed his shop. Often a tall, thin man stood outside. I didn't know him then – in those days we didn't talk much to older people and certainly not to one from "the other side". He seemed a pleasant man, though, and for a teenager, impressions endure.

When he gave the interview to BBC Radio Ulster, he had no intention of becoming a hero, or becoming a worldwide voice for peace. He was what he was – a sincere Christian, a grieving father, and a decent man talking.

It wasn't just Gordon himself; it was also the strength of his entire family, especially his wife. Joan's resilience has never been fully appreciated. She is a deeply spiritual and supportive woman. Gordon was at pains to point this out repeatedly in every conversation and in every interview I ever did with him.

I was lucky, on occasions, to visit Gordon and Joan in their home when I came back to Enniskillen a few years later. Indeed he often came to see me in The Graan for a chat. It was always an uplifting experience, a real blessing.

The talk was never of violence and death but rather of the power of God's word to heal. I never came away from meeting the Wilsons without feeling refreshed in a deeply spiritual way. Joan was and is a rock of faith. She had to endure even more tragedy when Gordon died.

As a couple they steadfastly believed in God's care, even though it hadn't been easy for them to recognise his presence.

We know about Marie's terrible death in the Enniskillen bomb in 1987. We also remember that tragedy struck again when her brother, Peter, was killed in a car accident. On that morning I was in South Africa and could only speak to the family on the phone. When Gordon himself died so suddenly and so quietly he left a huge vacuum in all our lives.

Many memories of Gordon come back to me. One that remains vivid takes me back to the BBC studios in Enniskillen. I was doing an extended 45-minute interview with Gordon for my series *Be My Guest*. As always, he was inspiring in a quiet, common-sense sort of way. The interview was due for transmission a week later.

When we finished, Gordon called me aside. He asked for prayers, sincere prayers, as he was about to meet leading members of the Provisional IRA later in the afternoon. He also apologised, and this is the measure of the man, that he wasn't able to speak about it on the tape, and therefore made the interview out of date before it was transmitted.

After their meeting I met Gordon and I rarely saw him so dejected. Not only had he taken a huge risk by talking to the same organisation that murdered his lovely daughter, but he also risked losing many of his lifelong friends who were not so forgiving as he was. Worse still, when he met the IRA, Gordon felt they demeaned him and dismissed him without the courtesy of a decent discussion. It broke his spirits. He was devastated.

All I could say to him was that perhaps they were bluffing and that his arguments got through to them more effectively than they were prepared to admit. I was clutching at straws but I knew from experience that was how they worked.

When the IRA ceasefire was eventually called, I reminded Gordon that God often brings new life from dark moments. He understood then that his dialogue with the Provisionals was more fruitful then he realised.

He loved Enniskillen, though he was born in Co Leitrim. In bad times he did think of leaving his adopted town on more than one occasion because of bigotry. He told me in one of his last interviews that he thought of moving to Scotland, but couldn't contemplate life away from Fermanagh.

Gordon was a wise and politically alert man. He was a thinking man, not just a reactive, emotional man. Sometimes he pondered too long before he acted. His gut reaction was often lost as he pondered the possible interpretations of every word said and every deed done.

Probably the bravest thing he ever did was to take a seat in the Irish Senate. That made him vulnerable to cheap, personal attacks from the hard-line Unionists.

At Gordon's funeral the whole world mourned him, but apparently many of those in the Unionist Party did not. That is to their eternal shame. The paucity of official Unionist representation at his funeral was a scandal. Such a good man deserved better treatment from his own people.

I learned a crucial lesson about forgiveness from Gordon. One day in a peaceful conversation I asked him if he ever regretted his message of forgiveness on the night of Marie's murder. This is what he confided to me. He said that every night before sleeping he prayed to God to be able to forgive her killers again in the morning. Forgiveness was not a once-off decision but an ongoing daily decision that depended on God's grace and his acceptance of that grace. It was worth knowing Gordon for that insight alone.

Gordon Wilson, a Protestant from Leitrim, was catapulted by violence into the glare of publicity and he became a symbol of redemptive suffering. That's what made him an ordinary hero. He was no saint because, by his own admission, he was anxious, impatient, conservative, and reluctant to change. Yet those are the saints I love, saints who have to struggle. No one can deny that the Wilsons struggled, but their struggles were not in vain.

Enniskillen and Omagh, two towns in which I went to school, became synonymous with the evil of violence. Both bombings were so awful that they made decent people work even harder for peace. A crucial combination in bringing peace closer was the coming together of Hume, Adams, Reynolds and Major. For his part, Albert Reynolds would claim that President Bill Clinton was just as important as the others were.

I always liked Bill Clinton. I met him for the first time when he came to Belfast to encourage the peace process on a December day in the late 1990s. I'd known that Clinton was both brilliant and affable from talking to Albert Reynolds.

Albert recognised at once that Bill Clinton was really sincere in trying to bring peace to the North of Ireland. The president, like Albert, was willing to take risks, and Clinton more than once went against the advice of his political advisors, because he trusted Albert, to talk to Sinn Féin, who in turn could deliver the Provisionals. President Clinton ensured the right people got to America to call off the dogs of war, even though it displeased the British government. He did it anyway in the interests of peace.

For a politician who had tenuous connections with Ireland, he gave peace here a worldwide profile as well as top priority in his own schedule.

Clinton was a charismatic politician, as I witnessed first hand when he came to Enniskillen to open the Clinton Centre. The centre is built on the site of the school where the Cenotaph bomb killed so many innocent people, including Gordon Wilson's daughter, Marie, in 1987. It was named after Bill Clinton because of his part in the peace process. He visited it twice and I met him on both occasions. He impressed me each time. On his first visit he had work to do to win over his audience.

It was plain many of them didn't like him because of his sexual misdemeanours, alleged and otherwise. They didn't want to condone his lifestyle outside of politics. When he entered the room many were silently hostile to him. He went to the podium and without notes spoke eloquently for 20 minutes. He surprised us all by admitting he'd made many mistakes as president but one in particular haunted him. He hadn't intervened in Rwanda to prevent the murder of hundreds of thousands of innocent people there. He was prepared to admit his mistake. He apologised and promised he and Hillary would work with Rwandans in the cause of peace and reconciliation.

They had just been there to attend a groundbreaking conference at which both Hutus and Tutsis were present. They sat around in a large circle. He sat opposite Hillary. Of all the people in the circle there was only one person who was not disfigured, apart from the Clintons. Most of them were missing limbs, had badly scarred faces, no ears – all physically mutilated. He admitted he'd been shocked by the seriousness of their mutilation. All of them told their story of what happened. Each of them was determined it should never be allowed to happen again.

There was one extraordinarily good-looking woman in the circle. It puzzled observers that she seemed to have no disfigurement. When it came her turn to speak, everyone wondered why she was there at all. It transpired that she, her husband and their children were attacked and slashed to pieces by people who lived in their village all their lives. Then they slashed her back until they thought she was dead. Her husband and children were already dead.

When the attackers left, she came to and saw the mutilated bodies of her entire family beside her. She was so angry with God because she was alive. She couldn't understand how God could be so cruel to leave her alive when she was so badly mutilated and when her entire family was dead.

She was brought to hospital and spent months recovering from her ordeal. Not surprisingly, she suffered a nervous breakdown. During her recuperation she concluded God must have saved her for a reason.

She concluded the reason she was saved was because God wanted her to tell her story to anyone who would listen, and ensure such murders would never happen again. The woman with no visible injuries then revealed her back, mutilated beyond belief. Clinton promised he would spread her story wherever he went.

The audience in Enniskillen were beginning to warm to him now. There were tears in his eyes as he told the story.

Despite his reputation, Clinton was a leader I would trust more than George W Bush.

Another well known story of mass suffering comes from the writer Elie Wiesel, who survived the Nazi concentration camps. On one occasion, the Gestapo decided to make an example of three people. They took two adults and an emaciated child and threatened to hang them in front of the entire camp. Nobody thought they'd stoop so low.

At the appointed time the gallows were prepared and the three victims, including the young boy, were brought out. Everybody concentrated on the child. He was pale and biting his lips. The hangman refused to do the hanging on this occasion so three SS men replaced him.

The three victims were made stand on chairs. Their necks were placed in nooses at the same moment. The two adults cried out: "Long live liberty!" The child was silent.

Behind Elie Wiesel, somebody whispered angrily: "Where is God? Where is he?"

At a sign from the cruel officer in charge, the three chairs were kicked from under the victims. There was total silence as the whole camp looked on. On the horizon the sun was setting. Then everybody in the camp had to march past the gallows where the three people hung. The two adults were by now dead. Their tongues were swollen and blue. But the third rope was still moving because the child was too light to hang. For more than half an hour he hung there struggling between life and death, dying before the eyes of the people who walked by. He was still alive when Elie Wiesel passed by.

The same man asked again, "Where is God now?" Elie Wiesel replied, "Where is He? He is here. He is hanging on that gallows there."

Ultimately that is not an answer at all for those who have no faith or no vision of another world. Yet in the mystery of life and suffering, it is the only answer. Our God is a God who suffers with us. He is not just a God who looks on while the innocent suffer.

To live that out in the bits and pieces of our ordinary lives can be misunderstood. In fact I believe now that being misunderstood is a crucial part of the passion of daily life. To speak the truth is not easy. It causes division, friction and harsh judgement, as people like Gordon Wilson and Bill Clinton discovered.

There is another wonderful example from the life of Archbishop Helder Camera, a man who worked for the poor in Brazil at great personal cost to himself. He was condemned by his colleagues in the South American hierarchy and by the politicians. He said, "When I feed the poor, people call me a saint. When I ask why they are poor, people call me a Communist."

This is a perfect example of somebody causing division not of his own making simply by doing and saying what is right.

CHAPTER 18

ALL TOO HUMAN

I first heard of Eamonn Casey's impending scandal in an unusual manner. At the time, I co-hosted a late-night phone-in radio programme on 2FM. Every Wednesday, I travelled from Enniskillen to Montrose to do the show live. Gerry Wilson was the resident host and I joined him from 10.30 to 11.30. People phoned in with questions, mostly on a moral theme. It was a risky programme to do, because I had no idea who would phone in or what they'd ask. I had been broadcasting for 2FM since its opening day in 1979. Bill O'Donovan wanted me to try something different. Bill always had enormous faith in my ability, much more than I had myself. He wanted me to do different types of programmes and to get away from being seen as an expert on country music and Irish music. He wanted me to present a variety of programmes for the station but I didn't think it right – somebody else might have needed the work more than I did.

On another occasion he had a programme lined up for me, but senior management in RTÉ decided it wouldn't be fitting for a Catholic priest to present a programme in a secular field: so much for a priest-ridden society.

On the other hand, when I crossed the Border to work in Enniskillen, a quite different atmosphere prevailed. I wasn't a month living in Enniskillen when Jim Sheridan from BBC in Belfast contacted me and asked me to take on a programme which involved interviewing celebrities, called *Be My Guest*. I was simply Brian D'Arcy, a professional broadcaster and journalist. And ever since, I've had my own programme on BBC Radio Ulster: so much for the bastion of Unionism. Perceptions can be misleading.

Anyway, this was as near as I got to hosting a programme on 2FM that didn't come under the control of religious broadcasting in RTÉ.

On Wednesday at the end of the programme, I normally rushed off home. It was a three-hour journey back to Enniskillen and I always had an early start the next morning.

One night, just as I finished broadcasting, a phone call came off-air from a bishop. Bishops rarely phone me. This was very unusual. He'd just heard the programme and phoned for a chat. That's always dangerous.

It had come to his notice, he eventually got round to saying, that there was a scandal brewing around Eamonn Casey and that the *Irish Times* were going to publish it, at the earliest opportunity, possibly in their next issue. The bishop, off the record, wondered how the media would react and, more urgently, how should Bishop Casey handle it. As far as I can recollect, it's the only time a bishop asked me for an opinion on communications. I asked him one question: "Where is Bishop Casey?" He said the bishop had left the country.

"Where?"

"Somewhere," he replied, "most likely America, but I don't know."

"That's madness. Bring him back and don't let the story break without Bishop Eamonn being here to tell the facts, plain and simple, from his viewpoint. Don't let him run, because that will be a disaster," I advised.

"It's too late, he's gone," he answered.

"Well, I think that's madness. The sooner he comes back the better."

That was my gut instinct before I heard what the full facts were; it's still my opinion today. According to the bishop on the phone that night, the *Irish Times* knew about this story for some time and Eamonn Casey knew that they knew. He went to Rome to tender his resignation before the story broke. Rome, apparently, was reluctant to accept his resignation. One can only presume that he wasn't the first bishop to be in this position and one also presumes that they reckoned he could survive the crisis. Perhaps they were right. But Eamonn wasn't willing to chance it. He was adamant that he should resign, and after some time, again according to the bishop, his resignation was accepted. That in my view was also right and proper.

I repeated my advice that he should come out with his hands up and admit honestly the facts of the case. He should ask forgiveness if he had done wrong, and I believed the Irish people would understand and forgive him for what he'd done. Perhaps at a later stage he could come back and work as a priest in Ireland again. I knew his days as a bishop were over.

Most of this seemed to come as a shock to the bishop who unofficially sought my opinion. But in fairness, he said that he would think about it and acknowledged the sense in what I was saying.

Even then I had great sympathy for Eamonn Casey. It took me some time to get my head properly in order to see that more sympathy was due to Annie Murphy and most of all, to Peter, who had suffered the most injustice. Of course it would have been a shock to hear a bishop say, "Yes, I've had a relationship, I've had a child, it was wrong, but I would still like to be a priest. In fact I think I could be a better priest now because I would understand personally what it is to be forgiven by God and his people." But think of the good such honesty would have done in the long term.

As it turned out, the story broke within hours and the rest is history. I can't help thinking even today, if only it had been handled differently, would the Irish Church be in a different place now? We'll never know.

It had a shocking effect, not only on the Irish Church, but also on the whole of our society. It was the first chink in the armour of the bastion of clerical morality. It's remarkable how quickly the whole edifice crumbled after that first chink appeared. I don't think the scandal in itself was as grave as its repercussions became in Irish Church history. However, that was the way the cookie crumbled and we can't rewrite history.

I'm not as free to talk about the intimate details of Michael Cleary's relationship with Phyllis. The main reason is that I was involved in all kinds of negotiations after Michael's death, which have to remain confidential. Also, Michael was an exceptionally close friend of mine. We knew each other for more than 20 years. We worked in the same areas within Irish society, and we travelled up and down the country with the Jimmy Magee Allstars for all of those 20 years. Towards the end of his life he had his own radio programme and he talked to me a lot about the contents of the programme.

I also knew Phyllis since her time in Ballyfermot, and she was always protective of Michael. She constantly rang me up if we were travelling down the country, asking me to drive. She knew that Michael hadn't been to bed the night before, sometimes because of his priestly duties, sometimes because he was playing cards. But she always warned not to let him drive, because he'd had no sleep.

On one occasion I failed to take her advice – with almost disastrous consequences. The Jimmy Magee Allstars were playing in Fermoy in County Cork on a Monday night. Michael said he wanted to drive. He was a much speedier driver than I was. As far as Mick was concerned, I drove "like an old woman". He always had good cars and drove in the fast lane.

He had a little dog, whose name I can't remember now, but who was a constant friend to Michael, so much so that he licked Michael's face on long journeys to keep him awake.

On the night we went to Fermoy, after the show, Michael wanted to get home early so he insisted he'd drive. About 10 miles out the road the dog was busy licking his face to keep him awake. And then I noticed the car veering across the road. He came to a corner but the car drifted to the far hedge. I screamed at him and pulled the wheel and somehow got round the corner. I'd had enough. I told him to get out and get into the passenger's seat and sleep. I drove. That was when I discovered how uncomfortable it is to have a dog constantly licking your face. The dog obviously didn't know the difference between my clean-shaven face and Michael's bearded one. He had foul-smelling breath – the dog not Mick.

As we went around the country, Mick was always the star. It didn't bother me in the slightest because I wasn't in the same league. I called myself Mick Cleary's altar boy. We had a lot in common and he knew I had a constituency of people he could never reach. I was only too aware that he had a vast army of loyal fans throughout the country. He didn't see me as a threat because he was comfortable in himself. Both of us were well known in our own right. Many a time when I walked down a street in Dublin or in other parts of Ireland, people spoke to me as if they knew me, but they invariably called me Father Cleary. I was quite surprised that the same thing happened to him. He was called Father D'Arcy. We didn't look alike at all but obviously in the public's mind we were well known priests and whichever name came to mind first was what we were called.

When Dermot Morgan was beginning a career of making a living out of the foibles of the priesthood, he wasn't sure whether he would call his character Father Brian Trendy or Father Michael Cheery. As it so happened, through Kevin Marron, who promised him good publicity in the *Sunday World*, he chose Father Brian Trendy, to my cost. That's the character that in time grew into Father Ted. It's an indication of how closely identified Michael and myself were. But he was a more gifted, more charismatic – an infinitely better communicator – and more important figure altogether.

He was a gifted speaker, a good thinker, and a skilled entertainer. In the Jimmy Magee Allstars there were many megastars from the world of showbands who played regularly with us, people like Brendan Bowyer, Larry Cunningham, Joe Dolan and Dickie Rock, to mention just a few. They played in our matches, if you could call it playing, and they all performed on stage with the Allstars at the fundraising concert afterwards. In showbusiness it's a golden rule that whoever closes the bill is automatically the star of the show. That's a principle that applies the world over. The lesser acts open the show, big stars close them. Showbusiness being showbusiness, when we put on our concerts after the games around the country, the major stars disappeared into public houses and other places because they wanted to be last on the bill and claim to be the star of the show. Professionally that meant a lot to them. But you can't have five closing acts. So it was a conundrum for Jimmy Magee. One night Jimmy and myself had this brainwave. Put Michael Cleary on halfway through the show. We knew it would sort things out because both of us were only too well aware of how good a performer he was and how much the people loved him.

The next Monday night Michael Cleary went on early and did an abbreviated version of his show, about 15 minutes, and took the house down. Every performer who came after him died a death. He stole the show.

Jimmy Magee and myself often talk about this. Both of us listened to him telling the very same gags, the very same stories, for 20 years. And the last night I heard him, he was as funny as the first time. I knew every detail of the story, I knew every punch line, but it didn't matter. That's a real comedian. He made them funny every time because he could communicate with an audience and he could feed off the audience to make the stories funny in a relevant way every time he told them. He was a genius as an entertainer with a unique ability to captivate any audience anywhere.

After that we never had any trouble with our big stars. Everybody wanted on before Father Mick.

After the Eamonn Casey story broke, Michael and myself, as two high-profile priests, were very much in the spotlight. Newspapers were offering large sums of money to tempt people to come up with (for want of a better word) the dirt on either of us. The journalists in the *Sunday World* kept me informed of what other papers were trying to do. Thanks be to God there was no dirt to uncover.

Mick, being a close friend of Eamonn Casey's, had much more to do in the public eye defending his friend. That was when I began to notice that his judgement could be suspect. Some of the things he said on that occasion were not really relevant. Things like, "Well at least he didn't have an abortion." Of course it was the truth, but so what?

It was round this time too that both of us had to have serious chats about how we'd react if false accusations should be made against us. I had this doomsday scenario in my head, that if newspapers offered enough blood money they could get somebody to make an accusation that she'd had an affair with either of us or that we'd forced her to have an abortion. I pointed out the difficulty of proving innocence. For a long time Mick seemed unable to see this. And I couldn't understand how he couldn't see a real possibility staring him in the face. When you're in a vulnerable position you have to be careful about what you say and you have to make sure there is no room for doubt. Furthermore you don't go round picking fights, because if you do they'll come back to haunt you. Essentially what can you do about it? Then as now it's nearly impossible to disprove a false accusation, though I think we're in a better position today to do so. You hope that nobody is so evil or so malicious as to make false allegations and if they are you hope that the law will protect you.

Those were the kind of chats we had up and down the country; they were worrying times, and I thought at the time both of us were speaking honestly to each other.

I have to say now that I never really knew or even suspected that there was anything going on between Michael and Phyllis. I'm not a busybody. I have many friends who are women. And I'm not one who thinks that every relationship between a man and a woman is based on sex. There is such a thing as genuine friendship between human beings. I was quite convinced that was the relationship between Phyllis and Michael.

Phyllis, God be good to her now, was always nervous about the relationship. Frequently she insisted there was nothing going on between them and that people who thought so were malicious and unfair. She always gave that information to me voluntarily because it was none of my business to ask. Not only did she give it voluntarily; she gave it consistently over at least a 10-year period.

So after Michael's death, when Phyllis herself broke the news that they had been living for years as man and wife, I was absolutely and totally shocked.

I'm not saying she was wrong to disclose it. It was her life and if it was the truth she was quite entitled to say so. I'm just saying that I was shocked because it came like a bolt out of the blue. It was not what both of them insisted to me personally on many occasions while Mick was still alive, and right up to the time of Mick's death. To be honest, I didn't believe it. And I said so when I was asked to comment.

This – which I can now understand – annoyed Phyllis and I was the recipient of serious, abusive phone calls and faxes. I was told that I was not welcome in her house and that I couldn't have been a friend of Mick's. Again, I didn't think hers was a rational or fair reaction. Immediately after Mick's death I knew I wasn't wanted in their house. It was a pity because Mick had asked me to help Phyllis and her teenage son, Ross, in any way I could. I did my best but I couldn't intrude where I wasn't wanted. Both Phyllis and Ross cut off all communications with me, which was their perfect right, and I'm not complaining; I'm merely stating a fact. I was sorry that life had turned out the way it had for both Ross and Phyllis, who were grieving the loss of a father and partner, while trying to cope with a raging and often irrational controversy.

The end result is that I became as confused as they seemed to be during their life together. Not only that but with hindsight I now know something died inside me in 1993. I found it hard to trust anyone after it. Let me put that more honestly: I simply don't trust anyone implicitly ever since, not even close friends.

I was also friendly with the Cleary family, who didn't believe Phyllis's claims either. I'm not sure that the family was ever keen on Phyllis. That's only an impression. But the news came as a massive shock and disappointment to them.

Michael received glowing tributes at his funeral. Everyone seemed to want to get in on the act. Leading politicians had something to say; entertainers were there in abundance as they should have been; there was a huge array of priests, all wanting to take part in his funeral. In fact Michael had asked me to preach at his funeral, and as far as I know the family would have been happy with that. But he was a member of the archdiocese of Dublin and they arranged the liturgy and the preacher. I was just as happy. I was too lonely and too sad and wouldn't have done a good job.

I often wondered afterwards where they all disappeared to when Mick's reputation was in tatters.

That was when the family needed help, and I tried my best to give them some support when Mick's clerical "friends" ran for cover. After a long, acrimonious and not very helpful battle, DNA reports did show that Ross was Michael's son.

I was overcome with sadness again. Why didn't they tell me? Why were they so ashamed of their love? I hope I would have helped them in every way. It wouldn't have changed my opinion of Michael or Phyllis one iota. It surely would have brought them more happiness. It's unbelievably sad how they both lived and died so tragically. I don't know whether it was their own choices or a cruel system that destroyed them. But they both deserved better and Michael certainly should be remembered more positively than he is.

It still rankles with me that all the good Michael did is forgotten. I know the hours of dedicated service he gave to those in need. His life was pressurised and for the most part unhappy. Maybe that's why he spent so much of his life on stage. The plus point was that he loved being on stage and he loved helping people. He was used by Church authorities as a credible mouthpiece and because he was more vulnerable than any of us knew, he allowed himself to be used. That to me is the greatest tragedy of all.

Mick was more conservative than I was but he had a heart as big as a mountain. He never lacked compassion. While I didn't agree with much of what he said, I understood that he said it for all the right reasons. What became known as the X Case is a good example. In the X Case the Supreme Court ruled that an underage child could travel to Britain to have her pregnacy, as a result of rape, terminated. I disagreed vehemently with Mick over his stance on this particularly tragic case. I knew more about the true facts than he did and warned him that he had got it completely wrong. But somebody else was pulling the strings by then. Mick felt that he had to take a line on this, or maybe others told him what line to take. During our discussions I said that the compassion for which he was famous was gone. Mick accepted what I was saying, and it didn't disturb our friendship at all.

When he was dying he sent for me and we chatted, said Mass, prayed together, and I know I was a source of strength to him. A couple of days before he died, Phyllis asked me to visit him in St Vincent's because he was in his final hours. I drove from Enniskillen and although he could hardly speak he held on to my hand for an hour. Small consolations like that remain with me when doubts take over.

No matter what the public perception, I knew Mick to be a good man in many respects. There are others who should be able to testify to this but don't do it now. He was easily distracted and the lure of showbusiness was always a danger to him because there's always a shadow side to our best gifts. He didn't take the road less travelled as often as he should have.

He allowed himself to be used by so many. Most of them were parish priests up and down the country who depended on him to fill their churches. There was nobody could fill a church like Mick Cleary. All who heard him preach were not only entertained by him, but came away feeling better about themselves. They had got a practical spirituality that carried them through bad times and difficulties. I never hear that said about Mick Cleary now. Few of those countless parish priests ever said a good word about him when he got into trouble. Not even those who claimed to be close to him uttered many words publicly in his defence.

It's obviously wrong that his family suffered as much as they did. That is still a huge disappointment to me. It's only one of many disappointments I have about the Mick and Phyllis relationship. When a good friend dies it's hard enough to get over it, but when he's remembered only for his failures it's unjust. It's only the Father Cleary "scandal" that is talked about. In God's eyes we are worth more than the sum of our sins.

After his death Phyllis linked up with another *Sunday World* journalist, Paul Williams. The only row I've ever had with the *Sunday World* was about how they handled her story. They published an interview with Phyllis, which was subsequently expanded into a book. The *Sunday World* never told me what they were doing and I still believe they should have. On the Saturday night before it was published I was told about the story by the *Sunday Independent*, who asked me to comment on the revelations about Mick Cleary being published in the *Sunday World*. I hadn't a clue what they were talking about. Next day I was attending a silver jubilee Mass in Mount Argus and was doorstepped by an RTÉ camera crew. I'd had no time to prepare so I staggered through, not wanting to let Michael's name be destroyed and yet not willing to call Phyllis a liar. What I said was as honest as I could be. But it really was wrong, with hindsight, to defend Michael.

To this day I still blame the *Sunday World* that they didn't have the decency to trust me enough to tell me the truth so that I would have been better prepared to talk about the life of one of my closest friends. I'd been writing for them that time for 20 years, so surely they knew me well enough. Their excuse was that they knew I was a friend of Mick's and that I wouldn't agree with their doing it. I'm not sure that's a good excuse. It's a bit like don't let him spoil a good story with the facts.

Anyway that's in the past. It was the only time in 30 years that I seriously doubted whether I could continue writing for the *Sunday World*. Good organisation that they are, they realised I was hurt and admitted that they had been overly secretive about it.

I learned another lesson from all of this, as we must in life. Loyalty in the media doesn't apply when there's a good story. And maybe it shouldn't either. That's what news gathering has become.

In his will Michael left instructions that I should dispose of any monies left over after his wishes had been carried out. I was to use the money for charitable purposes. He told me before he died what the charitable purposes were. As far as I know there was no money left over but that's another story. I now think of Mick and Phyllis often, more in sadness than in joy. That's a pity. I had many a laugh with them. I hope Ross, their son, will have a better life than his parents.

Sometimes I console myself, though not very convincingly, that Michael didn't want to drag me into the messiness of his life. If I didn't know, he probably reasoned, then I couldn't carry the burden of it. The advice I would have given would have been clear: if you love each other, and you have a son, then you should marry Phyllis.

The same logic applies to Eamonn and Annie, but then it seems that their relationship was broken down beyond repair anyway.

Mick wanted to be a priest and knew he couldn't be both married and a priest. In generations to come we'll look back on the incident and realise it was a disgrace they couldn't live happily as a family with Mick continuing to be the gifted priest God wanted him to be.

As we drove around the country it was I who argued against mandatory celibacy while Mick made excuses for it. He used to say, "The pair of us couldn't do the work we're doing if we were married." But then Mick always had answers for questions. His biggest failing was that he never allowed himself to ask new questions.

Throughout his life, Mick was sharp, bright and practical. There's a lovely story he told me from his time in Ballyfermot with priests like Val Rogers and John Wall. Ballyfermot was then a developing urban community with its own problems. The priests did their best to visit the people in their homes. In a previous era there had been a parish priest in Ballyfermot who seemed to fall out with half the population. When priests visited houses they discovered that almost all the men in the parish weren't going to Mass because they'd fallen out with the canon. This was particularly frustrating to Father Rogers, the parish priest.

At a parish meeting one day he asked how they should approach it. Mick had the perfect answer. "When somebody tells you they have fallen out with the priest and don't go to Mass, there's a simple answer to it," he ventured. "Just ask them another question. Ask them did they ever fall out with the barman? They'll say yes. And you'll come in for the kill. Well I bet you didn't give up drink because you fell out with the barman." Brilliant.

Val felt easier on visitation now. Next day he was visiting a home. It was evening, and the news was on. The mother of the house welcomed him in. But there was a beer-bellied man slumped in an armchair watching television. He never even looked in Val's direction, never mind spoke to him. Val stood in the centre of the room. The man looked right, left and through him but still didn't speak. Val chanced a question: "Have I seen you at Mass recently?" The wife jumped in. "Don't mind him, Father, he's a good man but he fell out with the canon years ago and he's never been back at Mass since."

Val had the answer ready: "Do you drink?"

The man looked over the top of his glasses and replied, "I used to, but I fell out with the barman down in the pub and I've never taken a drink since."

It was Mick who told me that, even though it's against himself.

Mick was always good in an argument. I hate arguments, especially on television. I think they're pointless and counterproductive. Mick loved them and did his best to create one. He was in his element. He had ready answers to every question and had words, wit and wisdom as well. He was just a terrific communicator. We got on so well because we respected each other. He used to say to me, "They all think you're an innocent fella with that baby smile you have. Hold on to that smile, it will get you through anything."

At our showband Masses Mick had the best entertainers eating out of his hand. He had a way of getting through to them. We went to Las Vegas with the Jimmy Magee Allstars. When we were there we had Mass each day. None of them would go to Mick's room because he was a non-stop smoker. He smoked 80 or 90 cigarettes a day, almost always lighting one cigarette off the other. They preferred to come to my room for Mass and knew that Mick would join us. The Mass was always respectful but good fun. None of the boys would miss daily Mass in Las Vegas, even though they might not go to Mass on Sunday when they were at home. We told stories and prayed together; arguments were made and sometimes left hanging. Twenty-three entertainers went to Las Vegas and none of them missed a single Mass. That was down to Mick.

They knew that the Masses could never go on too long because Mick came dressed in a whitish alb and placed a packet of 20 Afton beside the altar to remind them that after 20 minutes he'd go for a smoke.

When I travelled round the country with Mick I saw many prominent businessmen and politicians speak with him. Mick helped many of them. I know who they are, and I never hear them say a good word about him. That disappoints me. It's the same with Eamonn Casey. Eamonn Casey made a huge mistake. He was unfair to Annie and even more unfair to Peter. Yet he too did marvellous work at home, in England and in the Third World. Does anyone remember?

Mick and Eamonn were larger-than-life characters whose sins and virtues were on a grand scale. There was a time when Irish people remembered the good that people did. It's a pity we've lost that balance.

CHAPTER 19

SOUL SEARCHING IN THE DESERT

The year 1994 was my silver jubilee of ordination. I did not want to celebrate it. There were too many clerical scandals in the air, particularly the Brendan Smyth affair. I knew from the letters I was receiving that this was only the tip of the iceberg and that once the boil was lanced, it could not be stopped.

My fear was that a TV show would suggest a celebratory programme to mark my jubilee. I knew there were plans. I didn't want that because I wasn't sure if I wanted to remain a priest. I needed to reflect quietly away from the public glare. Abuse of children by priests on a massive scale left me floundering.

I asked for some time again in Johannesburg. The provincial was accommodating, as there were a few priests who wanted home on holidays. "If you don't mind shifting from place to place, covering a month here and a month there, it would be very helpful." I didn't tell him why I wanted to be away.

As it happened, the day I was leaving for South Africa in 1994, two other significant things happened. Firstly, just as I was walking out the door of the monastery in Enniskillen, a UTV crew arrived and Chris Moore approached me. "We're doing a documentary on the Church and sexual abuse and we'd like you to say something before you go," he insisted.

"I really haven't time. I'm going off to South Africa today," I said and I thought it was a foolproof excuse.

"We really need to get this; just give me 10 minutes," he pleaded.

They were under the impression that in one of my *Sunday World* articles

I had defended priests who abused. They concluded I was making excuses for abusers. They wanted to film me defending abusers. On the contrary, I was quoting psychologists in America who said many abusers have been abused themselves.

The interview was cut short because it was obvious I wasn't giving them what they wanted. This turned out to be the major, award-winning documentary that exposed the whole, sick scandal of Brendan Smyth's evil escapades.

I wasn't used on the programme. But I was useful because they went to other senior clerics and baited them with, "Father Brian D'Arcy has spoken to us so you should put your side." It became a groundbreaking documentary, not only for its content but for the methods they used as well.

Another more pleasant experience happened that day too. When Albert Reynolds became Taoiseach, I was with the family in the Dáil and later in their home. He made a promise that evening to me which I didn't expect him to keep. "Brian, I'll bring you peace in the North before I finish," he said. I laughed nervously.

Now that I was heading to Africa, Kathleen and Albert wanted a family Mass in their home before I went.

The evening before I left, we were beginning Mass in their Ballsbridge home. It was that very day he was waiting on word from the Provisional IRA that they would call a ceasefire. In fact, the note containing the good news was delivered before I began the Mass, which now became a Mass of thanksgiving for peace. Albert had prayer cards printed with a special prayer for peace. His prayers were answered.

He asked me to be with him the next morning as the news was to be announced at 10 o'clock. I couldn't because I was on the plane to Johannesburg.

As I was getting off the plane in South Africa I saw the headline in the Johannesburg newspaper: "IRA chooses the South African way."

It was a changing time everywhere. In South Africa, in April 1994, the vast majority of people voted for the first time in their lives. The place that I thought had no hope of changing when I was there in 1988 now had a Black African president.

The delight showed on the people's faces: they had voted, they had got freedom. It was a country buoyed by hope. The change had been dramatic over six years. To an extent, that was what consoled me in my own life. Where change is possible there is always hope.

Wealth was behind the evil of apartheid, first legalised in South Africa during the 1940s. Sometimes we forget that there are many peoples who claim to be South African. There are the Afrikaners, who are of Dutch origin; there are the British, who come from a different background; there are the Blacks – and even among the Blacks, there are at least 10 very distinct tribes; there are Coloureds and there are Indians. They are all from the same nation and all claim to be South African.

However, it was a different colour altogether, namely gold, which was at the root of all their problems. In 1886 a prospector with the unlikely name of George Harrison found gold near Johannesburg. He sold his plot for £10 and was never heard of again. One mine alone, in the early 1990s, was turning a profit of one million rand per day. There is enough gold to keep them going until 2050. The reef that Harrison sold for £10 has produced 35,000 tons of gold.

Gold was at the root of the Boer War at the beginning of the 20th century. That was when the British invented concentration camps and 26,000 innocent people died.

I was in an area called Westonaria, a mining district. One of the parishioners wanted me to see how the mines worked. He handed me a slip of paper that got me on an official tour for free.

I drove up to the office, exactly as he told me, parked the car and went in. I didn't present any piece of paper at all, but booked in to go on the tour. Unfortunately I was late but an assistant brought me to the lift-shaft.

"Get into that cage, press that button, and in 20 minutes you'll meet the others in the mine. First, you'll have to change out of your normal clothes and into a special boiler suit and wellingtons, because it's exceptionally hot down there. When you're coming up, you'll have to stop half-way because, if you came up the whole way, the change in temperature would give you pneumonia. You'll get a new boiler suit and a shower. At the top you'll have another shower and change into your normal clothes." I asked no questions, did what I was told and looked forward to meeting the others.

The cage went down and down and down, miles into the bowels of the earth. I was standing on my own in complete darkness, except for a miner's hat with a light on it. This thing was hurtling down at speed. Panic. This was the end of the world. I really thought it was the end. Think how long it takes a lift to travel two miles, even going very fast. Down I went in complete darkness, holding on for dear life, not knowing where it would end. After an eternity it bumped to a halt, the cage opened and I walked out into this wall of heat and lights to see Black workers scurrying around in their underpants – hundreds and hundreds of them. Perspiration instantly bubbled out all over. Now I realised the reason for the special suit. It was so warm that the workers digging at the rock and shovelling it into trolleys were being hosed down to keep them working.

It takes two ton of rock to produce an ounce of gold in a rich seam. And the workers spend 12 hours a day quarrying the rock.

There was a non-stop trolley on pulleys to step on. I hung on for dear life, bent down as if riding a fast hobby horse – I kept low so as not to bang my head as I went through a myriad of passages. Eventually I reached the tour party. Most of them, I noticed, were Black people, unusual for tourists.

We saw every aspect of mining over a two-hour period. It was an eye-opener. We were brought through all the steps of gold extraction. They showed us the process of burning the rock at a very high temperature so that the gold melted. Then the gold was poured into a precast tray, the mould for a gold bar. A gold bar is a precise measurement of valuable, precious metal which we were allowed to view from a distance. We were thoroughly searched along the way to make sure we hadn't concealed any gold.

After two hours of walking, crawling and stumbling in tropical temperatures, I was dehydrated and totally exhausted. Think of what it was like for the workers digging there all day. All I could see was black shiny rock, Black skinny workers and floods of black, shiny water. I could never wear gold again.

Eventually we came up a level, showered and changed. Even then, I was afraid I was taking a heart attack as I was gasping for breath.

Having taken us through the whole mining process, they then showed us the marketing and manufacturing side of the gold industry. Once we reached the top we showered and changed again. Then we had a light lunch. I was sitting with a group of strangers who didn't look like tourists, tucking into a free lunch. The leader of the group came over to me: "You were late, I didn't get introduced to you."

I said I was a pastor at the church up the road.

"What have you to do with the new government?"

"I've nothing to do with the government," I answered. "I hope you don't mind me saying this but you'd need to be careful who you invite on that tour. I'm a reasonably fit person but, honestly, it was a shock to me how hard and difficult it was. If an elderly person came down they would die in it."

"What do you mean a tour?" he asked.

"I came on a tour."

"Oh no you didn't, that wasn't a tour. Who sent you down?"

"I asked at the office and they put me in the lift."

"No," he said, "that was a group of civil servants from the new government. They're thinking of nationalising the mines and we have to show them everything that happens in the process. We spent a long, long time trying to make sure they knew the whole process so they'd make a good judgement. We wondered how you could be a civil servant."

They didn't want the government to take over the mines and they were making it as difficult as they could for them. I got the best tour of a goldmine that anybody ever got and it was as near to hell as I ever want to be in this life.

Back in the parish they couldn't believe security could be so bad that I, in total innocence, got down on this highly confidential government delegation. It was a truly amazing experience but, as I say, one that I'd never want to repeat.

Everything was hopeful in South Africa at the time. First of all, it was wonderful to experience the changes that had taken place in six years. I remember writing, when I came back from South Africa in 1988, that this was an evil society which would never be overcome. I could see absolutely no hope for South Africa back then, yet, in six years, it changed absolutely and utterly. Perhaps nothing is impossible either in politics or in the Church.

Mandela went to jail yet never gave up hope. One of the things I learnt from him is that you're more likely to change things from within rather than from without.

I came slowly to realise that priesthood was the only calling for me but I wouldn't be the same, unquestioning priest ever again. Until then, I was reluctant to say anything which would disturb the clerical club. I had a sense of false loyalty to them and I felt guilty for saying anything bad about priests. But now, I was determined to speak the truth no matter what. I had to internalise the truth on my journey and live with it no matter how difficult it might be. It's much easier to be part of the herd, but fatally damaging in the long run.

I didn't want to be a part of a group which had enabled the abuse of children. I wouldn't want to be part of a group who covered up abuse. I saw I had a role as a priest but had to hold onto my integrity too. At least I could sleep at night knowing I stayed, not because I had to, but because I had a useful place in the institution.

I also gave myself the freedom to leave if I wanted – I'm not staying for family, for parents, for security, or because I have nowhere else to go. I'm really staying because it's what God wants. I came to that position of peace during long, lonely nights in a presbytery in Johannesburg.

South Africans go to bed early and rise early. The Mass, at six o'clock in the morning, was well attended. I went to bed at 10pm and got up at 5.30am. The Africans followed nature. When it got dark they went to bed and when it was light they got up. There were many long nights when I thought and prayed – a rare luxury in my life. I was on my own in a strange place, with no distractions and no houses to visit, because I didn't know anyone. It was a desert experience and very helpful. It changed the fundamentals of my life.

I spent some time in Westonaria, two weeks in Saulsville, a Black township, and two months in Maryville. It was a great experience really, almost like a United Nations of Churches. There were Croatians and Lebanese, Italians, Portuguese, Irish, English and French.

There were Blacks and Whites there too in 1994. There was a very good school run by the Assumption sisters in the parish, which had quickly become a mixed school. The church building was huge and held about 1,000 people. Maryville was a one-priest parish with four Masses every weekend: one on a Saturday evening and three on a Sunday. Three of those Masses were packed out. There were two married deacons in the parish, really lovely people. We'd preach in turns, one week in three. I said all the Masses. I did few weddings, fewer funerals and no baptisms at all. The deacons did all of that. They were well trained by the priests who were in the parish over the years.

I never counted a collection; there was a finance committee for that. If there was a finance meeting I'd chair the meeting. They made the decisions and budgeted their own money. They were an advanced group of people. There was an elected parish committee which ran everything. They took responsibility for the parish. They were gifted people, Blacks, Whites, wherever they were from, they all made a contribution. It was as big a parish as Mount Argus, yet I never had as much time off in my life.

I arrived in Maryville on a Friday night. On my second night in the parish there was a vigil Mass on the Saturday evening. I was a stranger depending on them to tell me what to do. A number of volunteers came into the sacristy beforehand. They were readers, Eucharistic ministers and a group of servers, maybe 20 in all. One of those who greeted me was dressed in a white alb, as a Eucharistic minister.

"You don't know me?" he asked.

"No, should I?"

"You should, but it's a long time since we met."

I don't want to reveal his name. I said, "You're not so-and-so are you?" And he said, "I am."

When I was a young student, this man was a priest in one of our monasteries. He was an able young priest who went to Africa to use his many talents. A short time after he went there, he met a girl, fell in love and left the priesthood to marry her. This was a big talking point in the early 70s.

His parents took it badly, and I played a small part in later years helping them to come to terms with his decision. I hadn't met him for at least 20 years.

"I want to thank you for all you did," he said. "I was able to go home and see my mother and father and they were able to come here and see their grandchildren."

He introduced me to his wife and his five children, some of whom were grown now. All of the family were involved in the parish, as Eucharistic ministers, readers and altar servers. His wife was a catechist. It struck me for the first time as he, a Eucharistic minister, was standing right beside me, during Mass, that there was no need for me to be there at all. He was as validly ordained a priest as I was.

He was also making a bigger contribution to the parish than if he'd remained a priest. Remember, I was in a position of should I stay or should I go at this stage. Eventually he invited me to their house and I spent a lot of time with them, had a few meals together and enjoyed their company.

The day before I left to come back to Ireland, his daughter, with her boyfriend, arrived into the presbytery to see me. We had a cup of tea and a chat and she thanked me for being so kind to her mother and father. She said, "There's a letter for you. There's no money in it, we know you don't accept money, but there's a letter in it and don't open it until you're on the plane."

She gave me a blue envelope with black writing on it, written in tidy, clear handwriting. I opened it on the plane. "Dear Father Brian, thank you for being so nice to my father when you were here. I know that when my father left the Passionists, the Passionists lost a very good priest, but I'd like you to know that we gained a wonderful father."

When I left, they weren't able to get another priest just at that point, so they had no priest at all, even though this man was ordained a priest. About three weeks after I came home, the secretary phoned me in Ireland to say they'd got a priest.

"Oh, I'm delighted. Who is he and what is he?" I asked.

And she said, "You're going to laugh at this. He and his wife are moving in tomorrow."

"How come?"

"He was an Anglican minister who became a Catholic and he's taking over here temporarily until another priest comes; his wife and one of his children are moving into our house tomorrow."

I thought of this friend of mine going to Mass at the weekend to see a married priest, who disagreed with women priests so much that he left his own Church, but who has been ordained a Catholic priest and is being allowed to remain a married man. Meanwhile, this other man who had given his early life to the Church was sidelined and could never say Mass. I knew instantly that was the end of the argument about compulsory celibacy.

It just doesn't make sense. When I saw two decent, loving human beings in front of me, the intellectual arguments disappeared. In Ireland, many of those people who left the priesthood are forbidden even to be ministers of the Eucharist. I realised it's all a power thing and nothing to do with spirituality. I still believe that to this day.

South Africa is a vast country, bigger than Germany, Holland, Belgium and France combined. The first time I was there I was impressed by two people I got to know very well during my short stay. One lived in the White part of the parish and the other five miles away in the Black township. Let me tell you how they each lived. We'll call the man in the White area Reginald. He was a hard grafter whose father came from Europe to work as a technician in the mines.

Through sheer hard work Reginald built up a business and was now a wealthy man. When I knew him he paid his workers, both Black and White, well. He told me when I visited him at Christmas that he'd given all his workers an extra week's pay as a bonus to celebrate Christmas. He owned valuable property. As far as I remember, he told me he owned 28 factories. Anyway, I knew that he had two Mercedes cars in the drive. He was a very solid worker in the parish and never flaunted his wealth.

The other man, whom we'll call John, lived in the same parish, but five miles away in a Black township. He was old and weather-beaten and I'm sure he's long dead now. He was a gaunt-looking man, underfed, though always cleanly dressed in clothes that were well out of date. He spoke English well, was gentle, very respectful and bowed repeatedly. He said, "Father" often.

John, too, was a pillar of the community. He told me who attended church and who didn't. He informed me of those who wanted to join, when they should be baptised and whether the person who was dead wanted a funeral Mass. He trained the altar servers and was an interpreter at Mass.

He lived in a two-roomed shack made of tin. There was a wire fence around it and only dirt roads leading up to it because he lived in the poorest part of the township. He had no car, couldn't drive, had never been in a plane in his life and never would be. He walked everywhere or took one of the ever-present taxis. He had a good family whom he reared well and was respected in the community.

Reginald and John were two very proud South Africans. Both were devout Catholics. Both were exceptionally good men by any reckoning. They both belonged to the same parish, yet they never met and never prayed in the same building.

When I wrote about them initially, I said that they probably never would pray in the same church. I don't know if they ever managed it, but nowadays they could if they wanted. I'm glad about that.

One of the examples of change in South Africa I experienced for myself when I was in Westonaria. The new government, the Black government, had offered an amnesty for people to hand in weapons. If they couldn't hand in weapons to police stations, they could hand them to a minister of religion.

In Westonaria one morning, the doorbell rang. Standing there was this young Black man with a sub-machine-gun in his hand. I nearly died. He saw that I was frightened and he blurted out, "I'm handing it in, I'm afraid to hand it in to the police, so I'm handing it in to you. You can hand it in for me."

He sped off and I couldn't get rid of the thing quickly enough. I went around to the police station with it immediately. I phoned and told them I was coming around with it in case they thought I was coming to attack the place. And they laughed out loud at me.

They were very friendly about it. They said, "Well, we weren't expecting too many to hand in arms. In three weeks this is the first one we've got and we know it will be the last one we'll get. It's so old that it couldn't have been used in recent years."

That was my contribution to peace in South Africa.

In common with the rest of the world I have enormous respect for Nelson Mandela. But I also grew to appreciate how difficult it must have been for FW de Klerk to lead his people in the direction he did. I remember being deeply impressed by the kind of religious experience he shared which changed him completely.

When he succeeded PW Botha in 1989, de Klerk was the favourite candidate of the right-wing members of the Nationalist Party. De Klerk had a religious experience that began at his inauguration service. He invited his favourite pastor to preach at the service and the pastor took a text from Jeremiah 23. He told the new president that he was "standing in the council chamber of God", to learn the will of God and that he should act upon the will of God alone. Furthermore he pointed out that he was now God's instrument. The new leader should heed the traditions of the people but should also have the courage to break new ground.

De Klerk admits he was shocked but deeply affected by the pastor's words and took them as coming directly from God himself. At the end of the service he asked his family to pray for him and told them he knew now he would be rejected by his own people but that he was chosen to walk a new road and that they must help him to do it.

By any standards it was an incredible religious experience, but it became more than an experience: it became a way of life. Later, he spoke about the service and how he felt a strong sense of calling. It wasn't an arrogant feeling, but he knew he had been singled out by God to do a job.

I've kept a quote from him and I wonder how many political leaders would accept this? "I do believe that God directs things on earth and as a result I had to accept that God wanted my election and I must realise that in my actions I have a responsibility to God. No matter what I do down here, I will have to answer to God and I must live according to that calling."

There is no doubt that he did take many initiatives that led to the dismantling of the horrible apartheid system. He had little choice because the world had become a smaller place and by the end of the 1980s South Africa was a pariah state that nobody respected. But to his credit he began discussions that led to the new South Africa. Many Afrikaners, some of whom still look upon him as a traitor, rejected de Klerk.

It's easier to recognise coincidence or providence in another country, but I'm absolutely convinced that peace in South Africa would not have come unless de Klerk and Mandela had been willing to be its agents. In other words they were the right men in the right place at the right time.

That thought keeps me going, not only when I think about peace in Ireland but also when I think about the future of the Church. I'm convinced God has a providential care that will carry us through. I've seen it in my life and in history too often. It's the reason why we need to reflect on our various journeys. I'm convinced that when we are most open to God's spirit, he will show us new ways of being Church which will be simple, helpful, uplifting and spiritual. It's a belief that keeps me going on many a dark day. Trust in God!

CHAPTER 20

TO WED OR NOT TO WED

In 1994, live on radio, Joe Duffy asked me if I had ever fallen in love with a woman. Many people were shocked by the question. To me it was no big deal. I was getting used to being 50 then and answered, "How could any normal man arrive in middle age without falling in love?" Of course I fell in love.

In recent years I haven't talked much about personal relationships of friendship and love in public because it's not fair either to myself or to my friends. I simply state the facts: I know what it is to love another human being who also loved me, but I have never known sexual love.

Love was an experience that was beautiful and holy and was never given sexual expression through making love. It annoys me that sex and love are so confused in the modern mind and so I make no apologies for saying that chaste love is possible and desirable.

For a couple committed to each other for life, sexual love is their greatest prayer. But there is another experience of intimacy that is not sexual intimacy. There are experiences of deep, loving friendships which are precious gifts from God and don't lead to sexual intercourse.

As a religious and priest, I'm not free to commit myself to anyone but God and therefore I cannot and should not mislead others or myself about that. I have found it hard and I know that those who loved me found it impossibly difficult too.

When I entered the monastery all those years ago, I knew in theory that I would have to give up sex and marriage. That was easy enough to do at 18. It was the sacrifice of intimacy and companionship that proved to be the real challenge. It took me a lifetime to recognise that God takes no pleasure in unnecessary loneliness.

As a novice and student the constant mantra by which we had to live was "to mortify your eyes". We were trained to walk with our heads bent down and our eyes cast to the ground. If for some reason we looked out a window during our novitiate, we had to confess in public before all the community that we had failed "to mortify our eyes".

In university I used to joke that I knew the girls there by their legs rather than by their faces. That's what mortifying the eyes does. Seriously though, it was unreal and an encouragement to live in denial. It was also part of the unspoken assumption that women were bad and would always be a danger to our purity. Think of the implications of that attitude being implanted in a teenager's young psyche. The practice was to suppress normal human emotions rather than to cope with them healthily.

Even now I struggle daily with the need for emotional maturity, friendship and integrity in my life. I don't always live up to my principles. But the struggle must go on. My first duty as a priest is to live in truth, to hold on to decency and honesty, to try to live the Gospel before preaching it.

Throughout my life I have had to come to terms with the fact that I need close friendship with women as well as men. When it comes to close friendships, it's important that boundaries are absolutely clear. It's unjust to mislead anyone, but particularly a woman, into believing that there is the possibility of a long-term, married relationship on offer. If I do that I should leave the priesthood or leave the relationship. It is unnecessary and harsh that I should have to make that choice, but with Church laws as they are, there is no other option. I used to think it was a pity. Now I consider it a scandal.

The most advantageous and challenging parts of my priesthood have been the genuinely good, loving friendships I have with women. There are women in my life that know me better than I know myself. They are the people who encourage me and drive me to be a better man. If I can be a better man there is every hope I will be a better priest. I can never thank them enough for their love and their patience. They are the greatest gifts God has given me, a holy communion.

I have also met women who took advantage of me because I tried to show a normal friendship and openness to them. A few women have tried to "own me". I find it uncomfortable and distressing, but I presume it is no different for anyone – man or woman – who is "not available". It's one of the risks of normal life.

It would be unfair to say there are many, but there have been some and it is always a difficult experience. That's why it is so important to have boundaries and honesty right from the beginning. The trouble is that no matter how honest you are with some people, they neither respect nor hear you.

A greater danger perhaps is that we priests use women. It is a terrible crime to destroy a woman's future or a woman's life for selfish reasons. Worse still is to keep a woman hanging on because we can't or won't make up our minds, or with the impossible hope that priests will be allowed to marry some day.

My greatest fear, apart from the horror of wasting a good person's life, is that I would end up a solitary, disillusioned, old bachelor. I never want to spend my energies being celibate instead of striving to be a good priest. I believe it's achievable to have close personal friendships with special people in our lives without crossing the boundaries, without abusing or misusing friends and without displeasing the loving God we'll all have to meet.

As with any of God's special gifts, we should be grateful for them but we must be scrupulous not to misuse them.

I know now that I would have been a far better priest and a far better human being had I been allowed to marry. That's a fact not a moan. Nothing in life is perfect and I hope I have tried my best to be as normal, as healthy a human as is possible in a situation that does not lend itself either to honesty or maturity.

I would have preferred to be able to choose both priesthood and marriage in the circumstances but couldn't and ended up making the choice for priesthood. I still don't know whether that was the right decision. But it was the best choice I could make at that time. Most days I don't regret the choice I made, but I do regret having to make it. I've been able to live with reasonable peace of mind. But the choice had to be made.

If I had drifted in life it would have been unhealthy and upsetting, not only to myself, but also to the person who was good enough to love me.

It was only when I really thought about it for this book that I realised the time I was closest to leaving was when my best friend in the Passionists, a one-time classmate for whom I have enormous respect, decided to leave and marry. We are still close friends. He and his wife are so good to be with and are obviously people who have grown together in love. When I meet them I enjoy their company but there is a great sadness in my life as I drive home to my single bed in the monastery. Perhaps I could have been as happy as they are and have done as much good work as they do had I decided to marry 25 years ago.

At times like this I console myself that in life we make the best decisions we can at the time. After a period of wrestling with their pain, my friends made an honest decision that took them to a wholesome place. I also made the best decision I could to remain a priest. I can only leave it with God, stop beating myself up, and hope I have done the right thing in God's eyes.

Now to get back to that famous disclosure on radio and its aftermath. It was a run-of-the-mill radio interview with Joe Duffy. At that time Joe was sharing the morning slot with Gay Byrne. He had moved on from being a reporter on the *Gay Byrne Show* to hosting the programme a few mornings a week.

I can't remember the reason Ann Farrell, the producer, asked me on the show. Maybe it was because I'd just come back from South Africa. As I've already mentioned, I'd gone there deliberately to rest, pray, reflect and most of all to avoid my silver jubilee as a priest at home.

The interview was typical Joe Duffy. He was informed, knew where he wanted to go, his questioning was gentle, conversational, but penetrating. As always with Joe, he knew the answer I was going to give before he asked the question. Skilfully and when it suited him, he slipped the question in. "Brian, you strike me as a very normal man. Have you ever fallen in love with a woman?"

I answered it as honestly as I could. Yes I had fallen in love. I added, as I always do, that thanks to the grace of God and my mother in Heaven, I had not broken my vows. I went on to explain to him that for a man just turned 50, it would be more than unusual not to have fallen in love given that I considered myself still a reasonably normal human being. I thought nothing more of it. At the end of the interview Joe thanked me graciously for being so honest.

The way things work in communications these days is that when people in radio or television know they have a story, they inform the papers. It's good publicity for them and helps in the ratings battles. And so the headline on the *Evening Herald* a couple of hours later was, "Fr Brian admits to falling in love."

I don't have a problem with journalists doing their job. But why do they make being in love sound so dirty? Journalists, like bishops and priests, seem to think all sexuality is bad. The next day it was all over the papers and once again I felt guilty, ashamed and a failure. By now it was "admits to affair". It was not an affair and I really resented them cheapening a good, painful and worthy decision.

When I saw the word "affair" in black-and-white it really did upset me. It sounded nefarious; it sounded dirty and it sounded to me as definitely sexual. It also had implications of being illicit. None of those things was part of any relationship I've ever had. I was so annoyed about it that I sought legal advice. I was told that in law I had a case but was it worth the hassle? Probably not.

The senior lawyers I spoke to confirmed that the legal definition of "affair" had all these connotations.

I need to be careful not to be too negative, because overall this was a positive, developmental time of my life that helped me to be in touch with myself and to experience a kind of emotional intimacy without a sexual intimacy. I was able to be with another without the usual masks and defences. I was free and safe to share fears, anxieties and failures as well as dreams and visions. I was able to grow emotionally.

To be fair to myself and to others, too, I need to say something more about "falling in love". In the modern world the words sex and love are taken to mean the same thing. I don't like it and I consider it demeaning to genuine love. Yet I have to live in the real world and I fully realise that when I "admit" to falling in love, the normal person's mind races to one conclusion: "He's had sex."

When people close to me presumed the same thing, I was horrified. Ever since, I've had to add that I never broke my vows. For some, that's not enough. So, at the risk of repeating myself, let me clarify it for any of you who are troubled by either salaciousness or scruples: I never had sex with any person.

I feel demeaned having to use such language and to write so publicly about something which should be nobody's business but mine. Yet I realise that, unless I tell it like it is, there will be those who will add two and two and get 22.

I also realise that it is part of being in the public eye these days, as well as part of talking publicly about personal issues, as I have tried to do all my life. Regrettably, it comes with the territory.

Many of my priest colleagues thought Joe Duffy's question was a very unfair one and were angry with me for answering it honestly. I should have protected myself from such intrusions, they argued. It meant that whoever was asked the question in future would be obliged to answer it in a straightforward way or be looked upon with suspicion.

Once again my family thought I was on the verge of leaving the priesthood. And those who worked with me closely, especially the laity who keep me going, were frightened that I had spoken too openly for my own good. Over the years they have learned, as I have, that most of these things are a one-day wonder. It took me months to come to terms with the public knowing so many details of my life. But gradually, people realised what I was doing and have supported me ever since. It took them some time to realise that priests are human and that falling in love is normal, even for priests and religious.

To be honest, I didn't find the question offensive at all. It really was a first though. Until then there were some areas private enough not to be asked about in public. A priest's love life was definitely a no-go area. But after Eamonn Casey and Michael Cleary the boundaries changed. If we priests had dogmatically spoken about how others should behave in bed and out of it, then people felt – rightly in my opinion – that they should know how chaste and how normal we ourselves were.

Joe had the right to ask me that straight question because of the scandals which had happened. Gay Byrne, 20 years before, asked a priest on the *Late Late* if he had ever fallen in love and the country was up in arms that he would ask such a question. But in the mid-1990s, Joe Duffy slipped the same question in and it was easy for him to do it, because of the breakdown of that image of the priest as one who didn't have problems, couldn't have problems and never wrestled with personal sin.

Eamonn Casey, Michael Cleary and in a totally different way Brendan Smyth, with a plethora of others, were priests with human foibles and failings. Even though I didn't want it put in that context, in people's minds that was the context in which Joe Duffy was able to quiz me. Priests were no longer seen as perfect.

The central issue should not be whether I fell in love but how I, or more properly we, handled the experience.

What I'm trying to say now is this. There is a context in which there are genuinely loving relationships for people who are celibate, which can be life-giving, spiritually uplifting and fulfilling, and are in no way scandalous. Thomas Merton put it perfectly when writing of his loving relationship with a young nurse: "I do not regret at all my love for her and am convinced it was a true gift from God and an inestimable help to me" (*Learning to Love*).

Five years after the Joe Duffy interview, *Would You Believe* did a programme about me and asked the very same question. I answered it in exactly the same way. This time it was edited into the end of the programme and once again was made to sound sensational, dirty and totally unworthy. I was so disappointed with *Would You Believe*, not for asking the question but for the way they edited it. What encouraged me greatly, though, was that many who watched the programme were as annoyed as I was with the editing.

In those few years people's attitudes changed. They now accepted that just because we take a vow of celibacy, it doesn't mean we become angels overnight without feelings or failings. Nowadays the vast majority of people are angry that priests can't marry. The harsh law of mandatory celibacy is fast becoming a scandal in itself.

Only recently I realised that St Clare and St Francis loved each other deeply. If they were living in the present time, they could have been on the front page of the tabloids. Yet they were two of the great founders of religious orders, the Poor Clares and the Franciscans. They were able to do it with such incredible beauty and yet, at the same time, they had to ensure they didn't let their love for each other degenerate into something that would spoil their great work. That's 800 years ago and things have hardly changed.

Wrestling with loving relationships should be part and parcel of a healthy celibate's life. Even those who choose celibacy, I believe, as human beings need close friendships. That doesn't mean a sexual intimacy. There's a recent study of priests in Australia who want to remain priests, but don't wish to remain celibate. These priests are working out of a theology that allows them to be sexually intimate and priests at the same time. I just don't understand how they justify it. It seems to be another hypocrisy that follows on from mandatory celibacy for priests in the Catholic Church.

Freely chosen celibacy is difficult but can lead to a singularly dedicated life. It is even more difficult if lived outside community. My experience is that even within community I have met very few healthy, mature men who are better people because they are celibate. In over 45 years of religious life, I could count on one hand the number of healthy, mature, well developed men for whom celibacy is as an enhancing gift.

The fact is that there is an ongoing debate throughout the world about the value of mandatory celibacy for Catholic priests, even though officially the Church has said there should be no debate about this issue. Obviously the Church is bringing itself into disrepute. You can't prevent a debate on an issue as vital as this. And why would anyone not discuss it if there are rational arguments to be heard?

There is a tradition of celibacy for Roman Catholic priests going back hundreds of years and it must be respected. There is also a long history of married Catholic priests and that's a position that deserves respect as well.

In my view the debate is already over. The Church has accepted the principle that there can be married priests in the Roman Catholic Church. There are considerable numbers of married Anglican ministers, most of whom disagreed with their own Church's policy of ordaining women, who became Catholics and were ordained as Roman Catholic priests whilst remaining married. They are active in parishes throughout the world and they maintain wives and families whilst continuing parish work. So there is nothing in principle against having married priests in the Church today. They already exist.

Voluntary celibacy is a treasure in the Church. Irrespective of any changes there will be many priests that will remain celibate. Even if mandatory celibacy is removed, some diocesan priests will still choose to be celibate. In my opinion, that would actually add to the standing of celibacy in the Church. If people are free to marry and on principle choose to remain celibate, then that in itself is a wonderful witness. On the other hand, mandatory celibacy has no worthwhile witness value at all. On the contrary it has turned the priesthood, in many people's minds, into a weird group of bachelors, to be viewed with suspicion.

There are married priests today, and for most of the Church's history, married clergy were part of the priesthood. Indeed Clement of Alexandria, who lived in the third century, refused to have unmarried clergy in his Church because it implied a rejection of the value of marriage.

It is worth outlining briefly the history of celibacy in the Church. According to the New Testament at least some of the apostles were married. Peter had a mother-in-law, for example. According to early writers in the Church (e.g. Eusebius) his wife was a first-century martyr. Philip had four daughters. Read the Gospel of Matthew or the First Letter to the Corinthians or even Timothy and Titus to discover repeated references to married priests and bishops. In fact, it is St Paul's opinion that bishops and priests should be good at running their own families before being accepted into priesthood.

Things began to change in the fourth century for many reasons. The arrival of early forms of monastic life was one of them. But there was also a view that sex was incompatible with holiness. This is clear in some early rules and regulations that laid down that a priest should abstain from sex with his wife on the night before he celebrated the Eucharist. They obviously had a bad theology of sex and an even worse theology of the Eucharist.

Later still other reasons emerged. It was easier to have control over single men. A priest who was married would have to listen to his wife and family. A bishop could manipulate a single man more easily.

Property was also an issue. Early on in the Church's history, Church property got confused with personal property. Customs were different then, and there are even instances of priesthood itself being handed down from father to son. Many claim that this was how St Patrick became a priest.

Underlying all of these arguments though is an emerging view that sex is tainted and that those who gave their lives to God as celibates were holier than people who married. This has been one of the great tragedies in the history of Catholicism.

It was after the Reformation, however, that the rule of celibacy was strictly enforced. This had much to do with counteracting Martin Luther's views and less to do with spirituality. It was at this time that mandatory celibacy became the badge of priesthood.

The theologian Dr Thomas O'Loughlin sums up the history of compulsory celibacy: "Celibacy is a classic example of how an idea from one period, if it gets lodged in law, can become self-perpetuating and eventually be seen as an ideal." That's why it's time to debate the value of, or necessity for, mandatory celibacy.

On a practical level, some of my best friends have left the priesthood to get married. It has been sad to see their talents and their vocations lost to the Church. Over 100,000 (at the very least) former priests were forced to make an unnecessary choice between the love of the priesthood and the love of a woman. There have been occasions when that same choice has stared me in the face. I never know if I made the right decision when I chose to stay a priest or if I would have been better to marry.

What I do know is that many of those who left would have become exceptional leaders in our Church today and we would not be in the mess we're in. They were leaders, they were compassionate, they were open and vulnerable and by that very fact were deeply spiritual men. Most of them were the cream of the priesthood. We rejected those gifted priests needlessly. We chose a man-made discipline instead of a God-given gift.

(*For an excellent academic treatment of the subject read *Celibate Clergy: The Need for Historical Debate*, by Dr Thomas O'Loughlin of the University of Wales, New Blackfriars, Volume 85, Issue 1000, November 2004)

Chapter 21

The Ultimate Betrayal

Sexual abuse destroys a child's life. The innocence that is every child's God-given right is lost forever and can never be recaptured. Even when the child (or indeed the adult, later in life) doesn't recognise the damage being done, the effects are always there. If the abuse is not disclosed in a safe, healthy environment, it will damage one's emotional life and relationships insidiously. It cripples by stealth and it does not go away of its own accord. It leaves a mark that defies description. The word indelible is often used, but it doesn't even begin to explain the utter destruction of the victim's confidence or the crippling and needless guilt.

As a child and again as a youth I was sexually abused and only years later was able to deal with the stigma. It shocked me to realise how hard I had to work to be normal, even though I thought I was just like everyone else. Thank God I have been able to cope with the trauma, but only when I shared the experience with professionals.

The abusers were both members of religious orders. Even though the abuse was minor by comparison to that inflicted on those I've journeyed with in later life, I know it destroyed a part of my innocence. The inner child always needs to be acknowledged.

For most of my life I was ashamed even to think about it, let alone speak about it. I convinced myself that it never happened at all. There are days when I am still disappointed with myself when I reflect on how I irrationally suppressed the abuse. I'm learning to be more forgiving though.

In other areas of my life, I am as honest as we human beings can be. I have an objective view of my faults, gifts, mistakes and little successes.

When I check with directors and counsellors, they frequently affirm my efforts at integrity. So why was this central area of my life allowed to fester in secrecy for so long? Why do I still occasionally dissolve in tears when I think about it?

That's part of the reason abuse is so damaging. The abuses make the victims carry the guilt for actions they couldn't prevent, had no control over and weren't responsible for.

That was the key for me. As soon as I realised that I wasn't to blame, that I couldn't have prevented it and that I was used and abused simply because I was vulnerable, innocent and gullible, I was able to talk about it and start on a road to healing that will probably continue for the rest of my life.

I have spoken in public about my experience as a victim of abuse only once. The reaction then was almost as damaging as the abuse itself.

It happened when Joe Jackson interviewed me for *Hot Press*. We talked deeply and personally for several hours, which left me drained and emotionally unsure. I always try to answer questions honestly and fully, but invariably when I read the written interview, I'm left wondering what the point of the interrogation was.

In the course of the interview, Jackson asked me a direct question: "Were you sexually abused as a child?" Whether he should have asked it is a moot point. But with priests now, anything goes. Whether I should have answered it honestly is another good question. But I was trying to deal with the effects of the abuse at the time and part of that healing was that I should not be ashamed, because I had done nothing wrong.

I answered honestly: "Yes, I was abused. I am dealing with it. I don't want to go into details and in the larger context of others' abuse it was relatively minor, even though the effects on me in later life are serious."

It was the truth with the minimum of embellishment.

He promised not to misuse the information in a headline-grabbing way. And I trusted him not to.

I don't blame Jackson for what happened, but of course it was used by the magazine to get headlines in *The Star* and subsequently in other publications.

I remember the moment I heard it on the radio. I was out walking early in the morning listening to the news on RTÉ and *What it Says in the Papers*. To hear it broadcast on radio that "Fr Brian D'Arcy admits he was sexually abused" absolutely paralysed me. I had to sit down in a ditch on the side of the road to regain my strength. I felt as if the entire country was judging me. The whole trauma of abuse enveloped me again. The word "admit" made me feel as if I was making a confession for some great wrong I had done.

I sat there for close to an hour unable to move and I started to cry. I was so frightened of the consequences because I had never spoken to my family about it and now they too were hearing it for the first time in a tabloid headline. A few close friends knew, and I had shared with some key members of my Passionist brethren for reasons that will become obvious. That sharing was misused by one or two of those present, though most of the brethren were kindness personified.

Those were the thoughts that crowded my mind and I knew my life would be the subject of discussion and ridicule on radio and in pubs throughout the country. Many of the emotions of abuse returned. The anger, the awful degrading sense of feeling dirty, the guilt that I didn't have the sense to know what was being done to me – all came back to haunt me.

I sat there quivering, afraid to go back to my community, most of whom didn't know about the abuse, either.

When I got to the monastery, it was never mentioned, even though it was all over the papers. To this day I don't know what they thought about it.

My family was on the phone to see if I was okay and were distraught they hadn't helped me more. I explained that they couldn't have helped me because they didn't know about it. I just hoped that I hadn't brought disgrace on them.

When I heard myself saying that, I got really angry. Why should the fact that two elderly men whom I trusted implicitly, and who took advantage of that trust to get their dirty kicks by abusing me, make me feel as if I had disgraced the family name?

Luckily, my family understood and continued to accept me as they always have – with love and loyalty.

I have never explained the details of the abuse and I find it difficult to do so even now. I find it difficult to talk about because a few days later I got an angry letter from a priest I knew and worked with, accusing me of inventing the abuse to attract sympathy towards myself. It was such a shocking accusation that it destroyed my trust in my own judgement. I simply could not conceive how anyone in his position could be so cruel and downright unfair. And he was not the only colleague who thought that.

When I settled down, I realised just how impossible it must be for those who are not priests to bring an accusation against a priest or religious. It convinced me that I should stop at nothing to help the victims of clerical sex abuse. I hope I have been true to that promise. If I have any influence I must use it to help the least-understood victims of all.

The priest who so cruelly and spitefully dismissed my disclosure of abuse was a Passionist, the same order as me. We had lived in the same community. I would have judged him to be a good man. Yet he obviously lived in total denial. That drained every drop of confidence and hope from me.

In all honesty, the man should have known better. He had given missions and retreats all over Ireland with one of the men who had abused me. He must have known the kind of man his companion was. With hindsight, perhaps he knew only too well and had good reason to do all in his power to suppress any discussion of the problem. I would love to challenge both the abuser and his defender now that I can talk about it, but, as is the way of these things, they are now dead.

The abuse began when I was a first-year student in Mount Argus. An older student, whom I trusted like a guardian angel during this crucial first year in student life when I was obviously lonely and struggling, asked me, as a special favour, to go to one of the priests in his cell – the name we gave the rooms in which we lived. He suggested I go after night prayers, about 10 pm, when all was silent in the monastery.

At the time students were not allowed even to speak to the priests of the community without the express permission of the director. In our naivety, we dismissed the rule as outdated. Only too late did I realise it was for my protection.

After night prayers, I went to this priest's cell. He explained that he was tired, feeling sick and exhausted after a series of school retreats. He asked me to come to his room each night after night prayers and to bring him a jug of hot water. It would be my way of helping his special work by taking such care of him during his rest period, he said. The older student confirmed it was okay to do this and that I should do all I could to help this "good old guy", as he referred to him.

That appealed to my natural instinct to help and, if I'm really honest, the need I had to be liked. So, I did exactly as I was told. The second night the priest poured himself a glass of whiskey and added a little of the hot water. He then explained he had a very sore leg and asked me to rub embrocation on it. I know now of course that this was the grooming process. I wish I'd known it then.

Each night he got more daring until he convinced me he was depending on me to get through the night. By now he was using me to facilitate his masturbation into a towel. One night he grabbed my genitals as I attempted to leave. That was the first time it dawned on me what this evil man was doing to me.

I ran out of the room in a panic and spent much of the night on my knees beside the bed thinking that I had offended God and afraid to sleep in case I died. The way I was brought up, the biggest tragedy in life is to die in the state of mortal sin.

The next day he sent for me again and tried to persuade me to continue coming to his room because I was the only student he'd trust to keep a secret. According to him I would make a great priest who would understand people. Since these were all the right things to say to an idealistic youth that would do anything to become a priest, I now know he was a skilled and ruthless manipulator.

When I refused to help, he threatened to have me put out of the order. He could have done so because the community had an opportunity to assess all the students at regular meetings. To be turned down at one of these "chapters", as they were called, meant that a student would be sent home. For me that was the ultimate threat. Yet I am proud of myself now that I would not be involved in anything I knew to be a sin.

He held that threat over me for years and made regular approaches to me every time he came home from his retreats and missions – at which, undoubtedly, he preached with great fervour the necessity for "holy purity".

I never told anyone what had happened but I did warn other students never to go to his room at night. Of course this became another reason to beat myself up. Why didn't I tell others, especially my superiors? Firstly, I was afraid. Secondly, I thought I wouldn't have been believed. Thirdly, I would certainly have been sent home for destroying a reputable priest. Lastly, I would probably have been blamed for allowing him to abuse me. In short, as with every victim of clerical abuse at the time, the abusing priest would be defended and the victim ostracised.

The experience almost destroyed me. I was barely 18 at the time and an innocent abroad when it came to sex. I was many years ordained before I had the courage to disclose what happened. By then I was crippled with self-doubt and convinced that I wasn't good enough to be a priest. Most days I still think that.

The experience of mild abuse by a person I thought could do no wrong stayed with me all through student days and into priesthood. When anything happened to me or my family, I convinced myself it was all because of my "sinfulness". Even when my mother died a year and a half after the incident, I was close to a nervous breakdown. I used to awaken at night experiencing the awful visions, smells and sensations of those late-night encounters in his cell. It was an easy step to take my mother's death as a "fitting" punishment from God for my waywardness. Of course it was irrational and unnecessary, but that was how the shame of abuse haunted me.

Earlier in life when I was a 10-year-old boy attending school in Omagh, there was a Religious brother who was revered by many in the town. He never actually taught me but took a fancy to me. During lunch break, once or twice a week for a whole year, he would call me into his empty classroom and put me across his knee. He would convince me that I was a bad boy and needed spanking. He would then place me across his knee, face down, and fondle my bottom, spanking me, rubbing my buttocks and keeping me there for 20 minutes or more. I was so innocent that I never realised what he was doing. I thought I deserved this "punishment".

I couldn't even allow myself to think that the brother was doing anything wrong. It had to be me. I'd make confessions about "bad thoughts" and hoped the real "sin" was covered. It was always there and, after I left Omagh, I tried ever harder to be as sinless as I could possibly be.

It was when I tried to deal with the abuse that happened in Mount Argus that memories of those lunch-breaks eight years earlier came to life in most vivid ways. I was now experiencing confusion that seemed to be in my imagination, but wasn't. Why was it, I wondered, that my pants were always wet going back to class even though I hadn't been to the toilet? At long last I realised that the brother was being aroused and that the wet in my pants was from him. It's funny how the mind gently leads you to the truth when you're ready.

When I realised what had happened, that the spanking and fondling was to pleasure himself, I knew yet another religious had spotted the vulnerable and needy child and abused me for his pleasure. Even writing about it now turns my stomach.

It has taken me nearly 20 years to get even a basic sense of healing in my life for what were real but by no means the most serious forms of abuse. What must it be like for those victims who were repeatedly and ritually buggered, raped and defiled? And when the abuser is a priest or religious, not only life, but faith itself withers.

A final irony is that the Passionist who had abused me sent for me when he was dying in hospital. I was rector of Mount Argus at the time and he left instructions as to what I was to say at his funeral. Two days later I was the preacher at the service for the man who abused me as a student. I did and said exactly what he asked. Manipulator to the last.

"When they had a choice between protecting children and protecting the Church, they chose secrecy to protect the Church. They sacrificed the children for many, many years."

In 2003 that was the damning conclusion of the Massachusetts attorney general, Thomas F Reilly, after he finished an inquiry into the abuse of children by priests in the archdiocese of Boston since 1940. Of all the millions of words written about the sexual abuse of children by clerics, those words get to the heart of the matter most succinctly.

He concluded that more than 1,000 children had been sexually abused by 250 priests and other Church workers in one diocese alone. For Reilly, it was "the greatest tragedy to children in the history of the commonwealth".

It must be remembered that he examined reported cases only. He sifted through 30,000 pages of Church documents and 100 hours of grand jury testimony to come to that conclusion. It is difficult to calculate how many unreported cases there are. As we saw in the Ferns Report and in other inquiries in dioceses and religious orders across the world, the same pattern was revealed. Dublin will be no different.

I fail to understand why Church authorities the world over simply refuse to face up to this fact. It is not just "a few wayward priests" who have done the damage. Going back over a 50-year period there is enough evidence to suggest that it is more than 5 percent, and maybe close to 10 percent, of priests who have engaged in the abuse of children. Boston indicates a definite culture of acceptance of those who abused children. A thorough investigation into major dioceses and religious orders throughout the world would produce very similar results.

Mr Reilly went on to castigate successive bishops of Boston, including Cardinal Law, because they made a deliberate choice not to report the criminal behaviour of their priests to the authorities. He is certain that abuse had become part of the Church's institutional culture.

Reilly was categorical that the main problem lies with the hierarchy: "There is overwhelming evidence that for many years the cardinal and senior managers had direct, actual knowledge that substantial numbers of children in the archdiocese had been sexually abused by a substantial number of priests."

It couldn't be plainer than that. For many years I have believed that conclusion is accurate.

The attorney general's report is adamant: "Any claim by the cardinal or the archdiocese's senior management that they did not know about the abuse suffered by, or the continuing threat to, children in the archdiocese is simply not credible."

I've learned from personal experience that any attempt to speak the truth as one sees it, even when it is spoken out of love, will always be interpreted as disloyal. The closer one gets to the truth the more deep-rooted the denial and the rejection

There is an acceptance that those who criticise the Church are anti-Catholic. The Catholic Church prided itself on being "the perfect society". Well it wasn't and it isn't. And to question its structures, customs, practices and beliefs is not disloyal, but a duty.

I have to convince myself of that regularly when vicious letters arrive in the post. If I took them seriously I would have to conclude that the defenders of the Church are a sick and pathetic lot.

But of course that isn't true either. There are good and sensible people who are loyal to the Church, in that they will not be critical of it in public. There are also good people who love the Church enough to want to see rottenness excised, even if it means speaking out in public.

What annoyed many of my colleagues most was when I said that the institutions of the Roman Catholic Church, in this matter, are rotten to the core. I understand how hard it is to accept that Rome knew about abuse and did nothing. But the way Pope John Paul II handled the case of the founder of the Legionaries of Christ, for example, doesn't inspire confidence.

You will recall from the opening chapter of this book the story of the Spanish-looking priest who stood in our vegetable garden in Bellanaleck and told my father that he didn't earn enough money to send his son to the Legionaries of Christ. My father was gutted but he never told me.

After a decade-long investigation into accusations of sexual abuse, the Vatican in the spring of 2006 asked Fr Marcial Maciel Degollado, the founder the Legionaries of Christ, "to observe restrictions put on his ministry".

In Vatican speak it means that the investigation showed at least some of the accusations of sexual abuse against the 86-year-old Mexican priest were well founded. He will not be allowed to say public Masses, give lectures or other public presentations or give interviews for print or broadcast. In other words, because he's 86, he has been told to keep quiet, die in peace and repent for his past.

That's when a picture enters my head. It's of my father, an honest man leaning on his shovel trying to do two days' work in one to keep us going. In my memory he's being humiliated by a young Mexican priest with more money than holiness, telling him that his son is not good enough for his order. Now the founder of his order, at long last, has been told by the Vatican that his life was built on hypocrisy.

The sad part is that this same founder was praised and defended for years by Pope John Paul II, who even honoured Maciel. If you want to know why the sex-abuse scandals were handled badly by the Catholic Church, that's the reason. The clerical club, right to the very top, closed ranks and by their constant denials destroyed the credibility of our Church.

Rumours dogged the founder of the Legionaries as far back as 1956. Then he was deprived of his faculties to govern the order he had founded and was sent into exile in Madrid. Sex abuse wasn't the charge then; rather excessive control over seminarians, theft and drug abuse were. He was cleared in 1959 and restored as superior general.

The complaints of sexual abuse first surfaced in the 1990s when nine former members of his congregation alleged that they had been abused as seminarians by Maciel. A number of high-profile Irish priests left the order about that time. Perhaps they knew too much.

According to the allegations the boys were abused between the ages of 10 and 16, with Maciel telling them he had permission from Pope Pius XII to engage in sexual acts with them to relieve the pain of his stomach ulcer. How sick!

This is the man who accompanied John Paul II to Mexico in 1979, 1990 and 1993. Despite knowing that these accusations had been made against him, Pope John Paul publicly described him as "an efficacious guide to youth". And as late as 2004, John Paul II congratulated him for, "intense, generous, and fruitful priestly ministry."

It's a long way from shovelling spuds in Bellanaleck, but I thank God again that my family weren't well enough off for me to be part of a group like that.

Church leaders in Rome knew about the sexual abuse of children by clerics all over the world. But it's worse than that. It's utterly indefensible that somebody like Cardinal Bernard Law, who knowingly transferred priests accused of the sexual abuse of children, was then brought to Rome and made the archpriest of a Roman basilica. He still exerts a crucial influence over the American Church. Reward or punishment – make up your own mind.

In Philadelphia there was a deliberate policy of protecting priests, including some who raped many children, until the Statute of Limitations ran out. That's also a fact.

There is another reason why Church leaders, particularly bishops, cannot claim they didn't know the full implications of child abuse. In 1985 there was the famous Mouton-Doyle-Peterson Report entitled, *The Problem of Sexual Molestation by Roman Catholic Clergy*. It made clear precisely what was involved and how it should be dealt with. Incidentally, I mentioned Fr Doyle's report in 1985, the first time I wrote about clerical abuse in the *Sunday World*.

That report clearly warned the Church of trouble ahead, gave a clear outline of how grave the problem was, and laid down step-by-step procedures on how to deal with abusing priests. It also warned that dioceses could be made bankrupt because there were so many valid cases against them and stated in clear terms that an abusing cleric must never be admitted to ministry again.

The bishops were clearly told of both the extent of the problem and how best to deal with it, but they chose to ignore the advice. Worse still, the authors of the report were treated shamefully by Church authorities.

Fr Michael Peterson, a highly qualified psychologist, Fr Thomas Doyle, a canon law expert who was a secretary in the office of the Papal Nuncio in Washington, and Ray Mouton, an attorney, prepared and published their report at the request of the bishops.

They were confident that Cardinal Bernard Law, who then headed the committee which commissioned the report, would persuade the rest of the bishops to put it into action. What actually transpired was that the impact of the report was downplayed, and shortly afterwards Fr Doyle was removed as secretary to the papal nuncio and lost his teaching post in canon law at the Catholic University.

Claims since, by bishops all over the world, that had they known as much then as they know now they would have acted differently, ring hollow. The fact is they were told. They did know but did nothing because they thought they could get away with it.

All around the world, including Ireland, bishops deliberately protected men they knew to be criminals. The Church in justice should have handed abusers over to the civil authorities. Instead they protected them and enabled most of them to go on abusing other innocent children.

I appreciate that some Church leaders were acting with what they thought was compassion toward a troubled brother priest. They may even have thought it best to protect the good name of the Church. As far back as 1990 it was obvious that it was a false compassion to protect criminals in such a way. It was bad for the abuser, bad for the Church, and worst of all, it allowed abusers to go on destroying the lives of innocent children.

A real problem is that leaders who are so deeply compromised lose their moral voice and will never be trusted again. That's sad for the Church we love. It leaves Catholics angry and lost. They cannot trust their leaders, are not allowed to discuss the real issues that need changing, and are voiceless, leaderless and powerless. That's what sex abuse and the cover-ups have done.

Very often letters I receive put things more clearly than I can. In 2001, I got a letter from a "former" priest who poured his heart out from a single room, "somewhere in London". I don't know him and I have never met him. Yet I'm convinced his story is authentic from internal analysis of what he says. From personal experience, I can vouch that similar events took place in other orders.

He is now in his late 60s and was once a member of a religious order who "spent the best years of my life slaving up and down the country on missions, retreats, and was even, for a while, on the mission territory in Britain", he said with some cynicism.

"I am now a broken man living on the dole and fit for nothing," he continued. "And the reason I am here is because of the seldom-mentioned evil of Church politics.

"I'm lucky, I suppose, because even though I fell out with the Church, I never forgot God. That is why I never married. I made a promise and I would like to keep it until I meet my Maker in person.

"Let me start at the end, if I may. You seem to be unusual in that you are extremely outspoken about the Church's indifference to those children whom it failed to protect from predatory priests and brothers. I agree with you and that is why I am writing to you.

"Like yourself, I entered in the old days when we were snatched from our homes before we developed questioning minds. I left home at 17 and went straight into a novitiate. It was like a concentration camp. We were deprived of a loving family, we were humiliated and made feel as if we were dirt, we were starved of food, love and sleep, and only when we were broken were we finally allowed to move to the next stage.

"It was as a student that I first became suspicious. Often at night I was propositioned by an older priest who pretended he needed me to help him into bed. Being charitable I believed him. It was only when he wanted me to arouse him that I ran out of the room. When I mentioned it to the man in charge of students, he told me I was a liar.

"I made the biggest mistake of my life at that time. I stayed silent and I now know it was a sin to do so. Others must have been approached, too, but nobody ever mentioned it to me, or I to them. The culture of fear and secrecy was instilled in us.

"After ordination I was sent to houses where I was always the junior. I did what I was told and remained a 17-year-old boy in the body of a thirtysomething. I was immature and childish, but at the time everyone thought I was a 'nice young priest'.

"After 10 years as a priest, I was in a community where abuse of children was common. A group of young boys came to me after youth club and told me that three priests constantly brought them to their rooms and made them do horrible things. They bullied the children into silence. The children came to me simply because they thought they, and not the priests, were bad. They were extremely disturbed.

"I went to the superior and told him. He was furious with me and got in touch with the provincial, who had me sent for psychiatric care. I was put in a mental hospital for three weeks and when I came out, nobody had any respect for me. It was only when I found out from the children that the superior was one of the abusers that it began to make sense.

"I went to the provincial myself. He put me off by telling me that children always said this sort of thing. And anyway I wasn't in a fit condition to deal with such pressure. I was sent to Britain out of the way.

"I spoke to another priest and he advised me to go to the bishop. I went to see him, but he told me he knew the superior well, that he was a good man and an excellent confessor who 'upheld the moral teachings of the Church' and that I should not listen to children who often told lies about priests just to get notice. I was dismissed in 10 minutes.

"By now I was a nervous wreck. The children saw me as their only hope. And I was so brainwashed that I couldn't help them. I couldn't sleep at night and was again in need of psychiatric help. I can't believe that I didn't go to the gardaí. One of the children suggested that I should tell but I said it would be wrong to make it public.

"I trusted the Church to do the right thing. Now I know I was stupid.

"After repeatedly going to the provincial and the bishop, I got nowhere. And to my shame, I did the most cowardly thing of all. I left the priesthood and disappeared to America, sick and disillusioned.

"Nobody, not even my family, knew where I was. I worked there illegally until one night in a bar I met people from home. The next day I disappeared to England where I still live in fear in a small flat. Now that all the scandals have broken, I see what a complete failure I was. I let those boys down. I am tortured inside."

I have sympathy for that priest but I advised him to report it to the Garda even now. I wrote: "You have no choice. Tell the whole story to the Garda. You have a duty to those children who were abused. And you have a duty to ensure that those depraved former colleagues are brought to justice.

"You have been running too long. The only way you'll get peace of mind is to do the honourable thing, no matter what it costs you."

All of us in the clerical Church must take responsibility for what we have done and failed to do. We have become counter signs to the compassion of Christ, who blessed the little children. We now move from crisis to crisis. We hope that each new scandal will be the last so that we can "get back to normal".

It's an old clerical trick. Put your head down, say nothing and hope it will pass. It is precisely that attitude which has allowed the rape and abuse of innocent children by clerics for 50 years, at the very least.

Whatever other good we have done – and we have, thank God, done great good – we will be rightly remembered for the evil we have enabled. An institution claiming to represent Christ could serve no more evil purpose than to allow known, abusing priests and religious to continue in ministry.

What all the reports throughout the world agree on is that while the Church presents a public face of contrition, it ruthlessly obstructs the search for truth in practice. Every legal and canonical loophole is used to delay the search for the truth.

It's back to what Thomas Reilly said: it is more important to protect the Church than to recognise the wrong done to children.

Recently the policy has been to blame everything on the influx of gay priests. Gay priesthood and the pink presbyteries need to be examined, but they have very little to do with the child-abuse problem.

The clerical Church must look at the way it accepts, trains and prepares its new members. That's the crucial area nobody wants to talk about. Its propagation of unreal sexual morality, its refusal to allow priests to live in healthy marriages, its insistence on an all-male clerical club, its willingness to accept any kind of male into the priesthood rather than allow women to be ordained, and its encouragement of unhealthy sexual suppression, are at the centre of the problem. The result is that sexual deviants and criminal abusers find a cosy home in the priesthood.

That's what breaks my heart today. There are wonderful and good priests and religious in the Church as there always have been. But their lives, their dedication and their good works have been blighted because their colleagues betrayed the trust given them and Church leaders made an art form of defending the indefensible.

Can we seriously claim we didn't understand that raping a child was wrong? Does anyone need an expert to tell him that a cleric (or anyone else) who throws an innocent boy down on a dirty mattress and cruelly molests and buggers him is nothing less than a vicious criminal who should be put behind bars and should never be allowed to minister under any circumstances again?

Look back over the years. Church leaders who plead ignorance now were the very people who claimed to know so much about sex that they invaded every marriage bed in the land. They destroyed innumerable loving couples' marriages. They forced unfortunate people with failed marriages to live in misery, never to receive Communion again. Sex was their thing. It was wrong, dirty and forbidden. Much of our inability to see how wrong abuse is results from a distorted view of human sexuality, but they won't admit they were wrong or that they need help to get it right.

The irony is that those who put the institution's well-being ahead of the victims' rights destroyed the institution itself.

The laity will save the Church which we clerics have destroyed. The clerical monolith puts more importance on loyalty than it does on compassion. How un-Christlike is that?

The laity is rightly furious at the Church for protecting the abusers and dismissing their victims. Priests are angry with the Church authorities for hanging the foot soldiers out to dry, and angry with the media for presuming that everybody in a clerical collar is a secret sex abuser.

The morale of good priests is a vital part of the Church's future. Another letter from a priest makes that point abundantly clear. I prefer to use the thoughts of other priests because I have taken a stance on this issue and I need to listen to other voices to ensure a proper balance.

This letter was a reaction to what I'd written about priests being wrongly accused. I said then that whilst I understood what a devastating thing it is to be accused in the wrong of sexually abusing children, overall the balance of sympathy must always be with the victim. At present, priests are removed from their ministry as soon as an accusation is made before it's established whether it's true or false. The investigation comes later. Other professions do the same and see it simply as good practice.

In fairness it must be pointed out that a priest is different because his office and his home are the same place. When he loses his job, he loses his home. He also loses his good name, and even if the accusation is subsequently proved to be false, it is impossible for him to get his good name back. That is obviously unjust and needs to be addressed.

That's the background. The priest who wrote to me agreed with most of what I had written but it sparked something deep within him that has torn the heart out of his ministry.

He's 20 years a priest and had a tough time at school, where he was brutally treated by the religious who taught him; so much so that he resisted his vocation to the priesthood for as long as he could.

He's adamant that when he joined the priesthood he had no idea that a priest would abuse a child. Like most of us, he knew the Church had faults but also believed that the vast majority of those in the Church, including priests, try to bring a message of compassion to the world.

Gradually, he admits his innocence was shattered and "today I stand traumatised and devastated by our Church and its actions".

However, he did not agree with me that priests should feel a collective guilt for the sins of abusing priests. He detests the pain inflicted on innocent children, but he himself has always tried to carry out his duties as well as possible, respecting the dignity of each person.

Now he has lost hope in the Church and in the institution to which he gave his life. He finds it a cold and unloving place. He agrees with the guidelines to protect children and he agrees that what we did in the past was wrong. But he cannot agree with the sanctions against a priest when an accusation is made. He considers them medieval and ruthless.

"Why should priests be the only people to be hounded by the media, abandoned by his boss, and sometimes by his family and friends, and kicked out of his house while the alleged accusation is still under investigation?"

He sees the priesthood as a lonely life where the worldly rewards are practically nil. He's used by the institution when it suits and discarded when it doesn't suit.

He thinks that because I'm a member of a religious order and not a diocesan priest, I don't understand his fears fully.

He's right. It is much more difficult for a diocesan priest than it is for a religious. However, religious life is disintegrating too and simply because a group of men live under the same roof doesn't mean that they are a community or that there is a supportive framework for the lonely struggler. It's increasingly difficult to trust members of one's community to treat one's personal journey with respect.

The priest who wrote to me lives alone in a big, cold house, "trying to invent each day and knowing now that the Church I work for and love cares little for me". He feels that his bishop will toss him to the wolves to protect the institution, if needs be. "For me it is a cold, insecure and dangerous place to work. I have no more desire to work with children, young people or schools."

He says he writes his letter for the good priests who work 24/7 quietly and without pomp or ceremony. These are the men who respect their vows and duties but are "dying in an institution that cares little for its personnel".

His letter shocked me because his sense of failure and loss was tangible.

All priests who keep the show on the road need help and understanding, particularly from the laity. I know you will argue that the institutional Church was not very helpful to you when you were in trouble. I fully accept that. But most people, when they think about it, will understand that good priests who struggle alone find this a time of despair.

CHAPTER 22

THE LATE LATE SHOWDOWN

In November 1995 I was in the RTÉ canteen when John Masterson, the *Late Late* producer, approached me. He said there would be a *Late Late* special on the state of the Catholic Church and he and Gay would like me to be in the audience. I tried to put him off because the *Gerry Kelly Show*, the rival on Ulster Television, had asked me to have a discussion with the former priest Denis Bradley on the Bishop Casey and Michael Cleary affairs and, most of all, the Brendan Smyth scandal. I had agreed and for confidentiality couldn't tell John Masterson why I was putting him off.

The *Gerry Kelly Show* was to be aired a week before RTÉ's programme, so I told John to ring me on Monday and I'd give him an answer. I knew he'd have seen the UTV programme by then and I presumed he wouldn't want me.

The *Gerry Kelly Show* was excellent but much too short. Gerry knew they'd blown the opportunity of a really interesting programme because of fear. Fear that other religions wouldn't be interested. It was a bad call by the production team, and they knew it.

On Monday John rang. He was delighted the UTV effort was so feeble and insisted I should still be part of the audience for the *Late Late Show*.

On Friday I was recording a radio show and rushed over to the television centre just as the *Late Late* was going on air. I had no briefing, had very little time to reflect and was content to be a mere observer. There was a full audience of very able people. The first part was an excellent insight into how out-of-touch the crumbling institution was. I made a short intervention saying that the misuse of power was at the centre of our troubles, particularly the evil of clericalism best exemplified by our using the sacraments as weapons.

At the break, Gay asked me how I thought it was going. I told him he was giving too much time to priests and religious. There were articulate lay people in the audience, particularly women, who were holding back. Brilliant professional that he is, he took it up immediately. That was the most powerful section.

Throughout the night some wonderful people made contributions, but then to everyone's surprise, Cardinal Daly came on the show. I certainly had no idea he was listening to the debate upstairs in RTÉ. When he came on, there was instant hostility, mainly because he appeared to say, "You've had your say, now let's put this behind us and let the bishops get on with it."

The perception was that the cardinal was parachuted in to answer all questions. What was needed was a listening Church, not another run of the "we know best" authoritarian model. There was palpable anger in the audience. It was the same old patronising attitude. Anger in the audience grew to exploding point and it was disintegrating into a heckling, foot-stamping protest.

In fairness, Cardinal Daly was unaware of the extent of the hostility. He smiled at all the wrong places, answered questions no one was asking and silenced the very people who had given their lives to the Church and would still help in her hour of need, given the opportunity. That was why I felt I had to do something. I don't know if I was right or wrong and it doesn't matter. It would have mattered though if nobody had challenged the attitude that the institution can listen without hearing.

Some of the audience were beginning to stamp their feet and hiss at the cardinal. I thought that was a childish way to behave and when Gay Byrne, the host, looked over to me in the front row of the audience, I interrupted the cardinal.

"Cardinal," I said, "how come there are so many good priests and so many good lay people and yet nobody believes that they are seen as good? Nobody believes anything will be done. What's the problem with communications there?

"Most people looking at this tonight will say, 'That was a talk shop. It's nice to have a talk shop, but we will go to Mass on Sunday and next year and our parish will be the same.'

"So why can't we break that down? Why can't we do something on a practical level that will give people that hope and encouragement which you speak about so eloquently?"

The cardinal answered: "I wish I had some members of my own pastoral council here with me or some of my own clergy here to tell us about some of the things they are doing. I think some of us have been very hard on the clergy. There are some of them working very, very hard along the lines you desire. And getting there, too."

I said, "I don't think so, Cardinal. I don't think what you have said is fair. Cardinal Daly, you and I have had arguments many times before and I hope we will have them again in a friendly sort of way. But Cardinal Daly, what I'm trying to say is that I know there are good priests holding the Church together and I know there is a lot of goodness. But at the end of the day, the Church is perceived as heavy-handed and out of date and lacking in compassion. Now why is that? You can't dismiss it because it appears to criticise clergy."

He said: "Brian, if I may say so, the Church is also you, and I don't think anyone would regard you as lacking in compassion. But you are the Church; the caring face of the Church. And many other priests and a few bishops too. Just a few, but we are trying. Don't dismiss the whole clergy."

I answered, "I'm not dismissing it, Cardinal. That is precisely the point. Nor am I dismissing the whole clergy. But they have been let down."

Cardinal Daly said, "Yes, I have been let down. Bishop Bill [Murphy] and Bishop Willie [Walsh] have been let down, but what do we do about it? We go and try to do better."

I asked, "Perhaps the system is wrong. If you're hurting and I'm hurting, and it's a good thing that we should be hurting, and the people are hurting and the victims who have been abused are hurting, and those who feel they are locked outside the Church because of rules and regulations, they're hurting. If that is the truth, and you have admitted it and I have admitted it, where's the compassionate Church?"

The Cardinal replied: "The Church is in the compassion business day by day round the clock and priests who are living in ghettoised areas are the caring presence of the Lord for those people."

What you don't get from print are the anger in the voice, the passion of expression, the smile on the face, the tension of the moment, the applause of agreement, the hiss of disagreement. But as it reads, it's tame enough stuff, and quite frankly, I had said much more revolutionary things earlier in the programme and voiced far more critical opinions for 20 years in the *Sunday World*.

All hell broke loose as the programme came to an end. I remember nothing but hostility. Many of the audience thought they hadn't got a chance to speak and that it had been hijacked by clerics. Others were hoping for a "tidy" ending to help everyone through what was a horrible time in the Church with shocking revelations about priests, bishops, clerical and religious abusers. There were days at the time when I didn't want to listen to the news in the morning because of the litany of abuse and the scandalous response to that abuse.

The cardinal was spirited away to safety and Gay asked me if I wanted to go with him to settle our dispute. Many of the clergy leaving the studio were scathing in their insults to me. It was then that Maura Connolly, Gay's ever-efficient secretary, cornered me to take an urgent phone call. She said it was from a very disturbed caller who had asked for me.

I went to an extension and picked up the phone. On the other end was a suicidal woman who was crying uncontrollably. When she was a child, the chaplain of the hospital had ritually abused her each night. She had to stay in hospital for some months because of a serious illness. Each night the chaplain came round complete with stole and prayer-book, smiled and nodded to the sister in charge and pulled the curtains round the bed "to pray" for the child. In fact the vile abuser proceeded to prey on the innocent little girl trapped in her sick bed. He sexually abused her every night of the week for weeks on end on the pretence of blessing her.

By now I was tired, shocked and sickened. The dispute with the cardinal faded into nothingness as I tried to find the right word to keep this middle-aged, alcoholic woman from committing suicide. Eventually she promised me she would go to bed and contact me in Enniskillen in the morning.

Most of the audience had gone home and I wanted to do the same. Another caller wanted to speak to me. This time it was a man in his 30s who had spent the last year in a mental institution as a result of being abused as an altar boy in a Dublin monastery. The priest, he said, had moved on to greater things and refused even to acknowledge his victim's existence. He too felt aggrieved. The programme was upsetting for him and he felt like taking his life because he could detect no sign of change on the Church's part.

As I was speaking to this victim, Cardinal Daly and Jim Cantwell, the then press officer for the Catholic Church, walked out through reception. The cardinal had no idea who I was speaking to and, gentleman that he is, came over and shook hands with me before disappearing into the night, totally oblivious to the hidden pain our Church was causing.

Again I made arrangements for the caller to contact me on Saturday morning at home. I had the mother and the father of a headache. It was now after 2am and I had to drive home to Enniskillen. I arrived home at 4.30 and went to bed for a few hours, but couldn't sleep wondering how I was going to help the two victims. I never thought at all about the *Late Late* special.

On Saturday morning I got up before eight and went for a walk as usual. I turned on the RTÉ radio news to discover I was the news. The phone never stopped all day – the calls were mostly abusive, including one from a priest who claimed to speak on behalf of the priests of Armagh archdiocese. He was irrationally angry that I had dared to insult "our" cardinal by disagreeing with him in public. The tirade went on and on, ending with the promise that because of my "insubordination, no Passionist will ever preach in my archdiocese again".

The days following were difficult. I was trying to do something for the two victims who phoned, but was depressed beyond belief when a further eight victims got in touch within three days. I couldn't say anything about it, but those who thought I was being disloyal should have read my mail. They would have seen just how serious the problem really was.

Cardinal Daly, like me, wrongly thought it was a storm in a teacup. Whatever we thought, the people knew a boundary had been crossed. I cringe a little now when I read reports of the incident and I'm quoted as denying that the cardinal and I had clashed. Obviously I was living in denial. But not for long.

By Monday, I knew I had to think it out. Most of the hostile press accused me of ambushing the cardinal. Nothing was further from the truth. It was a spontaneous reaction at the end of a programme on which I had done more listening than speaking. In fact I didn't want to be there at all.

On Tuesday the debate had got out of hand and I rang Ara Coeli (the cardinal's residence in Armagh) for a chat. He wasn't available until Friday as he was out of the country. I made an appointment for Friday night.

I was working in the BBC all day and drove from Belfast to Armagh at the appointed time. "Look for the twin towers and come to the residence at the back of the cathedral," he advised. It was 9pm when I arrived, exactly one week after the *Late Late Show*.

The cardinal greeted me warmly, brought me into a small sittingroom with an electric fire and poured tea into delicate china cups. He looked tired, small, frail even, and for the first time I felt a tinge of guilt at upsetting a man at the end of his life. At least that is what I thought then.

Our chat was friendly and we both apologised for the hurt we'd caused each other, however unwittingly. Once again, he thought it was greatly exaggerated. There had been no row. It was just a spur-of-the-moment thing. I disagreed and explained that even though both of us thought it was not a row, the whole country perceived it as such.

I filled him in on the threat by his one of his priests to have all Passionists banned in his archdiocese. It was the only time he showed the flash of anger. He assured me it wouldn't happen and no self-appointed spokesman had a right to say such a thing. He was as good as his word and indeed a Passionist lectured at his request in Armagh, shortly afterwards. He asked that he be kept informed about any unfair treatment that might come my way from his priests as a result of the *Late Late*.

He then asked me why I was so disillusioned with the Church. I should be helping the Church in this time of trouble, he said. I explained that was precisely what I was trying to do and that unless we understood the terrible and justified anger that abuse generates, we would never find solutions. I tried to explain that the "good old days" were gone forever. We couldn't go on building clerical empires. The Church could be saved only by the laity. We had one chance left to do something and living in denial was not helping.

He was genuinely shocked, but not annoyed. How bad is the abuse, he wanted to know. Drawing on the hundreds of letters a week I was getting from the *Sunday World*, I tried to explain what it was like for a victim, and how much worse it was being abused by a priest, because you could not trust anyone afterwards, not even God. I was able to tell him about impending scandals in various dioceses and religious orders in Ireland. He was really grateful but I then realised he was sinking farther and farther into his chair.

The thought struck me that this lonely man, close to 80, with a bad heart and living on his own, was extremely vulnerable. I stopped at once, poured him a cup of tea and chatted about mutual friends as light-heartedly as I could. We parted, promising to pray for each other, which I still do, and drove back to Enniskillen hoping nothing would happen to him during the night. I would have been blamed for that too, no doubt.

The reaction of the media was fascinating.

The *Irish Times* opined that the "Father Brian Trendy" of the media was well and truly buried as a result of the television controversy. If I'm honest, I'll admit I was nonplussed by that comment. Sure, Dermot Morgan made a living out of the Brian Trendy priest but even though he took the name from me, he never implied my life supplied the script.

Kathy Sheridan wrote one of the most insightful articles in the *Irish Times*. "It was only as the show went into injury time," she wrote, "that a startled nation witnessed an awesome event – a priest breaching centuries of conditioning, throwing future advancement to the winds, to publicly challenge a cardinal. What made it particularly piquant was that virtually every viewer recognised Father Brian D'Arcy as the maverick priest. The 'Father Trendy' image had taken a dent earlier in the show when he confessed with obvious sincerity that the events of the past year had made him a different person."

That was the truth. I was so ashamed of what was happening in the Church that I seriously thought of leaving the priesthood on a matter of principle. How could I be part of something that not only abused children en masse but also actually suppressed the facts to protect the good name of the institution?

It was and is simply unforgivable that a priest would use his position to groom innocent boys and girls and then forcibly sexually abuse them. That many priests were allowed to continue raping children for decades by bishops and religious superiors, who moved them from parish to parish and from monastery to monastery, is a crime and a sin of such proportions that it demands the wrath of God. Is that what I gave my life to?

In 1995 I had just passed 50 years of age and completed 25 years in priesthood. Normally a silver jubilee is a time of celebration. For me it was nightmare. As I've already said, I went to Africa to think things out. I decided I still had to be a priest, even though every instinct told me to leave it behind me.

I promised myself that I would never again be the easygoing, acceptable face of the Church, foolishly defending the indefensible. I would stay with the intention of giving hope to those on the margins who are the real people of God. That is how I had the courage to challenge the cardinal, not to embarrass him but to give hope to those who love God but reject religion – or at least the squabbling institutions who claim the franchise.

Even the *Church of Ireland Gazette* got in on the act. "After last week's *Late Late*," they joked, "guess who will not be applying for a job in the hierarchy?" That said it all.

My friend of many years Fr Colm Kilcoyne thought it showed a twin-track Church – the Church of Cardinal Daly and the Church of Sr Maura Clune, who was one of the contributors on the *Late Late*. "Sr Maura Clune was so different to the Cardinal," he wrote. "Mostly in that the camera showed a woman listening as she was talking. That quality some people have of leaving spaces for you to dialogue in your heart with what they are saying. She was the one most at home talking about Jesus Christ. Her language was about relationship, not power."

I don't take any pride in saying that I don't think the worst is over for the Church even now. From my column I know that there is an underlying distrust of the Church. There are certainly many good people who will always stand by our Church. There are still enough good priests who work hard on the ground and who keep the faith alive in pockets where they work.

The danger is that many of them are growing old and tired. There is not enough of the under-40 generation with the ability and the enthusiasm to refound the Church from the roots up. That's where it needs to happen. That's why I would want to see a completely new kind of priest emerge. Sending them off to archaic seminaries where they will be taught dogmatically and initiated into the outdated and ultimately destructive clerical club is not the way to go about it.

More of the same, not surprisingly, leads to more of the same. I detect two main attitudes. The first and most prominent is disillusionment. Good people who have been hurt and let down, and who want to see reform, encounter what they perceive as clerical obstructionism. They meet men who are more and more removed from the world of their lived experience, with outdated methods of consulting and the power to squash real initiative. So the good people give up because they see no hope of change coming. They have more to do with their busy lives than to keep running into brick walls. But they would and do respond to anyone who tries to meet them half way.

The other group are those that have given up long ago. The Church has little to offer them, but they feel the need for some spirituality in their lives. All is not lost, but sadly, unless the clerical Church agrees to a new model of parish and community, time will run out. There is still enough goodwill around but we are fast running out of time.

The first thing we clerics must do is learn to listen and learn with humility.

In the 1980s, when I was a parish priest in Dublin, we consoled ourselves that, at least, we were getting the parents back for First Communion Masses. That was 20 years ago. Since then there has been a watering down in succeeding generations, so that soon, even parents will have no connection with the Church. Today it's obvious that fewer and fewer people are really committed to an active faith. The Catholic schools have an ever-diminishing Catholic ethos. With the influx of different cultures, that will change drastically and quickly. We haven't put anything in its place. We haven't trained married deacons; we haven't trained enough catechists who might hold classes in religion and faith and faith experience. We have priests who are elderly and further removed from under-40s and therefore less effective.

The clerical system strangled the life out of the best and brightest priests. The problem is obvious: when the best brains and those with humanity follow love out of the ministry, you are left with a huge vacuum in leadership skills.

Now we have a group of ageing men who were always safe, because they stayed and played safe, and a group of young men coming in who are older in mind than the men who are at the end of their days. From a leadership point of view the Church is in a perilous position, particularly in the Western world. It can be saved only by interested and educated laity. I'm telling you all of this to explain that I stayed hoping things would change.

Reeling in the Years is a popular programme on RTÉ television. It shows TV footage from the past, and the "cool generation" laugh at the haircuts and clothes from a decade ago, just as the new cool will laugh at us five years from now.

It's a programme that is beginning to haunt me. 1995 must have been an important year because they show it often. Each time they show the famous "fight" between Cardinal Daly and me on the *Late Late Show* of November 1995, it revives the passion of what has become a key moment in both television and religion in Ireland.

The weeks after the original airing brought the biggest reaction I ever had to deal with. Those wonderful people who helped me answer the letters told me more than 4,000 letters came to The Graan. They were long, well argued and largely helpful. I wish I had kept them, but I invariably destroy letters as soon as they are answered and anyway I'm meticulous about confidentiality.

What I can say is that three-quarters of the correspondents thought I was a saint and another quarter described me as the devil incarnate for daring to talk back to the cardinal. The most common reason given was that he was an old man and deserved respect. To this day I think I showed more respect for his ability and his position by debating with him. To ignore him because he was an old man (78 at the time but still Cardinal Archbishop of Armagh and Primate of All Ireland) would have been a terrible insult.

Every time I see it I wonder what all the fuss was about. I didn't see it as hugely controversial at that time, though I admit others did. Ever since, it is accepted that Cardinal Daly and I are enemies. We never were and I hope we are not now. He's a man I respect highly. When I was editor of *The Cross* in the early 70s, he was a regular contributor. When I worked in the Communications Centre, I synopsised and put into popular language the excellent pastoral letters he wrote for hierarchy on Life, Marriage and Justice. There were certainly areas of disagreement but I saw him as a dedicated, holy and highly intelligent churchman and I knew he respected my pastoral approach, though he was not as encouraging as his predecessor, Cardinal Ó Fiaich.

Three years later, in 1998, when Cardinal Daly published his own autobiography, he invited me to the launch and signed a copy for me. It reads, "For Brian, confrere and friend in union of ministry and prayer + Cathal B Cardinal Daly."

The Men in Black

Mrs Cranny, at
103 years of age,
attending the
beatification
ceremony for
Fr Charles of
Mount Argus

At Thomas Merton's
monastery in
Gethsemane,
Kentucky, 1989

Bekkersdal township, South Africa,
October 1994

One-armed bandit: trying to crack the system in Las Vegas!

Presenting a double platinum album to Peg Cunningham for sales of over 30,000 of *Give Up Yer Auld Sins*

The *Late Late Showband Special* – (from left) Eamonn Monaghan (Capitol Showband), myself, Brendan O'Brien (Dixies), Derek Dean (Freshmen), Paddy Cole, Joe Dolan, Joe McCarthy (Dixies), Sonny Knowles, Seán Dunphy and Earl Gill (Hoedowners), Eileen Kelly (Nevada)

The launch of Brian Carthy's book *A-Z of Country and Irish Stars*: (from left) Louise Morrissey, Trish and Brian Carthy, Philomena Begley and myself

The best of company: jostling for attention on a *Sunday World* billboard

A surprise party from 2FM marking my 25 years as a priest. Joe Dolan looks sceptical about the Divine D'Arcy Tour. It never happened!

Above left: Charley Pride

Above right: Kenny Rogers

Right: interviewing
George Jones

Below right: Ricky Skaggs
in Nashville

Below left: interviewing
Garth Brooks in Nashville
before he became a superstar

Above left: Beth Nielsen Chapman

Above right: Gretchen Peters

Left: Kimmie Rhodes

Below: Reba McEntire

Daniel O'Donnell and myself at the Novena of Hope in The Graan

Flanked by two of the gentlemen of popular music: Daniel and Cliff Richard

In Dungloe with Gay Byrne and Daniel.
Right: Mike Murphy
Below: Terry Wogan

Pop idol: Gilbert O'Sullivan

Simply the best: Tina Turner

Explaining Gaelic football to Alex
Ferguson in Croke Park, 1994

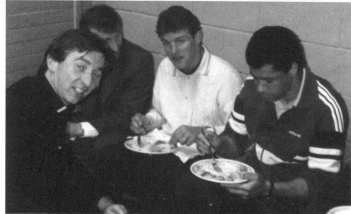

Above right:
congratulating Mickey
Harte, manager of the
2005 All-Ireland
champions, Tyrone, at
their homecoming in
Omagh

Left: with Kevin
Moran and Paul
McGrath

Enjoying the excellent company of a young David
O'Leary and family

With Fermanagh manager Charlie Mulgrew.
Guess who's showing the strain!

Soccer legend Niall Quinn preaches at the Novena of Hope in The Graan

With the Clones Cyclone, Barry McGuigan, while he was world champion

Chapter 23

Bono and that Question

The God of Surprises is one of my favourite books. Years ago the wisdom of Gerard Hughes gave me the freedom to let go of old Gods and be content merely to search for an ever-changing God – one I don't need to imprison in my tiny mind. The true God is so loving, so compassionate, so mighty, as to be beyond the oppressive rules and regulations of power-hungry legalists.

I need a more loving God, more just than the manipulative "Uncle George" or the spiteful "Policeman" of Hughes's book. Yet his naming of the false and frightening gods I was giving my life to made it easy for me to reject them. Instead, I had to discover a God of ever-new life, a God of second chances and third chances – the God of infinite opportunity.

Reflection helped me to "roll the stone back" which had entombed me in a dying institution, to accept new challenges and, like the disciples of old, not "to look for the living among the dead". It was the key to experiencing the risen Jesus walking the roads of life beside me, even when I don't recognise Him, and especially in that horrible decade of decadence.

Another favourite writer, Thomas Merton, once explained why he became a hermit living in the woods at a time when he was the most influential thinker in America. He described how he needed to be alone, in silence, and close to nature to experience a different God, the cosmic God.

"It is necessary to be present alone at the resurrection of day in solemn silence at which the sun appears, for at this moment all the affairs of cities, of governments, of war departments, are seen to be the bickering of mice," he wrote (*A Year with Thomas Merton*, SPCK London P127).

"The bickering of mice." What a wonderfully evocative description of the nonsense we Church people waste so much time and energy on! A s I grow older I've realised that God uses strange prophets to disturb our smugness. In my case it is usually the letters I get at the *Sunday World*. Most of them are heartbreaking stories of saintly people who think they are the rejects of society, when in fact they are God's closest friends.

To be fair, people who disagree with me also give me food for thought. By nature I'm not a confident man; I have to continually re-think what I'm about. My natural inclination is to be quiet and laid back and discern what is worth fighting for. But I know from experience that I will not be walked upon. I had to learn to stand up for myself but not in an angry, reactive way. It was a tough learning experience. There is a point beyond which I won't be pushed. I prefer a quiet life, but not at any price.

The conviction that I had to do something about my life happened in unusual circumstances. At the time I didn't recognise the impact of a throwaway remark from a man I admire but don't know very well. On the night it happened we were both guests on the *Late Late Show*.

Gay Byrne was the host and producer of the *Late Late Show* for more than 30 years. During that time it was consistently the most watched and the most influential programme in Ireland. His skill as an interviewer is world-renowned. By any standards he was unique and in his field brilliant. Ireland owes him so much. Like a wise uncle he prodded and guided us to think "out of the box", as it were.

When he decided to retire from the show, there was a final night of tributes and thanks. I was lucky enough to be invited on and to the party afterwards. We were either friends of Gay or people who had contributed regularly to the show over the years. The highlight of the night was when U2 presented Gay with a Harley-Davidson motorbike to thank him for his encouragement when they needed it most. It was an emotional climax to an emotional night.

RTÉ had erected a hospitality tent for the modest party. I didn't want to stay too long, as I had to make the lengthy journey to the North that night for the inevitable early start next morning.

As I was grabbing a plate of beef curry, I was chatting with friends from the entertainment industry who had been guests on the show. The Corrs, for example, were there. The always-pleasant Larry Mullan from U2 began to speak seriously to me. He sensed that life as a priest wasn't easy for me and wondered how I was managing to be so outspoken against the obvious failings of the institutional Church and still maintain a role as a priest.

As we were speaking, and by now many others were joining in the discussion, Bono came over. He was coming to greet the Corrs actually, but spotted me in the middle of the group. I don't want to give the impression that I know Bono very well, but I have met him on numerous occasions over 25 years now. He looked at me, listened to the conversation for a while and uttered the immortal words: "Why the f*** are you still a priest?"

He had a torrent of questions and comments, some serious, some funny, but in typical fashion, he got to the heart of the matter. For 20 minutes or so, I tried, unsuccessfully, to explain why I was still a priest. Bono wasn't being contentious or insulting. He was genuinely amazed that someone who had spoken and written as I had could remain a priest.

In his logic, I should have either got out or been put out. He explained that all the people who were friends of mine and were even more prominent than I was in an earlier era were now gone. He mentioned, among others, Bishop Casey and Fr Michael Cleary. "You're the last one standing," he whispered, almost guiltily.

The conversation fizzled out as it always does on such social occasions, with me trying to explain that being a priest and a member of a Church is not the same as being a member of a club, or a pop group for that matter.

But as I drove home that night, Bono's question had touched a raw, sensitive part of me. It was the question I hadn't really settled and I knew it was one I had to come to terms with before I could find peace. The thought of facing into it again terrified me.

I knew there was something "wrong" with my life. It wasn't something "sinful" – though as with everyone, there is sin involved and it would be a sin to do nothing about it. It was needless "busyness", a lack of awareness, a lostness, a dissipation of vocation, but most of all an unwillingness to think of what my role in Church and society should be.

I was being carried along.

Thomas Merton, shortly before he died, used to worry that he was "being diverted into a way that is not my way and is not going where I am called to go". I needed to find a way to keep my sanity and discover my freedom.

As I spoke about it with close friends, I noticed I cried often and easily. Tears are nothing to be ashamed of, but I've learned to listen to them. Loneliness is part of life and a healthy experience if we deal with it openly. However, I find if I suppress loneliness it will destroy me.

I value time alone, too, but I need relationships in order to grow. I've had to learn, painfully, to share my feelings and risk being vulnerable. There is no other way. Without relationship I will become a dysfunctional celibate, devoting more energy to protecting my vows than to simply being a decent human being and, hopefully, a helpful priest.

I knew I needed friends to help me through this one. There are lovely people in my life to whom I can turn in times of difficulty. I asked their advice and they were wise enough not to give it. They did however point out the areas of life I needed to reassess. Almost universally, they encouraged me to write it down.

I was totally against the idea of a book. At that point I had written several books, all compilations of articles, broadcasts and reflections. They sold remarkably well, most of them going into reprints, unheard of for books on religion. Another book? Not now!

But even the professionals thought the book a good idea. They reminded me that for a number of reasons I was in a privileged position.

I entered the monastery in 1962 and was a novice at the very time the Second Vatican Council started. Back in the 1960s, the Vatican Council was to be the great hope of the Church. Through it we were to dialogue with the world and even learn from it.

The 60s were a time of change in Church and society. It was the era of John F Kennedy, the Beatles, Pope John XXIII, Seán Lemass and everything positive, different and life-giving. John XXIII, hoping to take the Church out of the reactionary dark ages and help us to be relevant to the revolution, called the Vatican Council.

When I entered the monastery, training hadn't changed for centuries. We got the same training as novices had in 1860. The world had changed drastically since then and I knew as soon as I went to university that era was gone forever. In other words, I was struggling right from the beginning, and probably suppressed it because I wanted to be a Passionist and a priest.

I was ordained in 1969, and moved into a Church which had just dropped the Latin Mass and the "eat meat on Friday" mortal sin, and had begun to turn altars around to face the people. We were promised a new Church for a new world. Most of us looked forward with enthusiasm and hope. Others saw it as the end of their world. I remember an old priest in Mount Argus unable to cope with change saying, "I didn't leave the Church, the Church left me." It was that revolutionary. My generation was part of it and it was a privilege.

Furthermore, I've been chaplain to the entertainment industry all my life, which meant I spent the 1970s in dancehalls six nights a week. I was trained in communications, was editor of a religious magazine, and was a member of the National Union of Journalists. I wrote for pop magazines, first broadcast for radio 40 years ago and have been writing for the *Sunday World* every week for 30 years.

I was on one of the committees that prepared for the Pope's visit here in 1979 – surely, as discussed earlier, the greatest week in the history of the Catholic Church in Ireland. It seemed as if the Catholic Church had won the battle for the minds and hearts of the Irish people hands down. Yet anyone reading the signs of the time realised it was merely a temporary feelgood respite. Irish people have the capacity to rise for the big occasion – and slip back to their own world just as easily.

Personally, I've lived through both fame and notoriety feeling equally uncomfortable in both worlds.

In a few short years, it seems to me, I've been part of a Church in its most triumphalistic days and now I see that same institution barely surviving its own scandalous behaviour. I was superior of a monastery which had 83 members in the community in 1989 and will soon be disposed of because there are fewer than 20 ageing monks left in it.

I've survived the "Fr Trendy" joke and now the trendy wonder why I'm still a priest.

This book is an attempt to tell that story, reflect on it and try to answer that vital question: Why am I still a priest?

All these arguments persuaded me to leave some time aside for reflection. It was difficult to do in this age of priest shortage, but it was essential for me to do it anyway.

For years publishers have cajoled me to write a book. Showbiz connections and Church gossip would ensure a bestseller, they said. I always resisted because quite frankly I have more to do. Even though there are a little of both showbiz and Church gossip in this book, I hope there is something in it to encourage you to value your journey. That's the heart of it. If a journeyman priest like me feels the need to doubt, question, search, then I hope you can give yourself permission to do the same.

It is not a book about theology but about a life. Each of us has a precious story to meditate on and as John Shea, the theologian of storytelling, often says, all stories are true, some of them actually happened.

At least I can guarantee the stories here are true, but it is up to you to decide how much truth for you there is in them.

The poet TS Elliot warned us about wasting our lives. We have had the experience but missed the meaning was how he put it. This book is an attempt to connect some of the dots of experience in a complicated and full life.

About six years ago I was a contributor on Joe Duffy's *Liveline*. Because it is a phone-in programme, some people take it for granted that when you are on the programme you have actually rung asking to go on it. Funnily enough, even though I have been on the programme frequently with both Marian Finucane and Joe, I have never rung the programme. They have always contacted me to see if I would be willing to make a contribution. They never suggest what I should say; they merely tell me what they are talking about and ask if I would make a contribution.

It's risky because you never know who will phone in to argue or agree with you. On one occasion after I had spoken as honestly as I could about the position of the Church, a priest from the Midlands rang in to offer the opinion that I was nothing more than a spoiled priest.

This man never met me or spoke to me directly before or indeed since the programme. He is of course entitled to his opinion.

He went on to say it was obvious I never wanted to be a priest, that I shouldn't have been ordained, and if I had any credibility, I would have left the priesthood long ago.

The basis of his judgement was that I didn't agree with everything Pope John Paul II said, or more accurately, everything the priest himself believed.

Nevertheless it's a thought any self-respecting priest should contemplate at specific times throughout his life. Should I still be a priest? What gives me life? Am I still a priest simply because I have nowhere else to go, nothing else I can be?

It's a process I go through over a few days' reflection at least once a year. But it is also a question I ask myself as I go for morning walks to think and pray.

At times like this I have to let go and put myself entirely in God's hands. One of the psalms contains a verse that says, "My own judgement is darkness in the sight of God." That's it, exactly.

It's amazing. As soon as I settle myself to accept God's will, a peace comes back to my life. I'm not saying God is entirely satisfied with me – I honestly don't know. In another sense I don't care. I'm doing the best I can in the circumstances in which I find myself and I know that if I do that I can be assured of His love and support. I believe in God's love even though most days I simply cannot see how I deserve it.

There comes a time when I have to give up fussing about how I'm travelling through life and simply carry on to the next crossroads, knowing that when I arrive I'll have to choose again.

I need to learn that I will never reach Him by my own efforts or my own wisdom anyway. One of the keys to peace in the spiritual life was when I realised that I had to stop doing what other people expected me to do, including many of my superiors and spiritual directors. I also had to forget what other people do and learn to travel my own road. God inspires us as we travel our various journeys, but He sends us peace when we decide to do His will and His will alone.

The tough part of this message is that it usually leads to a cross. The hope that calms me is that it always leads to resurrection and new life.

This book is for people who've seen me on television and in the papers and wonder, "What makes him tick?" They realise I've been around for years, not agreeing with bishops and more at home at football matches or at pop concerts. I hope they'll see that, like everyone else, I'm on a journey. I may not be a typical priest, but everything in me is still a priest. Journalism is priesthood, entertainment is priesthood, sport is priesthood, and broadcasting is priesthood. Being a priest is using God's gifts to highlight God's compassion while still striving to be myself.

If I'm as honest as I should be, some people will recognise their own struggle and be encouraged to live with their own imperfection.

The Church must learn to welcome the wayward, because according to the Gospels, the lost sheep is important.

I bet Bono didn't realise what he started.

Chapter 24

Walking the Line

Every generation needs creative people to challenge our principles and our prejudices. The arts should encourage us to reflect on undreamed of possibilities. They do so through song – Kris Kristofferson has been creating a vision for me for 30 years or more. Kimmie Rhodes, Kieran Goss, Brendan Graham, Guy Clarke, Tom Russell, Gretchen Peters, Tom T Hall, Johnny Cash, Kate Campbell and Beth Nielsen Chapman are just a few of the writers who inspire me today. They write the real hymns.

Poets do it: from Kavanagh to Yeats to Brendan Kennelly to Heaney to Denis Riordan. Painters like Van Gogh and Craigie Aitcheson give life to my spirit. An occasional article or book, such as *The God of Surprises* by Gerard Hughes, has kept me sane in a mad world. I hope the odd article in the *Sunday World* over the past 30 years might have helped a lost soul along the way. God works mysteriously and wonderfully through anyone who endures the pain of being lost. And I pray this book will help someone to realise, "You're loved. Just because you're lost doesn't mean you're bad. You have to be lost to search meaningfully."

Patrick Kavanagh's insights inspire me when I realise that the ordinary is spirit-filled. Like myself, he was a bogman who walked to Mass on crispy ice of a Christmas morning. He was a bogman who recognised the God of the gaps, who found poetry in setting spuds, cutting turf and ricking hay. Those were not the topics of the poets I grew up with, but he made the ordinary sublime. He also preached a unique theology. How or where he got his insights I don't know. It must have been the Holy Spirit. Imagine how frustrated he must have been, locked into the small-mindedness of a country parish. It's no wonder he became a cranky old man, but poetry gave him his freedom, and is the real Kavanagh. Poets see things we don't see, express things we cannot express, understand feelings we don't understand and allow us to reach and express emotions we didn't know we had. They give us language and insight.

Kimmie Rhodes is a talented, thoughtful singer who writes challenging yet peaceful songs. Her concerts are a spiritual experience. I went to see her once in Lurgan. As well as being a lovely night, it gave me a good example of this changing Ireland. The concert was held in a former convent that is now a residence for young people from broken families, who find life difficult. Because there are no vocations the nuns moved out and the former convent became a place where dysfunctional adults could learn to be independent again.

There's an intimate little theatre that once was the nuns' chapel. It was a sobering experience when I thought of the irony. The nuns were gone, leaving not a single trace of their lives of virginal dedication. Yet an American lady with a couple of failed marriages, and one very fulfilling one, with her fruitful struggles and a freeing spirituality, used their chapel to evangelise a broken world. This is the word of the Lord. The word truly made flesh.

Kimmie gave me pause for thought on many occasions:

One night Kimmie and I were guests in the home of Kieran Goss and Annie in Sligo. We had pleasant, though deep, conversation in front of a roaring log fire. Songs and life were the topics. There were bypasses into religion, love, failure and humour. I must have been revealing more of myself than I knew because Kimmie gently borrowed Kieran's guitar and sang the song she thought put words on my searching.

Life has led me by the hand / Time has helped me understand
I'm headed to the promised land / With the heart of a believer.

I believe my dreams are safe / Faith that's blind will find its way
Doubts will leave me when hope remains / In the heart of a believer.

A star is just a ray of life / Finding its way through the night
It's travelled light years just to shine / For the heart of a believer

A pearl is just a grain of sand / A tree is just a seed that lands
Every miracle began / In the heart of a believer.

The *Heart of a Believer* was just enough to get me thinking on my journey home through the wet and windy winter night. By the time I arrived at The Graan, "A tree is just a seed that lands" blotted everything else out of my consciousness. Hope for the journey indeed. Sometimes the simplest inspiration gives me life.

Singer John Randall wrote in his 2005 Song of the Year, "I'm finding new faith in the arms of old friends/I'm walking among the living again."

After Kimmie's show in Lurgan that night, we took up the conversation again:

"You don't know how much your presence means to us entertainers when we come over here," she said reassuringly. "My husband and I were hoping you'd be here simply because you understand our life and our vocation. We feel at home when you're here. It doesn't matter where we are, we need people to make us feel at home and you do that."

It was a complete shock to me. I thought I was there to enjoy the music. She said I did more – I understood the music and thereby gave meaning to her search.

She continued: "Kris Kristofferson comes and you talk to him about his songs. For him to hear from a man of the cloth that you have given sermons about his songs makes his life worthwhile. A record company is interested only in a commercial success. Commercial success is necessary but the fact that you understand his thoughts makes his suffering, his pain, his struggle and his life worthwhile."

Johnny Cash was the same. He always asked to see me when he came here and in later years he asked me to introduce him on stage because he felt safe and fulfilled when I did it. He saw it as significant when "The Man in Black" introduced the world's most famous "Man in Black".

The last meeting I had with Johnny Cash was after I introduced him on stage in Ireland. As always when he came here, I got to as many of his gigs as I could. I always knew I was in the presence of a legend, but a vulnerable man too, whom I could not be sure of seeing again. It was his vulnerability that made him beautiful.

Walk the Line, the film of Cash's life, doesn't deal with the man I knew – the mature, focused and loving husband in the golden days of his life.

Each time we met – over a 30-year period – we talked more and more about life and less and less about music. My first conversation with the great man took place in Nashville in 1972 when he invited me to the premiere of his film *Gospel Road*. Religion was always central to his mission.

It is difficult to put Johnny Cash's talents into a single category. He wrote and performed far too many average country songs. But also he wrote and performed some great classics that will live forever. The more mature he became, the freer he became and the more powerful his music was. He told his stories in exactly the same down-home way, whether he was performing to a country audience or a rock audience. The fact that he was accepted into the Hall of Fame in both country music and rock music is a testament to his extraordinary appeal. Bob Dylan, Bruce Springsteen and Bono adored him. Johnny always called Bono "a true visionary". He appreciated his genius for prophecy before most. Johnny came to believe that his job as a writer and singer was messianic. That was why he dressed in black.

Kris Kristofferson told me that Johnny Cash was the spiritual father to a whole generation of musicians, himself included. He was the man who helped launch the career of Bob Dylan and persuaded Columbia Records to sign him. That's some legacy to music and to life.

In latter years Cash unquestionably recorded the best tracks of his career under the guidance of Rick Rubin. The voice wasn't what it used to be, the man's outward strength disappeared, but his vulnerability gave a depth to his music that was at once frightening and inspirational. His rendering of *Hurt* – which Cash himself reckoned to be the best anti-drug song ever written – is truly a masterpiece, full of excruciating tension as it highlights the fight between good and evil. What makes it outstanding is the certainty of redemption through weakness. Cash didn't want to record it at all because it was a pop song, but after listening to it more than 100 times, he knew the message he was determined to get across.

Cash lived the hurt in his own life. He and his great friend Waylon Jennings were rebel companions in the 1960s when they roomed together.

Tragically, both of them wrecked their bodies by substance abuse.

Fifteen years before his death, when Cash entered hospital for a bypass operation, Jennings came to visit him. Cash advised Jennings to have a medical examination, since, "You have lived every excess I have." Jennings did, and had to have emergency bypass surgery there and then. Both of them recuperated side by side and Cash admitted they both dreaded the arrival of their mutual friend Tom T Hall. If he saw them in this condition he would immortalise the pair in one of his brilliant story songs.

No mention of Cash would be complete without a tribute to his wife, June Carter, who died a few months before him. June Carter, according to Johnny's daughter, Rosanne, went to the man she loved each day and asked one simple question: "What can I do for you today, John?"

What she did for John was keep him alive. Over and over he paid tribute to her. He recognised each new day was a gift not only from God but also from June.

She was a vulnerable lady herself, who seemed to attract the flawed genius. She was a confidante and friend of Hank Williams. Williams had a back problem, for which doctors prescribed addictive, painkilling drugs. He died at the age of 29, having written some of the most poignant songs of the last century.

June also befriended Patsy Cline, another outstanding singer, who was addicted to alcohol before she was killed in a plane crash.

Elvis Presley was a friend, both at the most successful and at the most pathetic times of his life.

When June married Johnny Cash in 1968, most people thought he'd be dead before he was 40. She kept him alive past the three score and 10.

It was entirely predictable that when June died, Johnny wouldn't want to live without her. Four months after her death, he joined her in the heaven he was certain of going to. He told me once that he gave his life to God at the age of 12. He said, "Whenever I hand it over to Him, I have an inner peace that only He can give. When I try to run it myself I end up in a complete mess."

The last time we met he brought June and her sisters into a small room to ask God's blessing for the show they were about to perform. I always remember his final prayer: "God give me the strength to remember my weakness." That's how I like to remember him.

On one of his early visits to Ireland, we spoke at length about the value of music in communicating with young people. He believed, as I do, that the best songs express the values and doubts of their generation.

Johnny was so convinced of that fact that he volunteered to talk to me about his life and songs, if I would make a tape of it and distribute it to young people throughout the schools. We subsequently did three educational and highly entertaining tapes about his own music and other contemporary writers.

He was not proud of his early life and regretted the hurt he caused so many, especially his first wife, who as it happens, died just before the film *Walk the Line* was released.

Cash had many crises in his life but he maintained his honesty and his integrity. He struggled with life yet always believed. He was, as Kristofferson famously wrote in *Pilgrim Chapter 33*, "a prophet and a preacher . . . and a problem when he's stoned. He's a walking contradiction, partly truth and partly fiction . . . taking every wrong direction on his lonely way back home." In other words, human, just like me.

When it comes to people who have influenced me, Kris Kristofferson is near the top of the list. I am not just a fan; I'm mesmerised by his way with words and his ability to express emotional searching and sometimes emotional devastation.

As far back as 1970 I reviewed an album whose original name I can't recall now, but within months it was reissued under the title *Me and Bobby McGee*. His songs did something to me. They touched me in a way no other works had.

For nearly 40 years his songs have become old friends which get me through bad times. His imagery, his ability to capture feelings and his descriptions captivate me. I've been lucky enough to talk with the great man often enough to glean new insights into the suffering that produced them. Years ago he told me that the low times in his life produced the most powerful songs. When life is good, his songs are different. He needs to write from anger and despair. It's a cross to bear.

He has an unusual background for a songwriter in the country music tradition. His father was in the Air Force during World War Two and was later in charge of airlift operations during the Korean War. Kris was brought up in a base in Brownsville, Texas. A huge influence in his life was the Mexican nanny who looked after him like a mother. He spoke Spanish before he spoke English and she gave him insights into how the poor live and think. He was bright. Not many win a Rhodes scholarship. He did, and attended Merton College in Oxford. There he immersed himself in Literature, finishing with a PhD.

"For the first time in Oxford I got in touch with some wonderful, mind-blowing people like Shakespeare and William Blake," he told me, at a time when I wasn't too sure who Blake was.

"It was a great experience for me, but I went from there into the army carrying all of this inside me and I'm lucky I'm alive today. I did everything I could to be self-destructive. I spent three years in Germany and volunteered for Vietnam – I was absolutely suicidal."

I really liked his version of *Sunday Morning Coming Down*. What descriptions, what insights! The Johnny Cash version gave Kris his first taste of chart success.

He once told me that he considers *Jodie and the Kid* the first good, commercial song he ever wrote. At the time Kris brought his little daughter Tracey with him as he toured the bars trading songs. His then wife didn't see much future in their relationship, and before the final split, Kris took Tracey around with him to say goodbye to all the old guys they'd become familiar with.

"One old man saw us come in and said into his beer, 'Look, yonder comes Krissie and the kid.' I couldn't write it like that so I changed the name to Jodie," he recalls. I liked the song because there is a heartbreaking sense of loneliness about it.

The first time I saw Kris live was in the National Stadium in Dublin in the 1970s when the amazing Rita Coolidge was his wife. They sang *Help Me Make it through the Night* with passion.

The next time I met him was when Jim Aiken brought him to the RDS. It was a packed audience and I was backstage talking to Kris when Jim called me aside. He asked me to stay around, as there was bad news for Kris. His daughter – the very same Tracey of *Jodie and the Kid* – had been in a car smash somewhere in California. She was on life support, not expected to make it.

Kris was distraught. I'd never seen a hero so broken. We chatted for a while, and even got through a mouthful of prayers. The show was cancelled as he headed for America. It was a decade before I met him again. This time it was when he toured with lifelong buddy Johnny Cash. I was sitting round with the Cash crew when Kristofferson came in.

I asked him for an interview and he was delighted. Johnny left us and 20 minutes later we were locked in discussions about lyrics, melodies and meanings. Before turning on the tape I reminded him of the last time we met – obviously he had no idea who I was. I asked if Tracey had survived. His eyes opened and his face stiffened as the blood drained from him. I wanted the ground to open and swallow me.

After a few moments, he composed himself. He was thrilled that I remembered and he called his travelling companion into the conversation. "This is my manager now," he said, "the very same Tracey who survived the wreck."

It's amazing what's in the life of a song.

I have always found Kristofferson a courteous, shy, thoughtful man, especially if you can talk about his songs.

Another night I was chatting to him in the Ulster Hall in Belfast after a show. It must have gone on for an hour – and that was probably about only one song. The band were having a few beers and grew ever more noisy. It annoyed the hell out of Kris. You could see him thinking. Suddenly he shouted, "Can't you see I'm talking seriously to the man. If you want to party, go somewhere else."

Another side of a real human hero – the way I like them.

He insists he's not a religious man in any conventional sense but then so do most modern saints I meet. They have a real relationship with their personal God but don't want the encumbrances of organised religion. He's a Christian with a personal faith in Jesus and after all, he did write *Why Me, Lord?*, not to mention *One Day at a Time* – both of them in their own way expressions of faith.

The song that introduced Kristofferson to the widest audience of all was *Me and Bobby McGee*. The first hit version was by the late Roger Miller. At the time Miller was the biggest country star in the world. He came to Nashville to record, and Kristofferson, who had given up the academic life to follow his musical dream, volunteered to work the weekend as a cleaner just to get close to the legend.

"I was working in Columbia Studios and Miller rolled in," Kristofferson remembers. "He was all over the place. Those were the days when Miller was a living testament to better life by chemicals. He rattled. He was climbing the walls. He pulled out a suitcase and pretended to talk into a phone. He didn't record a thing. He was high. A short time later he remembered me and invited me to Los Angeles to write new songs for him. In fact we spent all day, every day, by the pool and not one song was written.

"We were on the plane back home and Roger said to me, 'I hear you have a good song; let's hear it.' I taught him *Me and Bobby McGee* on the flight to Nashville. We went into the studio and recorded it and that was the start of big stars recording my material. I owe a lot to Roger Miller."

Janis Joplin also had a million-seller with the very same song and that's the version Kris prefers, but then he adored Janis anyway and was rocked to his foundations when she fell victim to her crazy lifestyle and died.

He was always close to Johnny Cash. There's a wonderful story about their first meeting. Cash lived a quiet, guarded life in Hendersonville, near Nashville, especially after he and June were married. Kristofferson sent him songs but didn't even get a reply. Cash "wasn't listening", as they say. So Kristofferson hired a helicopter and piloted it himself. He landed on Cash's lawn. June thought they were being robbed and phoned the police. Cash, though, was more impressed. He thought that if a songwriter was that proud of his material, he deserved to be listened to. It was the beginning of a long, close friendship between the giants of songwriting in the 20th century. Cash protected Kristofferson.

When Cash died Kristofferson penned a tribute, which highlighted the point I am making about songwriters being modern-day prophets: "Johnny Cash has always seemed larger than life to me. He's a true American hero, beloved the world over, as much for his kindness and compassion and championing of the underdog as for the power of his art.

He's been my inspiration, my faithful friend, my oasis of unconditional love and support. His fierce independence and free spirit, balanced with his love of family, children and his fellow man would stand as a shining example of the best of what it means to be human. And he was damned funny, even in the darkest times."

If I were ever asked to write a tribute to a hero like Kristofferson, it would be pretty damned close to that.

There were only a few artists in the world I would liked to have met and didn't. I hadn't met Frank Sinatra but towards the end of his life I did and heard him perform. He was still magical and even though the voice wasn't what it used to be, his insight into the power of lyrics was amazing.

The only artist that I really wanted to meet and didn't was Elvis Presley. He had been so much a part of my youth and I adored his music, his charisma. Then in the early 1990s I went on a trip to Nashville.

One morning I booked a one-day, cheap flight to Memphis. When I arrived I went directly to Graceland, the home where Elvis lived in supposed luxury for the greater part of his life.

The omens weren't good when I got there. It had all the hallmarks of a professionally run tourist attraction. It was a smaller house than I imagined. But then in our mind's eye the word mansion had its own connotation. Obviously in Tennessee mansions didn't mean the Big House.

Instead of having a human guide taking tourists from room to room in groups, we were handed a Walkman containing all the information about the house, which I was able to control myself. And so I spent the next three hours going pensively from room to room listening to the commentary and taking it all in. As the tour progressed, I got sadder and sadder. I saw the room downstairs which had carpet on the floor, up the walls and across the ceiling. This was the place Elvis met and sang with many of his buddies.

The bedrooms, the studio and the TV room all looked so ordinary by our standards today. I had to keep reminding myself that Elvis was almost 20 years dead by this time and Graceland had been a luxurious place by the standards of the 1960s. I was impressed though by those who were in charge of Graceland at that time. It wasn't cheap or tatty. It wasn't a rushed tour and you had time to look at the significant memorabilia in the house, all of which brought the hero of my youth back to life. The songs he sang, the memories they evoked, the poignancy that a huge superstar actually led such an ordinary, sad life. By some standards it may have been a wasted life too.

Colonel Tom Parker usurped his talent. Elvis was used by this man for his own ends, to finance Parker's drug addiction.

Outside were Elvis's jet planes, and the room where he died had over 260 gold discs decorating the walls, yet despite such success he died lonely and tragically in August 1977.

It was the little graveyard out in the garden, however, which really got to me. There his mother's memorial lay alongside Elvis's own. There was even a memorial to his twin brother, who died at birth.

I have often been ashamed to admit this, but I sat in a corner and cried my eyes out. I wasn't the only one crying and that was a comfort. To this day I don't know what the tears were about. They probably were about Elvis but they were more likely to have been about my own lost youth.

I love Brendan Kennelly's writings. Brendan, in one of his works, has a theory that memory is all-important. As long as we are remembered, we never die. He links it into Christ's death and His plea on the night before He died: "Do this in memory of Me."

As an example of memory keeping someone alive, Brendan wrote a beautiful poem about his father. He remembers him dancing in the kitchen and whistling his own music of dance. It's a magnificent memory – evocative, real and not at all deathly. It makes his point brilliantly that when we remember we keep the person alive and furthermore the memories we ourselves leave behind will keep us alive.

In that sense Elvis really is alive. Graceland evoked for me very precious and wonderful memories of a rebel singing music, the kind I'd never heard before that stirred something inside me that is still alive to this day.

Richard Thompson wrote *From Galway to Graceland*, which Eleanor Shanley performs to perfection. Every time I hear that song with its mysterious and almost ridiculous storyline, I find myself back in Graceland on a sunny afternoon, on my own in a corner, crying for a man I never met.

Later that evening in Memphis, Al Gore, who was then vice-president, was on a walkabout visit. I shook hands with him and if you were to put a gun to my head at this moment and asked me to describe what he looks like, I could not utter a single sentence from memory.

Later still I visited BB King's great Blues House in Downtown Memphis. It was a wonderful night and the music as always was superb, but the loneliness of a fallen hero, lying in a graveyard, with tourists sifting through his memorabilia, said everything there is to say about the passing of fame. As the old Latin phrase used to have it, *sic transit gloria mundi*. That roughly translated means, everything in this world is transient.

CHAPTER 25

LOOK BACK IN ANGER

In recent years, most of my friends within the priesthood think I have got angrier. They may be right. I appreciate it when people give me an honest opinion. It forces me to look at my life in a more objective way. Over the years I have developed a sense of who to listen to and who to ignore. I have a couple of really genuine friends, priests, who know to offer an encouraging word when it is needed and also to offer a questioning word when it's more appropriate. The same is true of my many friends who are not priests.

There are others, however, who make comments which are not sincere. So whether they are complimentary or critical doesn't really matter. They are not worth giving a second thought to.

For the past two years I have been thinking deeply about whether it is anger or genuine concern for the people of God which is my main motivation. For the same reason I asked psychologists to assess every line of this book before publication.

I began by looking back at 35 years of priesthood. One of the advantages of being in journalism is that it is possible for me to look back at how I have developed during that period. I can check what I said in 1970. It is still there in black and white.

I was genuinely frustrated and disappointed to read that the things I say now are similar to what I said in the 1970s. The disappointment came from the fact that I have spent my life trying to open up a dialogue about priesthood and the Church's pastoral care of people, but nothing much has changed. That sounds like a wasted life.

I unearthed a cutting from the *Irish Press* (now defunct) reporting on a talk I'd given to the National Conference of Priests in Galway. The Bishop of Galway was Eamonn Casey and in response to my talk he gave an assurance to the delegates that he personally would give as much consideration to a statement from the Conference of Priests as he would a directive from Rome. The chairman of the priests' conference was Monsignor Larry Ryan, who later became a bishop himself. He complained that the bishops took no notice of what the conference said, even though its members were the democratically elected representatives of the priests of Ireland.

Imagine what kind of Church we'd have now if the bishops had listened to what their own priests were saying in the mid-1970s.

I have many regrets. How could I have not seen through the nonsense that went on in my own order and in my own Church? Why was I so utterly naïve that I didn't even question the ridiculous rules and regulations? How did it take me so long to see that beating myself on the backside while saying prayers, far from being virtuous, was actually a sick practice without merit or excuse? Why did I not object to the sexual perversion I had to endure? Why did I allow the abusive priest to convince me he had the power to stop me from being ordained if I ever revealed his secret? Wouldn't you think a student at university would have more sense, more cop on?

I read back over what I had said to the priests' conference in 1978. I told the meeting that the Church of the 1970s was irrelevant to many members of the younger generation. The young people, I warned, had an image of the Church as a sterile institution led by middle- and upper-class clerics who preach a religion which has nothing to do with the world they face day in and day out.

I concluded that the young generation, even in the 1970s, were years ahead of the institutional Church. They knew that many of the attitudes we cling to were not essential to a relationship with God. "The world changes and because we are seen to be irrelevant, it is taking shape without us. That is not only a betrayal of Christ; it is a betrayal of the world which we are called to save and bless."

Obviously it wasn't a very effective piece of communication because I could say the exact same thing today and it would still apply. Furthermore it was the last time I was asked either to attend or address the Conference of Priests of Ireland.

When I looked up old copies of *The Cross* that I edited, it was no different.

What frustrated me even more was that many of the editorials I wrote for *The Cross* in the early 1970s show that I really did have a clear picture of what was relevant and irrelevant within the Church. Some people might think this was an unusual insight back then. I wouldn't be so self-satisfied about it myself. What frightens me is that even though I knew what was wrong, I didn't do much about it, other than point it out. I stayed within the organisation and too often defended what was obviously indefensible. That's a terrible burden on my conscience now.

What makes it more culpable is that I wasn't a priest confined to a small parish. I was, from an early age, frequently quoted in newspapers and on radio. I had access to the media and regularly met the famous and the powerful.

One of those famous, powerful people was Mother Teresa. I'll never forget the first time I met her. She had a look which was at once piercing and gentle: a look which said there is no sham in my life and there ought to be none in yours either. She had travelled back from South America. Her entire luggage consisted of one plastic bag – a prayer book and a sari.

Mother Teresa was born Agnes Gonxha in Skopje, Albania (then Yugoslavia), on August 27th, 1910. Eighteen years later, she entered the Loreto order in Rathfarnham, Dublin.

After her profession she taught in India until what she calls her "day of inspiration" on September 10th, 1946. While travelling on a train to a retreat, she was inspired to devote her entire life to the poor.

She got permission to do so and two years later was allowed to leave the Loreto Sisters to work full-time with the poor. One year after that she got her first companion and on the 7th of October, 1950, the order of the

Missionaries of Charity was born.

In October 1979, she received the Nobel Peace Prize. Her acceptance speech ruffled a few feathers. She condemned abortion as the great sin of selfishness in Western society.

I interviewed her five or six times in all. Towards the end, age and work had taken their toll. She told me of an American benefactor who visited her in Calcutta. She was cleaning a leprous wound on a poor person's foot. "I wouldn't do what you're doing for a million dollars," he said. "Neither would I," answered Mother Teresa, "But I do it for the love of Jesus."

In the last chat we had, in Knock, she told me that she had suffered from crippling doubts for long periods of her life. She wondered if she was doing the right thing and found it hard to see where God was in the midst of so much poverty and suffering. That was a great comfort to me. Mother Teresa had doubts bordering on despair? It was at that moment that I saw her real sanctity, her true heroism. No journey is without crises.

I once had a dream which I found revealing. Let me put it in its context. I had a number of important meetings in Dublin that brought back memories of the capital and the years I spent there. In the afternoon there was a meeting with members of my order about "New Directions". Younger members of the congregation were wondering if the present form of religious life wasn't dying rapidly. There was a suggestion that a number of us should get together and live a new form of religious life.

I was the one who spoke most loudly about the death of religious life as we know it. I asked, "Does anybody know any example of where religious life is working?" Some people answered honestly and accepted that my question was honest and valid. I insisted that what passes for religious life now is not really religious life. It's not even a healthy life; the sense of community is not there. We are like a group of bachelors living together. It was very painful for me to say those things and even more disturbing that so many agreed.

After a short break the chairperson insisted we should choose a direction. I suggested that each of us say exactly whether he wanted to be part of the new community or not. I admitted I was at the stage in life where I couldn't commit myself to a new form of religious life but I passionately supported anyone who wanted to make that choice. A number of those present were young enough to change radically. They should be the ones to actually decide whether to make the change or not. In a year or two they will be too tired and too old and too caught up within a system to do anything about it.

A number of people agreed that they would like to do something while a number of others agreed with me that they were too old to be involved.

I also had a later meeting with the *Sunday World* about future projects. I ended the night by seeing a play about life in Rwanda. I spent the journey home thinking about all those different aspects of life. Rwanda made our discussion about religious life seem futile.

That's what was in my head when I got to Enniskillen at 1am, exhausted. I worked for a while at my desk and fell into bed.

That was the context of the dream. I saw myself back as a young man standing in a crowded sacristy in Mount Argus. It was Holy Saturday night and I was preparing to be main celebrant at the Easter Vigil. Even standing looking at myself in the dream I was saying, I've been doing this a long time. I have been the main celebrant at the Easter Vigil for over 30 years. I work hard to make it meaningful for the people as well as for myself.

In the dream I was standing in a black Passionist habit. Everybody else was dressed in white albs. The time was 9pm. In my head the vigil was supposed to start at 9.30 but everybody was walking to the altar at nine. I could not find a white alb to fit me. I felt as if I was squeezed into it.

The community were puzzled because I wasn't joining them. I was getting very frustrated yet seemed calm on the outside. Eventually I went to another room to look for a suitable alb. When I came back, the sacristy was empty. I could hear sounds coming from the altar. They were speaking in German, a language I don't know. Remember, this is a dream. While I was still looking for an alb two or three agitated people came into the sacristy asking why I was not out on the sanctuary. It was a disaster out there. Funnily enough I didn't recognise any of the people. But they were youngish. The dream became more and more frustrating as I decided I wasn't joining them. I simply turned and walked away, still in a black habit. It was then that I woke up.

I was disturbed when I woke up. It was time to get up but I couldn't physically get out of bed.

The overwhelming sense at the end of the dream was that I had let people down. I think it came from me admitting earlier that I didn't see a future for religious life but also didn't feel able to join a new form of religious life. The fact that I didn't go out to the sanctuary implied to me when I woke up that I didn't want to be part of new life. That thought haunted me for quite some time. I couldn't celebrate the Resurrection. I think for me the black habit was significant and not being able to fit into a white alb was also significant.

The sense that I had let people down was very strong. I was confused by it. I didn't know whether I was letting people down now in my present life or that I let people down by not leaving when I was as young as in my dream. The tight-fitting alb indicated that I was more an altar boy than a priest – a man being forced to act like a child.

I was choosing death over new life. If you're not at home in your position, then don't stay in it. Choose life, not death. That's the whole point of resurrection for Christians: don't choose a death-giving situation. Look for where there is life. Christ said after the Resurrection, why do you look for the living among the dead? You won't find it there. Look for life, nurture it and choose life. You may need to go through death to get life – in fact you almost always do. But unless you can see life at the other side of death, don't choose death. I've learned to respect my dreams. They reveal the unconscious.

I am blessed to live in the unspoiled countryside of Fermanagh. Spring is my favourite time of year. That's when nature dresses herself with a lush, verdant, multicoloured carpet and death takes on life again.

Everyone should have a corner which to him or her is heaven. Mine is a soft chair in the community chapel at The Graan in Enniskillen. The chair is positioned beside a delightful, large, round window in the shape of the rising sun. The window is a modern form of stained glass with a pattern that allows soothing shades of light to slip through but doesn't distort the magnificence of God's beautiful creation outside.

Alpha and Omega, the beginning and the end, are subtly insinuated into the design. There are wheat colours to remind me of bread; purple grapes become the wine of Eucharist.

When I was planning our new monastery at The Graan, I asked the architect to help me make a statement about what our prayer room should be. As I sit beside the window I recognise the many presences of God; in the tabernacle, in our prayers, in the Word of God. But when I swivel the chair to look out through the window, I see a real presence of God in a Fermanagh countryside.

As far as the eye can see there are rolling hills, each one with a personality of its own. There are wonderful trees, blossoming hedge groves, pink apple blossoms and lush grass in which even good-sized calves hide.

Then there's the tree. It's just an ordinary tree standing majestically in the valley of the field. From where I sit I have the unusual experience of looking down on the tree. In spring it's dressed like a model. Leaves, each one different, make it rounded, full, symmetrical, but imperfect enough to be naturally beautiful.

A few weeks ago it was naked and skeletal. Six weeks on, the leaves will pale to a tired yellow and then turn a sleepy brown before returning to a bony skeleton in October. The miracle is that it will be magnificent and beautiful in every season.

I've watched if for years now, giving food for thought and food to birds no matter how it looks. It gives me perspective in the troubles of life and priesthood and the Church. Life comes and life goes on – yours, mine and nature's. Each of us is a work of art, a canvas coloured uniquely by God as He writes straight on crooked lines; imperfect enough to be beautiful and yet loved for what we are.

In November the tree will remind me that beauty passes. At Christmas a white frost will purify its profile in honour of the God who made it. And in February it will stand in expectation of its buds, leaves and clothing returning.

One morning I shared what the tree meant to me with the rest of the community as we prayed. It so happened that the Gospel on that particular day was from John (16:28). "I came from the Father and have come into the world and now I leave the world and go to the Father." What a stark and accurate summary of what life is for a believer! We come and we go.

The leaves on the tree spoke the same truth as God's inspired Word. The words and the picture merging allowed God to penetrate a burdened heart. I can only hope that at some point in my life I will be able to recognise that my little life can become like the lovely, green leaves dressing the tree. But I also know that life will pass, the tree will remain and God will find other people's gifts to dress it.

As I shared my thoughts with the two lovely men praying with me, I became aware that this was the very day my mother died over 40 years ago. And I remembered how many were blessed by her short life. To leave behind a good memory is a sacred gift, whether we're gods, trees, monks or mothers.

When we prayed about it we agreed that many in authority give the Church a bad name. The People of God is a more gentle family to belong to. But we do need to belong somewhere. We can't do it on our own. Eucharist, Communion, means union with. Our lives are short. It's a simple process. "I came from the Father and I've come into the world and now I leave the world and go to the Father" (John 16:28). Like leaves on trees. Like saviours on crosses. Like me and you on our journey.

Chapter 26

Masters of the Airwaves

In 40 years of broadcasting, I've met and worked with most of the legendary names here and in Britain. Most of the greats were Irish.

The late Eamonn Andrews paved the way for Irish broadcasters in Britain. In my youth I got up in the middle of the night to listen to him commentate on world heavyweight title fights. It seemed a glamorous and important job, bringing a sense of pride to know an Irishman was *that* important.

He moved through journalism with the BBC and ITV to become the host of the hugely popular *This is Your Life*. When I got to meet Eamonn later he was, like many of the great broadcasters, a shy man away from the camera and the microphone, but became a different personality as soon as he got on air. He didn't like talking about his glamorous life and would much rather talk about normal life in a quiet corner away from the limelight. The hallmark of really successful broadcasters, communicators and people in the public eye is that they know when to come alive and when to switch off. Artists who are never off the stage are a bore to be with. Eamonn Andrews was never a bore.

Another advantage I have is that I grew up, professionally, with many of the top broadcasters on these islands. I have freelanced in RTÉ and BBC for close to 40 years.

I broadcast with 2FM on the day it first aired, May 31st, 1979, and continued with that station for more then 15 years.

I've worked regularly alongside such luminaries as Gay Byrne, Mike Murphy, Treasa Davison, Ruth Buchanan, Pat Kenny, Ronan Collins,

Marty Whelan, Larry Gogan, Alan Corcoran, Paschal Mooney, Gerry Wilson, Aonghus McAnally, Maxi, Marian Finucane, Joe Duffy, Henry Kelly, Derek Davis, Mary Kennedy, Brendan Balfe and Val Joyce. All of them were contemporaries and I have been part of their programmes and they have been part of my life since the 1970s.

I learned from each of them and some might admit to learning a little from me. The nature of broadcasting is that every time you go into a studio you learn something new; you never take success for granted. Live shows are the best. The adrenalin does wonders for the pace of broadcasting. On Millennium night, I hosted a five-hour live show for BBC Radio Ulster. I was in my element. Later when I chaired a live current-affairs programme for BBC Choice I revelled in the discussions. *Straight Talking with Brian D'Arcy* was my favourite programme for two years.

You cannot prepare enough for broadcasting. Recently I was part of RTÉ's radio team at the State funeral for Charles Haughey. I sat up most of the night reading background material even though I knew I would use less than six or seven minutes of it during the entire service. I could have talked for 70 minutes if necessary. That's the only way I can relax and feel confident – be on top of my subject.

Many broadcasters don't write scripts for music programmes. I need to have the programme fully mapped out so that I have pace and balance. Random selections rarely work. It's the same whether I'm doing a 90-second broadcast on *Pause for Thought* on BBC Radio 2, or an hour-long broadcast for BBC Radio Ulster.

Pause for Thought (PFT) on Terry's *Wake up with Wogan* is by far the best thing I've done on radio. I do over 30 spots a year on what is now the biggest radio show in Europe with over 8,000,000 listeners daily. The feedback is incredible, mostly from people who never enter church, mosque or synagogue. Terry's listeners are unique. The producers are all fans of Terry (and his producer Paul Walters) and we on *PFT* borrow them for a few minutes every morning. What makes it really worthwhile is that Terry and Paul (as well as Alan Boyd, more recently) make me so welcome and make me feel part of the show. To do *PFT* well I have to listen to the whole show, so that I am across the running banter.

I get hundreds of requests for scripts and every summer dozens of English visitors call at The Graan, just because it's mentioned so often on *Wake up with Wogan*.

I now do the show from my bedroom, on ISDN phone line or, as Terry puts it, "Here's the man who won't even get out of bed to talk to us."

A couple of years ago when it was dangerous even to talk to the British army, I got an invitation to a party in a nearby barracks. I had to go but wondered why I was being asked. I was met at the entrance by the major in charge.

"I'm delighted you're here, Fr Brian, just to repay what you did for me," the major said.

That kind of talk could get one shot.

"When I was appointed to Enniskillen," he continued, "I knew nothing about the place. I was driving to the South of England, wondering what I could tell my worried wife about Enniskillen. Then I heard this voice on Terry Wogan giving a vivid description of what a beautiful place Enniskillen was. I pulled into a lay-by and took copious notes of what you said. When I got home I was able to make a glowing report on the town and how privileged I was to get this appointment. You'll never know what you did for my marriage that morning. I was determined to make contact with you as soon as I arrived here to thank you personally."

Such is the power of radio.

Terry always makes a helpful little joke which sets me up positively. When he's not on – he does take holidays often these days – I have to work harder to win over the listener. I've been doing *PFT* for 16 years now and if I never preached a sermon in church I still would have spoken to more people than a 1,000-year-old missioner. What a privilege! I'll come back to Terry later in a different context.

I'm often asked who is the broadcaster I admire the most.

The broadcaster I listened to most was the late Alistair Cooke. His *Letter from America* ran for close on 60 years. He was over 90 when he stopped broadcasting, weeks before he died. I still have tapes of his programme, which I listen to frequently. His style, his delivery, the pictures he paints, the gentleness with which he makes serious points and most of all the flow of language are inspiring no matter how often I hear them. For honest, basic professionalism, talking to microphone, no-one comes close to Alistair Cooke.

It's a cliché to say that the pictures are better on radio, but it is true. I spend hours most days in my car. I listen to sports events, particularly soccer matches, night after night, as I travel around the country. Now I would much prefer to listen to a soccer match on radio than to watch it on television. It's just that the pictures I have in my head are more interesting than the actual pictures on television.

Gay Byrne is another professional whom I admire. He's a consummate broadcaster, well prepared, professional, but most of all highly aware of what listeners want. For all the years I've known Gay, he is always a pleasure to meet – a man of knowledge, of wisdom and as far as I'm concerned, unfailingly helpful.

I can never forget what he did to help me when I was restoring Mount Argus. Without my appearance on the *Late Late* at the start of the campaign and his continued support throughout, it would have been next to impossible to achieve.

On the weekend after that appearance in October 1983, thousands came to look at Mount Argus, from every county in Ireland. The first day brought IR£60,000 in the post and by the end of the week, IR£250,000; all as a result of one, short *Late Late Show* appearance. That's just a hint of the power Gay Byrne's *Late Late Show* had.

Even today whenever I visit his neighbours John McColgan and Moya Doherty in their Howth home, Gay and Kathleen arrive with the welcoming, encouraging word.

One of the absolute gentlemen in broadcasting whom I've had the privilege of knowing all my life is Larry Gogan. Larry is the best pop DJ I've ever heard. Apart from that he's a shy, kind and good man who has been a friend, a colleague, a helper and an inspiration since I first met him in 1968.

The broadcaster most people ask me about today is Terry Wogan. Even other broadcasters are fascinated by his genius and want to know what he's like to work with.

My friendship with Terry goes back for more years than I can recall. It certainly predates his going to England. I kept in touch with him all those years. I've worked in the studio with him, talked with him, gone for cups of coffee, and enjoyed his company. Terry Wogan is not only the best broadcaster I've ever met, he's also one of the kindest people I've ever met.

Not many know this but Terry is, first of all, a frighteningly well read man. I've never talked to Terry Wogan without being astonished and a little bit bemused at the breadth of his knowledge and ashamed at how little I know. He can speak French, German and Spanish excellently. And of course he uses the English language as nobody else can. That's because he reads insatiably. Not only is he well read but he has a memory like an elephant. He can remember large chunks of Latin as well as long passages of poetry from his school days in Crescent College in Limerick and later in Belvedere College in Dublin.

Off air he's a thinker and philosopher. As my father often said, it takes an educated man to play the fool. And you'd be very naïve indeed if you took Terry Wogan for a fool. Far from it. His ability as an intellectual broadcaster has never been fully utilised.

When I was editor of *The Cross*, in 1972, I did an interview with Terry in which he outlined his philosophy of broadcasting. It's still valid 35 years later, even though the medium has revolutionised itself in the meantime.

"The trick in broadcasting is to stay around long enough to become a habit." I've learned the truth in that nugget of wisdom after years of wondering whether the next controller will hire me.

In the interview with *The Cross*, he praised the broadcasting style of his colleague Jimmy Young. But notice what he considers important:

"Jimmy is the same every day – the voice, the style, the humour are always the same. He may not feel as good some days as he is on others but the average listener isn't going to notice. And so the woman listening in Burnley living in a flat, not knowing the woman next door, with her mother 100 miles away, her husband gone out to work and the child crying in the kitchen, knows that she can switch on and there's Jimmy Young exactly the same and he's always there as a companion when everyone else is away."

As I've mentioned, Terry Wogan now has 8,000,000 listeners tuning into his radio programme every morning. He has become the reliable companion to those who are hassled by life; to people who want to get away from the bickering of the *Today* programme on BBC Radio 4, or whatever local row there is on morning radio across Britain. More and more people today listen to Terry Wogan simply because he is an escape from the boredom of the rows we have to endure daily.

Terry never scripts his morning shows, but he's quick to admit that he has the best scriptwriters in the world – his listeners. I've often sat in the studio waiting to go on air for *Pause for Thought* and heard the continual hum of the printer, running off hundreds of emails from all over the world. The producers, Paul Walters and, more recently, Alan Boyd, spend their time going through emails and selecting the most suitable for broadcast. I'm often jealous, as dozens of wonderful scripts are dumped into the wastepaper basket because there is no time to use them.

Not only is Terry the king of broadcasting, a professional who can make the *Eurovision Song Contest* interesting – something close to a miracle – he is also a friend. He is helpful, encouraging, insightful, and always interested in the affairs of Ireland. What's more, he never forgets his friends. Most days when I speak to him he continues to ask for his old friends, many of whom were on air before he went to England at all.

I've also had the privilege of being a guest in his home with Helen and the children and you could not meet a more normal or more welcoming family. When people ask me what is Terry Wogan like, I always answer with the same words: Terry Wogan is the best broadcaster I've ever worked with and one of the most loyal friends I have. He is a colleague, a friend and a hero.

Terry Wogan was the first person to explain to me the essence of good radio broadcasting. He pointed out that everyone should be able to broadcast on radio, because everyone is able to talk on the phone. Think about that. Each of us has a conversational style that is exactly right for radio, which we use day in and day out on the phone. Yet if somebody thrusts a microphone in front of us, we "put on" a voice. Terry suggested that I talk to the listeners as if making a personal telephone call. That's sound advice. You are speaking to a mass audience made up of groups of two or three.

"Think of those small groups, not the millions. That's why I never work from a script. If I wrote it down my sincerity would be gone. If I'm wishing somebody a happy birthday, then I wish them with all the joy and enthusiasm I can muster at that moment. To do anything else would make it all sound flat.

"In the course of a two-hour programme you're always going to say something you wished you hadn't, or you will wish you had said it differently. You have to put your mistakes aside."

Terry thinks deeply about life. He has gone on record as saying he finds it hard to believe in God. I'm not going to argue with his sincere convictions. All I know is that in practice, he's a better Christian than most of us who are supposed to be the professionals. Helen is a religious person. I believe Terry is much closer to God than he realises, and anyway who'd want to be in Heaven if Terry wasn't there? Not me.

What is vitally important to me is that he is helpful to me as a religious broadcaster, and indeed to all those who contribute to *Pause for Thought*. People of all faiths agree that if you have something reasonable to say, Terry will make it easier to say. He goes out of his way to get the best out of me.

Obviously Terry Wogan is the one I've worked most closely with and from whom I've learned most. As I look back now on a lifetime of broadcasting and television work, however, I can't think of a single person that I would not broadcast with again. There are a few I've refused to go on air with and never would. But of all those I've gone on air with, I cannot think of one that I wouldn't go on with again. I mightn't approach it in the same way but I never met one who was so unfair that I wouldn't work with them again.

Broadcasters and journalists who last the pace are always well prepared, thorough, fair and professional in their approach. Those who aren't are soon found out.

It is often said about me that I'm always looking for notice or that I look for the attention of the media. After 40 years I don't need to defend my role. Others say I am not a real priest because I write and broadcast. I see communication as part of my priestly work and an essential part of it at that.

At those times in my life when it seemed much easier to leave the active ministry I was offered, on many occasions, full-time posts in broadcasting and on national papers, in Ireland and Britain. Some senior producers in BBC would have been well pleased if I'd broadcast with them full-time. I always resisted. Broadcasting, journalism, chaplaincy to the entertainment industry, and interest in sport and music are all part of my priestly life.

There are many ways to be a priest. One of them is to run a parish, which I've done. Another is to present a programme or write a column for the *Sunday World*. These days my biggest congregations are on radio, the World Wide Web and the *Sunday World*. It's about finding the most effective way to be in the marketplace.

The central question for me is not, "What do I want to do with my life?" It is one of the many questions but not the central one. The central one is, "Where does God want me to be?"

Looking back on my life there have been so many providential twists and turns that I am convinced God brought me to this place.

I wish I could say I trust God blindly, or that believing comes easily. It does not. I wrestle, fight, twist, turn and look for different ways to satisfy my conscience. But eventually I come back to the fact that priesthood is in the marrow of my bones. I am convinced if I left the structure of priesthood tomorrow, I would continue almost every single one of my priestly activities no matter where I was, including broadcasting and journalism.

Chapter 27

Dutch Encouragement

In the 1980s, I spent the best part of my years raising two-and-a-half million pounds to restore Mount Argus and now I'm part of a committee which will downsize to a smaller building. That's some movement in 20 years.

Just when Mount Argus faces a crisis because of a lack of vocations, we have been told that another miracle has been attributed to Blessed Charles's intercession which means canonisation as a saint.

When the news came through, I was asked to preach at a thanksgiving novena in Mount Argus. I felt I had to try to do something special.

But when I sat down to write a sermon about Fr Charles, I found I had absolutely nothing new to say. The thought of coming back to Mount Argus frightened me.

It was then I accidentally saw an advertisement for cheap flights to Amsterdam. And I recognised instantly that "Charlie" was guiding me. I did something I never do. I booked a flight with an overnight stay in Amsterdam. A nurse in Enniskillen, who has great devotion to Blessed Charles, had a friend in Holland. She got the instructions. I went to Amsterdam airport, caught a train and three hours later ended up in Sittard, the nearest large town to his birthplace.

There, a taxi driver took me to Munstergeelen and that is how I got to the wee country place Fr Charles came from. There I discovered his house and the little church, a delightful oasis of peace. It was heavenly. And I knew that I would get the inspiration to tell, not what I wanted to say, but what Fr Charles wanted people to hear.

Father Charles Houben's family were so poor that they couldn't come to his ordination. He never saw them again because he was sent to England and then to Mount Argus and never got home or had the privilege of seeing his home place after he was ordained.

I'm sure that he left home thinking he was an insignificant person in his village and would be forgotten in a week. But now, 150 years later, there are 2,000 candles burning in his memory at his shrine.

I sat and prayed most of the morning. I talked to everybody who came in and there were many, most of whom came on bicycles. He's not forgotten.

I met the local priest and he was most welcoming. He was the priest responsible for pushing the miracle now accepted for the canonisation of Blessed Charles. He knew the sick man from seeing him at morning Mass and was the one who blessed him with a relic of Blessed Charles. The priest brought me to the house of the miraculously cured man.

It struck me how fitting it was that I should visit the home of Blessed Charles and discover how, step by step, God led him from an obscure village to Heaven, via Ireland.

I'm sure many a day Fr Charles, walking the corridors of Mount Argus, yearned to do what I did – go back and spend a morning in the little peaceful village where he grew up. But he gave his life to God and accepted the consequences.

I thought of my own journey and how he had helped me.

I had seen the trip to Holland as a diversion, but it proved to be providential.

In Holland I had one spare day and the tourist office suggested I visit Van Gogh's museum. It was the first time I'd ever gone to a gallery displaying the original works of a major artist. I love Van Gogh; I love his struggle.

His early works are dark, literally dark, not just dark subjects but dark colours. Yet even in those early days he focused on a chink of light somewhere in the picture. The best example I know of is *The Potato Workers*, which was one of his first works. It was slated by the critics of the time but has now been recognised as a masterpiece. This family with their big, gnarly hands, uncouth features and earthy, too, sit around the table eating spuds out of their hands.

In the cosiness of this little dark room, there is poverty for a start, but they're close to the earth and close to each other. They are eating from their hands the fruit of the earth which they produced out of their own land. Van Gogh said that their features are animal-like, to highlight their earthiness. And how did he manage to light it? He had an oil lamp sitting just above them. His genius is that he used the light of the oil lamp to highlight the spuds, the significant faces and the gnarly hands, the important aspects of his work. There is a light even in the darkest events.

My eyes wanted to search through the picture but the light drew me back to the dark faces. It reminded me of a more cerebral picture that hung in our house, in Bellanaleck – *The Angelus* – when the potato diggers stopped to pray.

At 16 Van Gogh began to work in The Hague as a junior assistant in an art dealer's firm. During that period he developed an eye for the genuinely artistic paintings, but had no business flair at all. He was transferred to London and became so interested in religion that he was asked to leave his employment. He wanted to become a missionary.

He then became a Protestant minister but abandoned that as a career because he couldn't agree with much of what the Church preached. Then he went to work as a lay preacher in a Belgian mining district and became so involved with the impoverished inhabitants that his licence to preach was not extended.

At this point, his brother Theo suggested that he might try art, at the age of 27. In the beginning he was largely self-taught, and even then he carried his missionary zeal into his new career.

Although Van Gogh painted for only 10 years, in that period he did 1,100 drawings and 900 finished paintings. He moved from dark colours to bright colours in his short career as an artist, from the age of 27 to 37.

Initially, he was untrained. He studied Rembrandt, another Dutchman. There's one beautiful self-portrait inspired by Rembrandt's *Pietà*, where Mary receives the body of her dead son. *Pietà* means faithful to the end – as all mothers are. In many of Rembrandt's paintings there are faces of people who were helpful to him in life. But Van Gogh loved Rembrandt's *Pietà* and painted a version of it from memory. And whose face did he put on the Christ, the dead body? His own, but it's a living face, actually. That's just how he saw himself – wasted, a failure, taken down from the Cross, consumed by death. At least he must have felt that Jesus, also broken and a failure, would understand and care for him.

Amazingly, Van Gogh did 39 self-portraits. I didn't see them all, but in the ones I saw, there is a pattern of obvious deterioration. In the early ones he's vibrant but, progressively, the eyes and the face become more haggard, more lost. His way of crying for help was through his self-portraits. He viewed himself getting old and haggard and lost. Towards the end, a medical person would recognise utter depression in his demeanour. He couldn't express himself through words, but he painted how he felt in his self-portraits.

Towards the end of his life he entered an asylum. He had an unhappy time there, but nevertheless painted the wonderful scenes he saw from his window. Even though he was locked behind the walls of the asylum, he still saw the beauty of nature through his hospital window.

One of my favourites is *Almond Blossom*. It was painted for his nephew, Theo's son, as a gift at his birth.

On July 27th, 1890, Van Gogh shot himself in the chest with a pistol in the fields close to Auvers where he had been living after leaving the asylum. He died two days later with Theo at his side. Shortly before, he had painted the wonderful *Wheatfield under Thunder Clouds*. Experts say that in the beauty of the *Wheatfield*, his impending death is foretold in the darkening thunder clouds in the blue sky.

Van Gogh's story is a classic one of misunderstanding, poverty and appreciation after death. He lived from 1853 to 1890, just 37 years. Most of those years were spent wrestling with failure. His brother Theo stayed loyal to him. But even that took its toll and he died less than a year after Vincent shot himself.

In 10 years Vincent sold only one of his paintings. Now they are all close to priceless.

Van Gogh preached through his paintings. Amazingly, he painted 30 canvases on the parable of the sower. One is so powerful, and helpful to me, that I have a print framed on my wall. It speaks to me of my life as a priest today. It gives me hope.

There is a dark, foreboding figure in the forefront surrounded by death. There's a dead tree, but there are also little green shoots visible in the tree trunk. That's almost one half of the picture. That's the part which I found immediately striking. The other part is a huge sun, one of his striking yellow suns for which he is famous. It's almost like a Communion host rising, like a resurrection – the rising sun and the Rising Son. It is an early-Christian way of symbolising the Rising Son with the rising sun.

There's the blue sea and most of all the golden harvest field in the background, confirming that there is life after death. But most importantly, the sower continues to sow seeds, even though everything around him is dead. He keeps on sowing especially when it seems futile. That's the importance of the golden harvest behind him – the seeds produce a harvest that the sower will never see. That's our duty as religious leaders today: to keep on sowing seeds so that God can reap the harvest in God's good time. We don't have to see the results of our work.

So many of the works in the Van Gogh museum gave me an awareness of the value of working blindly for a future I won't experience for myself. It was a Godsend, reminding me of the importance of having a direction and a vision for the future, when there is no obvious sign of hope for that future. In life we sow, we plant, and God brings in the harvest.

I know all of this is a long way from the bogs of Bellanaleck. But it gave me hope to recognise that everything in life is a journey which makes sense from different perspectives. Also it's worth recognising that the journeys we think we're making for the first time are as old as time itself. All we have to do is to trust the journey and leave the past behind us, rather than clinging to death. The green shoot will eventually have a rising sun and a harvest field, though we won't be around to see it.

Father Charles and Van Gogh were two Dutchmen saying the same thing, from very different religious backgrounds. Charles, the sower, gave himself to God and became the seed out of which other things grew.

It's interesting that God can use so many gifts in so many different ways. I got enthusiastic about *A Different Journey* having watched "failures" like Charles and Van Gogh. All I can do is live with integrity – try to hold integrity in the middle of chaos. I have to be myself, be honest, tell the truth and later generations will know there were people in the Church, lay and clerical, who did care. At best, the story of my life will be a footnote to the struggle.

There is a theologian called Henry Nouwen, another Dutchman. Much of his writing is about his journey of self-discovery. There are some wonderful sections in his writing that have been very helpful to me in my life.

Personally I find it difficult to identify with a God locked in an institution but I can identify with God in day-to-day events in life.

Henry Nouwen was a bright young priest who taught in Louvain University in his early days, but found no fulfilment there. He then lectured in various universities in America with little or no sense of purpose.

In a midlife crisis, he worked in South America with some of the emerging Christian communities. He liked it at the beginning but later ran out of steam. He was lucky to meet Jean Vanier, the founder of the L'Arche movement.

Jean Vanier himself was an eminent philosopher who understood the value of holistic living. He brought together handicapped people with people who were not handicapped to live in community, side by side. L'Arche is a hugely successful worldwide movement where people befriend either a physically or mentally handicapped person.

Henry Nouwen willingly joined the L'Arche movement. For the first time he found companions on that painful journey to deep happiness. He discovered the gift of love, to complement the gift of intelligence. During his time in L'Arche he wrote some of the most spiritual works of the last century.

Being a Dutchman, Henry Nouwen knew the works of Rembrandt well. There is a famous Rembrandt work called *Return of the Prodigal Son*. It's in the museum in St Petersburg. He got permission from the museum to spend weeks contemplating and meditating in front of this painting. He then put his emotional and spiritual journey in book form.

Rembrandt's use of symbols was intriguing. He repeatedly used the face of a woman who was helpful to him throughout difficult periods in his life. It's almost like a code. It was the same with hands. Different hands appear in his works indicating what he wants to portray at that time.

As Henry Nouwen meditated on the painting, he became aware of the significance of the characters. The face of the prodigal father, who represents God, is the face of a kindly old mentor of Rembrandt in real life.

At an earlier stage of his life Rembrandt painted a picture of the Prodigal Son. He was so arrogant that he used his own face to represent the Prodigal Son. Rembrandt apparently wasn't always a pleasant person; in fact he was hard on people who befriended him. I think at least two of his partners committed suicide and many would say that it was the pressure of living with Rembrandt that drove them in that direction. Tragedy followed him.

From being the artist who was most successful in the palaces across Europe, he was almost friendless in mid-life. It was at this time that he painted *Return of the Prodigal Son*.

In this one the face of the Prodigal Son is not visible because Rembrandt is chastened and repentant. But the face of the kindly old man is. The hands on the back of the Prodigal Son become a vital statement. Once again they are recognisable hands from his life. One is a gentle woman's hand and one is a supportive, male hand. He was saying that God is both feminine and masculine. The strong, firm hand on his back is God the supporter. The lovely, feminine hand on his shoulder is God the encourager, the forgiver. The specific gifts of men and women are highlighted in this ability to forgive and to give courage for the journeys.

The pilgrim's feet are visible. One is sandalled and one is bare. The latter is the penitent pilgrim looking for forgiveness while the sandalled foot represents journeys still to be made. Receiving forgiveness is not the end of the journey. There are shady characters in the background, one of whom is the Prodigal Son's brother.

If you ever want to realise what reconciliation entails, read Nouwen's book. In it you will discover the real meaning of the Gospel, repentance, forgiveness, kindness and the role of the prodigal brother, who couldn't accept that his life was important.

For Nouwen, relationships were a struggle. Towards the end of his life he accepted he was gay. Perhaps it was the feminine hand that sparked his journey into self-awareness, in safety, but it was only when he accepted himself as he really was that he found happiness.

A film company asked him to produce a video of his *Return of the Prodigal Son*. He was on his way from America to St Petersburg but stopped off in Holland to see his aged father, a strict authoritarian.

When he was with the father, whom he thought he might never see again, Henry himself took a heart attack and died. He never got to make that film of *Return of the Prodigal Son*.

Life can be a series of coincidences which, when the dots are joined, reveals God's providence. Circles become complete with hindsight.

CHAPTER 28

DISCOVERING GOD'S CALL

Working in the North, as I have done for almost 20 years now, makes ecumenism a real priority.

I have been blessed to have worked closely with many exemplary men and women from many different religions and faiths. Dr Bert Tosh in the BBC religion department in Belfast is a close friend with whom I have much in common.

My near neighbours and very close friends Archdeacon Cecil Pringle and his wife, Hilary, were responsible for one of the genuinely deep religious experiences of my life. Cecil, as rector of Rossorry Church of Ireland, invited me as rector of The Graan to preach in his church in January 2004. It is less than a mile from our monastery to his church but it took 95 years for us to share our pulpits. When I preached in Rossorry, I realised my family background had prepared me well.

Bellanaleck was a country village of 40 houses as I was growing up. Neither my mother nor my father would have been able to spell ecumenism, but they lived it. In our humble house by the side of the road, Mrs Moore was as welcome to a cup of tea as was Mrs Murphy. My mother's motto all her life was, "It doesn't matter which church you go to on Sunday as long as you go to some church."

When her neighbours were sick, she often took their children into our house. We hadn't much but we shared what we had. And I was always aware that the clear spring water we got by the bucket from Thorntons' well was given to us freely and generously. Even a cup of water given graciously is one of the keys for a Christian to enter heaven.

On my father's birthday, our house was usually full of children. My father's birthday was on the 12th of July and my mother looked after our neighbours' children while parents went to march.

The journey from The Graan to Rossorry was literally and metaphorically an uphill one.

Some Protestant people could not see their way to be present at the prayer service. I respected their integrity. I don't regard such principled people as enemies; far from it. I see them as friends and in that friendship, God's spirit is present, leading us down roads we cannot predict. A few fundamentalists held a protest and others wrote to the papers objecting, but the vast majority welcomed the opportunity to move on.

To me the real scandal is that our various Churches don't nurture goodness. Instead we emphasise our differences. I believe we should appreciate some simple truths:

All of us, whatever our differences, believe in the same God.

That same God loves us, saves us, died for us and lives again as the source of all our hope.

It will be the same God we all meet when we leave this world. He is the maker who will judge us justly, mercifully and compassionately when we die.

The same God recognises the hurts we have, the love we have for our families, and He cries with us in our times of sadness and sickness.

That same God has blessed us with many gifts. At the end of our days, a patch of earth six feet by three feet will do us, unless of course we are cremated, in which case a decent-sized matchbox will do.

That's the countryman's ecumenism, the kind that begins with good neighbourliness. It was bred in me as I grew up going to school on a bus with my Protestant neighbours and friends. And although we went to different schools, we lived side by side when we came home from school. Integrated education is helpful, but sectarian ghettos are the real problem.

It was practical ecumenism that allowed me to visit my sick neighbours when I came back to Enniskillen as a priest years later.

There was one woman, Mrs Black, who was gravely ill in her old age. I sat with her in hospital and prayed with her. The next day, I was visiting again when I met her Church of Ireland minister on his way out from visiting her.

"It's only a waste of time my going in there," the minister said. "I went in to Mrs Black and I prayed with her for 20 minutes and at the end I said, 'Do you know who I am?' And she said, 'I do indeed, you're Father Brian, that's who you are.' So," he joked, "there's no point in me coming here at all. You get the credit."

Today all our Churches are in danger of being relegated to relics of the past. It is my experience that people, and particularly younger people, have grown tired of the clichéd rhetoric of "the two communities". Isn't it petulant of us to think that when we speak of two communities we mean Protestant and Catholic? If we were really Christian, would we not divide communities into rich/poor or believers/non-believers?

Soon we will be grateful that people are believers. What particular brand of Christianity will be of little importance. I look forward to that day.

I am bitterly disappointed when the leaders of our Churches fail to agree on a theology that would allow us to share the Lord's Table. I look forward to the day when at interfaith weddings we can celebrate a Eucharist as the centre of the service, as a symbol of unity rather than a reminder of our divisions.

Ordinary people are voting with their feet, and telling us: we want to be together; to overcome hatred; to transcend community boundaries; to be peacemakers; to be believers praying together.

I regard sectarianism as the single greatest evil which kills the spirit of friendship. We cannot allow ourselves to become prisoners of sectarianism. We must cross barriers daily to ensure that the evil of sectarianism does not strangle us forever.

We should thank God for our differences and praise God for what we have in common. We should encourage goodness wherever we recognise it and begin by recognising our own goodness.

Over 40 years ago I was part of a Church that was a powerful, triumphalistic, too-proud sham. I believed and trusted the Church. I thought it stood for virtue and against evil. Now I find myself still standing – just about – when the powerful and popular have been exposed as whited sepulchres, and when the lost and lonely have still a loving God to call on.

Sometimes on my way out of Dublin I travel through the Phoenix Park. For old times' sake I turn to see the papal cross. I did so again on a beautiful June day in 2006 when there was talk that Pope Benedict might visit us soon. The sun glistened on the cross. It has stood the test of time well. I went up to the foot of the cross and looked out across the massive plain that is the Phoenix Park. It brought back memories of standing on the exact spot on September 29th 1979, and I felt nostalgic and sad.

In my mind's eye I could see once again the million-plus people stretched across the plains, all neatly fenced in to manageable squares on a beautiful day when the atmosphere was as close to heavenly as you can get on this earth

It was the high point of the Catholic Church in Ireland. Since then things have deteriorated year on year. Now it seems a happy memory but an irrelevant one.

It was sins of the clergy which destroyed the Church. We have nobody to blame but ourselves and we must take responsibility for it. Now we clerics say the Church belongs to the people and you have to help us. Well, it didn't belong to the people when it was a matter of power.

I see everything I worked for collapse and I see my order and my priesthood dying. It is only a belief that the Passion gives meaning to failure and becomes the gateway to an unknown, new life, which keeps me going. It's not much but most days it's enough.

We clerics must honestly face up to our responsibilities. We must take our share of the blame. We supported an oppressive form of clericalism. We put pious names on it, like loyalty and prudence. It was nothing of the sort. Cowardice and careerism are more apt words.

We allowed power freaks to control us. We played the clerical game. If we were more honest, we'd recognise our failures, accept responsibility and do something about them.

The Church is all the people of God. It's important members are not those wearing mitres, robes and collars, but the marginalised, rejected, voiceless, suffering victims.

That's why the Church, as we knew it, is dying. It has few vocations and no credibility. It is not enough to examine sex abuse itself. We simply must purge the system which allowed abusers to thrive. Nothing less will do. Let the people decide who will be their priest, whether he/she should marry and what sort of community/Church we should have. Let the laity make decisions about how their money is spent. Let's dismantle clericalism, which is not part of God's plan and has become an obstacle to the working out of that plan. Let's begin by accepting healthy, married men into priesthood. It's no big deal; the principle is already accepted when married Anglican ministers are ordained as Roman Catholic priests. There is no obstacle apart from the intransigence and arrogance of the clerical club.

How we can change the Church and make it relevant for an era that is radically different is still the question we need to answer today. The leaders of the Church don't want to lose parish structures because they have become the foundation of power structures. We priests are not as relevant to people's lives any more. By and large, people do without us, except that we're handy for the big wedding, the First Communion and the funeral. The younger generation don't buy into the traditional roles. In all honesty we're not really relevant to their lives.

I look forward to the day when all priests, and not just a handful of converts, will be allowed to marry. That will be the first step to healthy relationships within the Church. We may even regain some semblance of credibility.

I still meet many of those men who had to leave priesthood in order to marry. I admire their courage and their goodwill towards the Church. What a difference it would make if there was an invitation to those men to return to active ministry! If married priesthood is an already accepted principle why shouldn't there be an invitation to those men who have given the best years of their lives to the Church as active priests?

Those of us who remained often directed more energy to remaining celibate than to being good priests. The sad, safe, aloof, ageing bachelor priest is a testament to stoicism, but hardly an attractive vocation model.

Hardly a day goes by that I don't receive letters from wonderfully articulate, marvellously dedicated but extremely angry women. They argue with clarity and cogency that they are being patronised by this men-only club. They seethe when they are arrogantly squelched by heavy-handed authoritarianism.

That's what annoys so many of the women who contact me. They are still treated as if their role is to "help priests to run the Church better".

One woman put it graphically: "My parish priest told me that I could serve God by cleaning the church, arranging the flowers, making tea for the bishop at confirmation and occasionally by reading and giving out Communion at Mass."

It's the "pray, pay and obey" system of abuse all over again. Women now realise that they will never be allowed to serve as priests as long as the men-only club can do without them. They know that any kind of man is preferred to them. It's not a question of ability, but virility.

It has finally dawned on most intelligent women that they will never become priests, because men have power. They will not be allowed to crack the all-male power base which the priesthood is at present. For most women now, it is no longer a question of good public relations. It is a question of justice – plain and simple.

It is, women say, indefensible that the all-male priesthood should have the only say on this matter. To add insult to injury, the principle is not even up for discussion.

How could anyone with a reasonable argument to make not engage in respectful dialogue? To dismiss half the population of the world as being unworthy and unable to serve God and their community as priest is unwise, unhealthy and unjust. It is a scandal and probably one of the main reasons why God sends so few vocations to the Church in the Western world.

There is still a good supply of vocations to the male priesthood in poorer countries where women are still treated as inferiors. That's no coincidence.

There are those in authority who say that the Catholic Church *can't* ordain women because Jesus chose an all-male priesthood and because tradition says there have never been women priests. But the majority of theologians (many of whom are now women) and scripture scholars say their arguments don't hold water.

First of all, the Scriptures reflect the times in which they were written. (Slavery is justified in the Old and New Testaments. Does that mean we should never have fought for its abolition?)

Women in those times were second-class citizens and it would have been inconceivable for them to be in positions of leadership in such a society. Jesus went out of his way to proclaim the dignity of women even when it scandalised the religious leaders of His time.

We live in different times now and, women argue, if Jesus were alive today He would be the first to give them their proper place in the Church. He would not condemn them to the slavery of second-class citizenship. He would welcome their giftedness and would use their unique qualities to spread His message of love and redemption to a world in such dire need of compassion.

Furthermore, Jesus made the Eucharist the central act of worship. Yet more and more of His people are deprived of Mass because of a lack of priests while Church authorities continue to bar one half of the world's population from the priesthood.

Sadly, even the most dedicated are getting the message now. You won't get into our club, not now, not ever. In short, you might well be the saviours of our Church, but we'll still hold onto power. That's what I hear the still-interested women say and it saddens me.

But one must always live in hope. We are a risen people. I believe new life will come despite the deadwood and despite male intransigence.

I met a friend from my past recently. He's a happily married man with two grown children. He's been successful in his profession and will retire shortly. He and his wife have plans to work voluntarily for their community and to live a simple, comfortable, relaxed life. They are both spiritual people who have adjusted well to change. They are obviously happy, fulfilled and at peace.

My friend was once a priest like myself, only he was much better than me. He retired from active ministry and married the woman he loved. It was a difficult decision for both of them – and for their families too. Looking at them now, it was truly a holy, inspired choice on their life's journey.

Had my friend stayed he would have been a good priest, but his life would have been very different. For a start, there would not have been any possibility of retirement. He would be working not less than 12 hectic hours a day, seven days a week, and be on call 24/7. He would typically live on his own, cater for himself and be in charge of a parish with multiple churches and schools.

He would have given the best years of his life to the priesthood in the certainty that in his middle and old age another crop of capable curates would do the donkey work for him. Now as a priest he would find himself doing the donkey work with not a curate in sight. He would be a good and dedicated priest but tired, overworked and, if he thinks at all, frustrated. In other words he would be part of the priesthood in crisis.

He would not be the happy, mature, emotionally healthy man he now is, thanks to his own openness and his wife's wisdom and love.

Many of his classmates tell him what it's like to be a priest today.

Looking around, a normal priest is aware that a large proportion of his parishioners don't attend church regularly. They come for baptisms, weddings and funerals. They don't need the Church at other times. He knows he's irrelevant to their lives – most of the time anyway. They haven't lost faith in God; they have just given up on the Church as they experience it.

The young see him as a relic from the past. They have no sense of what all this religion thing means. It's not that they are switched off by the Church; it's more that they were never switched on. So much for Catholic schools with their so-called Catholic ethos.

My friend knows that married couples make up their own minds about sexual morality. They plan their families as effectively as they can and he knows they are right, but he dare not say so. It's the "sin" no-one mentions; an unnecessary battle that couldn't be won. There'll be no dialogue, no discussion, just silence. It's a good example of common sense from the people and communal denial by the Church.

When he speaks with priests my friend finds two distinct trends. One group, usually the very old and the very young, see no problem. Their way of coping is to deny the problem exists. He understands the old men because they'll hang on for a few years and die peacefully. Who would argue with the "as long as I get my day out of it, I'll be alright" mentality in a 70-year-old?

The young baffle him because he can't understand why they became priests in today's climate and how they came out of training with such blinkered, intransigent views. Even in his day he was taught that faith is not a static condition but a way of being on pilgrimage. Ideals have to be proclaimed, but should never be made requirements for sacraments. It's common sense and good pastoral care.

Today's priest knows there won't be a dramatic surge of vocations. He willingly spends days at conferences discussing the latest in-word, "clustering". He'll cut back on Masses, stand in for a neighbouring priest who gets sick and help out with penitential services which he knows are of little use. When he allows himself to think at all, he knows the game's up. And if he had the courage, he would tell his clustering meeting what he really feels:

> It's not the number of Masses that counts. It's the quality of them.

> Our preaching is out of date. Our experiences don't match our congregations' experiences. We live in two different worlds: a good man expounding irrelevant spirituality; good people dying in a spiritual famine.

> There should be general absolution of sins on special occasions. There is no need to stick with a formula which was once helpful but is no longer meaningful. Churches are full of repentant people if only we were brave enough to reach out to them in a compassionate way. There is no limit to God's compassion.

> Priests don't have to be single and celibate. If some want it that way let them choose it. But don't confine the gift of priesthood to males with imposed vows of celibacy.

> Allow priests to marry and also ordain men who are married.

> Every living parish/community has many good, qualified and willing married men and women who would give a fixed number of years to

presiding at Eucharist and to serving their communities as priests. In the early Church, leaders were always chosen from within, not imposed from above. Humbly use the gifts God gives us.

Make a stand against the imposition of "safe" bishops from Rome. Fight against those who undo the reforms of the Second Vatican Council, which was the work of the Spirit.

Don't make a virtue out of passivity. It is not "loyal" to suppress or ignore real problems.

Listen to the people. Give them real power. Trust them with money. Trust their commitment. They have a right and duty to talk about what disturbs them. The Vatican Council said so over 40 years ago: "By reason of the knowledge, competence or pre-eminence which they have, the laity are empowered – indeed sometimes obliged – to manifest their opinion on those things which pertain to the good of the Church" (*Lumen Gentium*). Truth will set us free. Today in the Church to speak the truth is to be accused of disloyalty.

Invite back to active ministry all those who left the priesthood to marry. Thousands would willingly come back, enriching the priesthood and entire Church with new gifts and experiences.

Welcome women to genuine leadership roles. Allow them to preach the Word at Mass. They are forbidden to do so now.

Get real and find new ways to get bums back on church seats. It can be done. Good preachers and lively liturgies still enthral, inspire and attract.

Encourage people to experiment with new models of parishes, new ways to pray and new forms of religious life, including men and women living together.

Scrap the seniority rule in most dioceses, whereby a man, if he lives long enough, will be imposed on a parish, no matter how unstable or unsuitable he is. It's institutionalism gone mad.

How about giving half our wealth to the poor – for a start – and experience what it's like to be poor and powerless ourselves? People who have to beg don't have to be told how to be humble, how to dialogue or how to compromise. It would also remove the main fear in relation to a married clergy – that they and their wives will eat up parish money.

Learn a new sexual morality from married people. At present, no matter what we say, we act as if we believe sex is bad. Look at the damage we've done to ourselves and others living out that falsehood. Sex is good and is a gift from God.

Welcome those who can't be perfect into Church to pray with us when the Spirit moves them. Encourage, rather than stifle, the Spirit. Welcome those in second relationships; those who find it hard to believe; other religions; anyone who is searching. There's a place for all of them in God's house.

Let the laity have a say in who they want as their priest/leader and let priests and laity appoint their bishops.

Honest conversation and discussion can only bring us forward. There are still good people who want a Church they can own and be proud of. Some of us narrow-minded, frightened, jaded clerics are strangling the Spirit and killing the Church.

I don't expect you to agree with all of what I've said. But I've had so much encouragement from laity and so much grief from some clerics recently that I've been thinking, praying, reflecting and pondering the future. I don't mean to hurt anyone, but I make no apology for the challenge offered. It's part of trying to be faithful to the prophetic calling of the Gospel.

I'm often asked if I see any hope for religion in Ireland. I'm convinced that if we look to our Irish roots we'll find a solution because we have an innate spirituality. Look at our history. Long before Christianity we had burial rituals and Celtic gods. I love Brian Friel's play *Dancing at Lughnasa*.

It explores the relationships of families and communities, but also the tension between Celtic mythology, superstition and customs imposed by Rome.

When we look at where the Church is going today and how we can get through the present mess, it's best to look on the positive side and search for the gifts already in the community of believers.

St Paul saw the need for at least five great gifts to build up the infant community of his time. One of the most important is prophecy.

As I look around in society and in Church, genuine prophets are at a premium. Sometimes we mistakenly think prophets are people who foretell the future. This isn't the true biblical sense of the word. It's difficult to get a precise definition of a prophet but prophets are essentially people who can read the signs of the times under the guidance of the Spirit. They really listen to the voice of God speaking all around them. A prophet is one who reads the present well enough to be able to plan for the future. In biblical history prophets were invariably non-institutional people.

There's always a tension between a prophet and the institutional Church. The prophet initially suffers rejection, but passion for justice and integrity eventually win out, though not always during the prophet's own life. Prophets are necessary, but are uncomfortable to be around.

Answering God's call is the centre of our spiritual journey. Discovering God's call can be more difficult still. I take great comfort from one of my heroes in the Old Testament. Amos was a small farmer who came from a tiny village in the hills. He lived in the middle of the eighth century BC and had no formal training.

Amos had a call from God, and the small farmer, with no training, became a prophet. He was so convinced of what he was doing that he left his farm and his country. Like many a small farmer before him, Amos was a simple man but he wasn't stupid. In fact he was the first prophet to commit his work to writing and he was a brilliant communicator, a gift which got him into trouble. People understood what he was saying and clarity can be dangerous.

All around him there was the equivalent of the Celtic Tiger. Israel then was at the highest point of its prosperity. The land was productive, the cities were elegantly built and the rich had their winter and summer villas.

However, Amos knew that there was also widespread corruption. The poor were exploited and sold into slavery. There was a show of outward religion but no justice. Amos didn't like it one little bit. He said, "I hate and despise your feasts . . . Let me have no more of the den of your chanting . . . but let justice flow like water, and integrity like an unfailing stream" (Amos 5:24).

The priests accused him of being disloyal. It's an old trick to attack the prophet who opposes the status quo. But it didn't work with Amos; he told them straight – loyalty to the word of God has priority over any other loyalty in life.

The small farmer, the ordinary layman with no training, was effective because he got his priorities right.

I am utterly convinced that as soon as we begin to listen to the prophets of today, God will inspire and bless us with new forms of Church.

Another great gift, and according to St Paul probably the most important gift, is the gift of being an apostle. Again it's a peculiar term that we can't easily identify with today. An apostle, in biblical terms, is one who is sent on a mission. The apostles got their authority by being witnesses to the risen Lord. They were sent to spread that message. Because of what they saw, heard and experienced they had vision and conviction. Mary Magdalene was the first apostle, and the one sent by Jesus to convince the 12 men. Mary Magdalene, despite the bad press she gets in second-rate novels these days, is often called "the apostle to apostles".

Apostles have an authority and are usually sent by their communities to start new foundations: to plough a field that somebody else will plant. Apostles are selfless people who have nothing to lose and are willing to give all for the cause. Their belief in the risen Lord and in the values of the Gospel is greater than their own self-interest. Apostles are rare and precious.

Pope Paul VI thought the gift most needed by the Church was evangelism. The mark of a genuine evangelist is the spreading of good news. The word again leaves a bad taste in the mouth because of so-called evangelists who tell us we are all damned. They are not evangelists; they are fundamentalists. True evangelists in the Gospel sense welcome and invite. The sheer joy of their own life will attract people to follow Jesus. We Catholics are shy about the word evangelist because most of us were baptised in infancy and are often wrongly presumed to base our lives on the Gospel of Jesus. Evangelism begins with a conversion experience – the recognition that the way of life we are leading is not what Jesus wants. We recognise there are other values in life worth making sacrifices for. We are willing to spread the good news that Jesus suffered, died and rose again out of sheer love for us.

Another gift St Paul sees as essential, and one that I would deem as the fourth essential gift, is that of being a pastor. It's not the same as being an administrator, which is another gift, and a necessary one, but secondary at best. Pastors today, namely priests, usually spend their lives as managers of huge plants made up of churches, schools, finances, etc. Administrators are necessary but are not pastors (1 Corinthians: 12).

For me, a central part of the gift of being a pastor is compassion. Many others would say spiritual direction and growth are central to the pastor's role and I wouldn't disagree with that. But the gift most lacking from us pastors today is a genuine compassion for people on a journey who are struggling to find a direction. So much of our life is spent applying rules from on high; so little is spent actually listening to people's journeys and encouraging them on their journeys.

A pastor has to understand his own humanity and his own journey as well as human relationships, family life and indeed communication. Most of us are not good pastors, simply because we don't spend enough time developing our own humanity and our own spiritual life.

But I don't want to confine the gift of pastoring to those who are ordained. Far from it. The hope for the Church is that those people with immense compassion and wonderful ability to lead us on a spiritual life are clearly among the non-ordained. That's why for the past 20 years, I have insisted that any spiritual direction and counselling I get is from a qualified woman.

The last gift I will mention here is one that embraces a whole host of gifts summed up in 1 Corinthians 12:28. I'll gather them together under the general gift of teaching. It's extraordinary that the more effort the Catholic Church in Ireland has put into Catholic education, the less Catholic most of the pupils have become. A serious review must be made of what we call Catholic education. I'm not speaking against it here; I'm merely asking for a debate on what it should be.

Surely a central part of it ought to be helping students to grow as spiritual people rather than instilling greed for material wealth. I have nothing against Celtic tigers and the abolition of poverty but we know it has left a spiritual poverty in its wake. This is where the true gift of teaching is required. It will include adult religious education which is not just learning about what you can't do but is about being imbued with the Scriptures and spiritual writings. I have no doubt, for example, that at least 20 people in every congregation I preach to on a Sunday could preach and teach better than I can. I look forward to a time when they will be able to share those gifts with the wider community.

Those are just some of the gifts already present in our communities which we fail to recognise, much less avail of. But they are a source of great hope to me.*

(*There are many books worth reading on this topic. I found *The Price of Peoplehood* by Richard Rohr very accessible.)

CHAPTER 29

RECOGNITION WHERE DUE

I always like to encourage ordinary people to do something different with their lives. I don't see myself as talented or gifted, but I know if I keep using my gifts, I will get the opportunity to use them in an even greater way.

Today most of the stars that pioneered the showband industry and were huge personalities in the 60s and 70s are long forgotten. Many of them are dead. Occasionally they are remembered nostalgically and with fondness. On one occasion I was part of a group who made a serious attempt to honour them officially.

I was talking to President Mary McAleese and her husband, Dr Martin, about old times in Ireland. The President knew of my role as chaplain and was anxious to hear some of the stories associated with the characters in the showbands.

She recalled that in their youth Martin and herself often danced to these bands in Belfast and throughout the North. She remembered fondly the great entertainers and the happy nights they had in otherwise dreary times. She also described, hilariously, how her aunts looked forward for weeks to a night out dancing to the showbands and the excitement as they prepared for these special occasions.

It was Dr Martin who wondered if we could get some of them together and honour them officially at Áras an Uachtaráin. I gave it a little thought and, at Dr Martin's prompting, we got together Jimmy Magee, Jim Aiken and Hugh Hardy (himself a showband manager and promoter). I came along to provide contacts with people long forgotten. As a result we were able to hand a list of about 200 invitees whom the President could contact.

She took the initiative and organised a special day to honour the showband legends in Áras an Uachtaráin. The President sent the invitations and almost all the recipients turned up to be greeted personally by President McAleese and Dr Martin. They had photographs taken with her and spent an afternoon in the beautiful rooms of the Áras, meeting old friends, sipping drinks and eating more tasty sandwiches than they ever got in cold halls across the country.

The highlight of the day was an address by President McAleese. I had some small part to play in it because she invited me for a cup of tea in the Áras one Sunday and in the kitchen I reminded her of the essential aspects of the industry. That was all she needed. On the day she spoke brilliantly for 20 minutes about the showband era.

Of course she remembered her courting days and the part that the bands played in solidifying their relationship and marriage. She thanked them for that. She recalled in her usual, humorous way the excitement of getting ready to go out to a dance. Her aunts fitting on the glamorous fishnet stockings of the day and making sure that the seams were absolutely straight, in line with the stiletto heel and up the calf of the leg. She talked about the dances, the non-drinking halls, the marquees.

On one famous occasion Larry Cunningham and the Mighty Avons played in a village called Leitrim in County Down. Larry at the time had a huge hit with *Lovely Leitrim*. It was written about the county Leitrim but locals thought it might be about the village Leitrim in County Down.

All of the village and half the county turned up for the dance. So much so that at midnight they had to take the sides off the marquee so that the crowds could spill into the field. More people arrived and then the late Charlie McBrien, legendary manager of the Mighty Avons, thought of a better idea. He moved his table with the money out to the gate of the field and charged them just to get into the field. It wouldn't happen now.

President McAleese recalled the political troubles and how the bands helped to brighten up people's lives. She paid special tribute to the murdered members of the Miami Showband.

She remembered some of the industries that grew around her own home place as a result of the showbands – the petrol stations, hairdressers and draperies with their new blouses and skirts. Not to mention shoe shops and the ever-present bottles of perfume. She concluded with a special tribute to the bands. "Times have changed now," she said, "but the stars of the past are not forgotten. This day is simply to say a sincere thank you to the thousands of musicians, managers and promoters who helped brighten up those dark days of long ago.

"They brought life, enthusiasm, joy and glamour to every parish in the country. They helped thousands of couples to meet and marry. They gave us memories that should never die when, with their swirling brass and electric guitars, they had us dancing all night long.

"To you and your families, on behalf of the Irish nation, I say a heartfelt thanks. You are not forgotten."

It was a day full of nostalgia for those who turned up, many of whom had not met in more than 20 years. The usual stories were told and people went home happy that they had been remembered by the President of Ireland. As long as we're remembered, we never die.

What surprised me most was the huge number of letters of thanks that were subsequently sent to the President and the members of the committee. The officials in the President's office told me the percentage of people who wrote to thank them for this special day was extraordinary.

Two major stars, Brendan Grace and Brendan Shine, who have performed on the biggest stages in the world, went out of their way to say this was the proudest day of their showbusiness lives.

It was so successful that we organised two more equally nostalgic days in the Áras with President McAleese and Dr Martin.

It's typical of President McAleese to honour Irish people whom others have forgotten. She does this not only with showband stars but also with former sporting stars. We should never forget where we came from. It's a quality often lacking in the Ireland of Celtic Tigers.

One superstar who never forgets his past is Daniel O'Donnell. It's well known that Daniel and I are good friends. Most people tease me about Daniel: "Come on, give us the dirt on him. He couldn't be as good and as nice as he appears." I've known him now for 30 years, maybe more, and what you see is what you get.

And I'll tell you more. Most of the good he does, nobody hears about.

Everyone knows of the incredible work he did for the Romanian orphanages. But what people don't know is that Daniel probably knows the name of every "special" person in Ireland. When he's touring, he'll have a list of people to visit before the show. He's like the perfect priest, actually, and his dedication to the sick and handicapped, in particular, puts my priestly work to shame.

He has a vocational conviction that he should use his gifts to help others. He realises he is blessed and recognises the call to use his talent positively. Many entertainers have the same sense of duty. As with most of us, it's part guilt, part goodness.

In the early days I knew his sister Margo better than I knew him, because she was one of the earliest showband stars.

As a young boy Daniel never displayed any special gifts or talents. I knew him as an upcoming, struggling singer playing at dances in small venues. He'd grown up so quickly, I'd forgotten who he was. I realised one night he was Margo's brother – which is what he was then, Margo's brother – when he played in the Irish Club in Dublin. I thought he was personable, knew how to handle an audience, sang well; and whereas the band wasn't great, it was good enough to get by.

It so happened that Seán Reilly, who had been the manager of the Hillbillies Showband, was a close friend of mine. He is an honest, hard-working manager who volunteered to help me with the gigs to raise money for Mount Argus. Seán phoned me next day: "I've been asked to get involved managing a young singer that Mick Clerkin is going to take on, Margo's brother. What do you know about him?"

I was able to tell Seán that I'd been to see Daniel in the Irish Club the previous night.

"What do you think of him?"

"He's very good. Looks well, sings well but the band needs to change. Make sure he doesn't drink and that he's really dedicated to the business. He'll never make a massive fortune, but he'll make a good living out of it."

How wrong can you be? I knew he'd "make a good living out of it", because Margo had a unique ability to communicate with her audience. The people loved her. She had the X-factor. And I just saw the same quality in Daniel. But I never thought he would become the world superstar he is today. It's nice to be wrong about some things. Seán is still his manager and both of them are still close friends.

Early in his career I went to the *Sunday World* to alert them to Daniel's potential impact on the scene once Seán got involved. If we wanted to be first, we should do something on him, I advised. Bill Stuart, the deputy editor, who always wanted to help Irish talent, agreed. I wrote a double-page spread on Daniel in the *Sunday World* in 1986 – the first such recognition of him in a national newspaper. He's turned out to be one of the most impressive ambassadors ever in Irish music.

Daniel's a huge star in America yet there's no fuss about it in the media. In Branson his shows fill out quicker than those of any other star. He has the unusual title of "Number One Bus Artist in America". Only the Americans could come up with it! It means that more fans use buses to travel to see Daniel than any other artist in America.

Branson is the new Nashville but is closer in concept to Las Vegas. In the theatres the artists do three or four shows a day, yet Daniel books out instantly. The big country stars all want to appear with him. Some of them even come to Ireland to appear on his shows.

For a number of years there was a festival in his home village of Kincasslagh. On the final night a surprise guest would close the festival. Not even Daniel knew who this star would be. I usually introduced them because I could keep a secret. One of the stars I was most proud to introduce was Loretta Lynn, who was the subject of the Oscar-winning film *The Coalminer's Daughter*. She's a wonderful singer/songwriter with an amazing story to tell. Her sister is Crystal Gayle.

Loretta's story is unreal. Hailing from the Kentucky mountains and born into a poor family, she married an older man as a teenager and had six children before she was 21. She was rearing her children at home when she began to sing. When she was 26 her career took off. The award-winning *The Coalminer's Daughter* was the true story of her troubled life.

She has always been Daniel's idol, and the festival organisers, with Daniel's sister Kathleen, managed to get her to come to Donegal, a magnificent achievement. Of course he didn't know this would happen and never suspected this world-famous singer would come to a tent in his village. I was given the "task" of looking after Loretta and keeping her under wraps. It was a pleasant duty, I can assure you. Loretta Lynn was great. For me it was heaven to be in the same room with her, chatting about songs, her husband, Mooney, and her late singing partner, Conway Twitty. It was a wild, wintry night and we still had to smuggle her through the rain and into a marquee which was swaying in the storm, without being seen by anyone, especially Daniel.

She could have blown home to America that night, it was so wild. She had a magnificent emerald-green, ankle-length dress, specially made for the occasion and she looked a picture as she stood shivering backstage while Daniel warmed up the audience.

The big introduction was about to take place. Daniel had his eyes closed on stage as the countdown began. At zero he opened his eyes – Loretta walked out and Daniel fainted. I was trying to hold him up. He just couldn't believe that here, in his home village, in a tent, on a windy October night, in an emerald-green dress, stood the "Coalminer's Daughter", Loretta Lynn.

He tried to talk but couldn't. Luckily I was able to talk about Loretta Lynn to the audience, off the top of my head, for five minutes, while Daniel regained his composure. It was one of those marvellous, magical nights. I suppose if you asked Daniel what was the greatest night of his life, I think that, apart from his wedding, the night Loretta came to town would be right up there.

I suspect that the last night of the last Kincasslagh Festival would come into contention too. That night I introduced Cliff Richard to Daniel and the people of Kincasslagh. Daniel and Cliff have become friends who visit each other's homes and even record together. Cliff thinks Daniel has developed into a skilled artist, while Daniel has always taken Cliff as his model. They are both well respected artists who believe Christians should help the underprivileged.

I chatted to Cliff for a couple of hours in Daniel's house and then introduced him on stage as a surprise for Daniel. It must have been strange for Cliff, but true professional that he is, he sang his heart out to the backing of John Staunton's acoustic guitar. He shook hands and signed autographs – a superstar totally at home in a tent.

I once did a BBC interview with Cliff as part of my *Be My Guest* series. During the live interview I asked him, cheekily, "Were you ever close to marrying anyone?"

He admitted he nearly married Sue Barker. And he added, "I still think she's a wonderful person. I was wrestling with that decision. I was somewhat older than her and I was a bachelor all of my life. I thought I was too set in my ways. I didn't know if I could live with one person for the rest of my life and I dreaded ruining her life. The dilemma just paralysed me. I went out to dinner with friends of mine who were a happily married couple. I asked them, 'How do you know when you've met the right person?'"

They asked him to talk about it. He told them everything. At the end they were puzzled. Cliff did his best to explain his dilemma: "As far as I know my dilemma is this – could I live the rest of my life with this one person? Would I be doing her an injustice? Would I be happy with the one person? Or would she be happy with me? I can't answer the question could I live with one person for the rest of my life.

"Their answer was insightful and enlightening: 'Cliff, you'll never answer that question because it's the wrong question. The question you must ask yourself is could you live the rest of your life *without* that person.'

"When I went home and thought about it, I came to the conclusion that I could live the rest of my life without Sue. I knew then it would not be proper to marry her and I didn't."

It's good to learn from other people's journeys, as well as our own.

I thought for a long time that Daniel might not marry. Luckily he met Majella. As everybody knows, Majella had a previous marriage that was annulled. Neither Daniel nor I had anything to do with that process. It was Majella's own decision about her own life.

I was really happy for Daniel and Majella as I love to see those who search finding peace. We had such a lovely day at their wedding, which was planned meticulously around the Mass and the religious service. That was the centre of their day and they let every guest know that. By now I've heard thousands of speeches at weddings, but Daniel's speech that day was the best from a groom I've ever heard.

There were several hundred people at the wedding. Daniel first thanked God for the gift that Majella was to him on this day. He thanked his family, especially his mother, and other important people who helped him in his life. He then thanked Majella's first husband: "Whatever happens between people happens between people, but he has always been a kind man to me. Not only that, he and Majella have two beautiful, teenage children who are the delight of my life."

It's that kind of thoughtfulness which marks him out as special. His patience is amazing. I think he gives far too much of himself to his fans and the more he gives the more is demanded. His fans are loyal but a small minority seem to think they own him. But then who am I to tell him what's wrong with his life? Daniel's a really good person and one I'm proud to call a friend.

Daniel has, in my memory, been the most successful Irish home-grown solo artist. He started from a humble showband background but has developed, with Seán Reilly, a most professional stage show that can take its place in Branson, Sydney Opera House, Albert Hall or Carnegie Hall.

At one stage the British Country Music Association banned his records from the charts. They had to, because no other artist could get into the charts. Daniel outsold them all.

When people criticise him I always ask if they have ever been to his show. You might not be a fan but if you can recognise professionalism you'll have to respect his show.

Sometimes I think that if he were a drug addict, a drunkard and a sex maniac he'd be the darling of the media. But because they can't knock him, they laugh at him. As a matter of fact, I haven't heard a bank manager laugh at Daniel O'Donnell in a long time.

I get a certain pleasure when I've been at the birth of an idea which developed into a worldwide success. Daniel is certainly one of those successes. I had no insight that the young man I saw performing nervously in the Irish Club in 1985 would, within less than a decade, become a multimillionaire, a world star and the perfect ambassador for the Irish entertainment industry.

I had the same sense of pride in a show which grew out of an interlude act in the *Eurovision Song Contest*. I'd better start at the beginning.

When I went to work in the Communications Centre in the mid-1970s, we had to produce programmes to studio conditions to ensure the participants on the course understood what it was like in the real world of television. Part of each segment of training was that the students produced an actual programme. It included writing, scripting, camera work, sound operating, editing and directing. To ensure that the highest standards were maintained, we hired in auxiliary staff, on a freelance basis, to help us out. From my contacts in RTÉ, I had two cameramen I used regularly. At the time, and I'm sure they would have no problem admitting this, both were struggling cameramen in RTÉ. One was Shay Healy. He went on to become a famous journalist, and then moved on to writing songs and performing himself. Eventually he won worldwide acclaim as the composer of *What's Another Year?* for Johnny Logan. Shay is still writing and recently wrote and produced a brand new musical, *The Wiremen*, at the Gaiety Theatre.

Another man who was even more in need of a helping hand then was John McColgan. John was a budding disc jockey in the early days of RTÉ Radio 1. He was always interested in television. To ensure he learned the trade well, he got a job as a cameraman in RTÉ. I was living in Greystones at the time and driving into Booterstown every morning. On many occasions when John was standing at the bus stop waiting on a lift, I brought him into town. If there was a spare job going, John was the man I hired as a cameraman and I was glad to give him a few pounds – and they were only a few pounds – to augment his wages.

Later, John became a producer in RTÉ and eventually became head of entertainment there. Then he went to England to head up morning television.

When I was doing *Morning Reflections* in the early days of 2FM with my great friends Ronan Collins and Bill O'Donovan there were a number of very able production assistants. One of them was Moya Doherty. I've known Moya since those early days and always knew she was a talented, capable and professional lady.

When John McColgan went to England, Moya Doherty also went over as part of a *TV AM* programme. I always made sure to meet them when I was over working with Terry Wogan on the BBC. My routine was to have an early breakfast after the show with Terry and a light lunch with John and Moya whenever we could manage it. In time, Moya and John returned to senior positions in RTÉ. As a result, Moya was chosen to be the producer of the *Eurovision Song Contest* from the Point Theatre in Dublin.

Long before the contest, Moya and John were excited about their interval act. They explained that Bill Whelan was writing the music for it and that it would revolutionise Irish dancing. They were both enthusiastic and slightly secretive about a new dancer they were using who worked mainly in America with The Chieftains. His name was Michael Flatley.

In the early stages of production, John and Moya invited me to run an eye over the ambitious interval act. I could see it was stunning.

Then two days before the *Eurovision*, Bill Whelan, Moya and John invited me to watch a final rehearsal of the interval act. There and then I told Bill he was going to have his first number one. John and Moya wondered if it could be expanded into a show. The consensus was it could but that they'd wait to see how it went down in Europe on the night.

As the world now knows, *Riverdance* was the most famous act ever to appear on *Eurovision*, even though it was never entered in the contest.

John and Moya struggled hard to find backers for their show and risked everything in the process. Their success on stages across the world, including China, is the most richly deserved in our showbusiness history. It could not happen to two better and more generous people than John McColgan and Moya Doherty. Again it was rewarding to be in at the beginning of something which revolutionised Irish dancing and introduced a new, self-confident Ireland to the world. They are still friends of mine who continually update me on their plans.

In life, the combination of talent, luck, dedication and sheer hard work doesn't always achieve the success it deserves. In their case it eventually did. That's where the hope lies.

Artists help us shake off the shackles of the past, encourage us to mature, and support us in making our vision become reality. They nurture the best gifts we have. Would that our Churches were so freeing, so uplifting.

Chapter 30

The Prodigal Father

There is a stark-looking Van Gogh painting which looks like it's black-and-white but can't be, because in my memory I recall colours. It's a still life of a large, open Bible. It is not a well-thumbed Bible; but it's perfect looking, sitting on a sturdy stand, rather like a heavy-bound Latin Mass book from the old days. On the table alongside the Bible is a randomly placed novel – a small, insignificant-looking book compared to the weighty Bible.

In a corner are two brass candlesticks and two half-burned but quenched candles. No light in a Van Gogh picture? That must be significant. Darkness, hopelessness, must have been part of his plan. A guide pointed out that the painting came about after a row with his father, a Protestant minister and preacher of the Word of God.

The novel in question is a recognisable bestseller of the time, written in French. The title meant nothing to me until it was pointed out that it was a story of family scandal. Van Gogh thought it an important novel because it dealt with human frailty in a realistic way. His father tried to prevent him reading the novel, because of its sexual innuendo. Van Gogh is highlighting the connection between the Bible and the subject matter of the novel.

The chapter of the Bible on display is also significant. Isaiah 53 predicts the Passion of Christ, beginning with the line, "He took our infirmities and bore our sorrows." Van Gogh was adamant that the problems and failures of life, which the novel highlighted, had a solution in the pages of the Bible, so there is a connection. Church people, like his father, too often quenched the light in God's Word. Van Gogh realised that and wished to convey that the Passion of Christ is relevant in today's world. No suffering is wasted. "He took our infirmities and bore our sorrows."

The obvious prediction of the passion in Isaiah 53 gave the work special meaning for me as a Passionist. There was a real connection there. The Passion that Jesus endured was life-giving and gives us a spiritually enriching way to handle the failures in our life. Van Gogh, in what might be dismissed as an ordinary still life, showed he had a grasp of a healthy theology of the Passion.

Father Charles, when he blessed sick people, always told them a simple story from the Passion narrative. He too was convinced that the Passion of Jesus ensures that suffering is not wasted because the Passion of Jesus changed everything. It's no longer just the Passion of Jesus but rather the suffering, death and resurrection of Jesus in a single mystery.

Jesus died on the Cross between two thieves, a failure. The Messiah, the most powerful one, died without power. God took the failure of the Passion and made something powerful out of it. "Into Your hands I commend My spirit," Christ said. Because He put His life in God's hands, God was able to use the failure, the brokenness, and the vulnerability of His Passion, not to glorify suffering and death, but to redeem it.

Passionists are not the only people who should preach the Passion; the whole Church should. So why then is the Church afraid of brokenness? Why should the Church be afraid of death when we understand the significance of the empty tomb? The tomb was not always empty; there was a dead body in it. Now it's empty and Jesus is risen. Through death, new life came.

It's the same for the Church today. We need to recognise that we must let the past go to find new life in the new directions we'll inevitably take. Why should the Church be afraid of failure? It's out of such failures that new life emerges. For that reason I welcome the death of much of the institutional Church as we now know it; only in death can new life come.

I don't wish to see the Church disappear, nor will it. Christ said, "I will be with you all days until the end of time," so the Church won't disappear. Yet this institution that we make a god of is collapsing. Our task is somehow, despite the brokenness and the scandals, to be able to recognise that unless the grain of wheat dies, it cannot produce a good harvest. Let's admit that the structures as we know them are a millstone round our necks; let us give them a dignified death and let's see where the green shoots thrive.

God gives new life through our brokenness, our vulnerability. That is the meaning of Charles Houben's life. Poor old Father Charles was the antithesis of what an accepted, good Passionist should be. Yet of all the Passionists who lived in Ireland over the past 150 years, he is the only saint we have. In the eyes of the world a failure, in God's eyes a saint.

As Passionists, our calling is to walk with people along their Way of the Cross. To suffer with people, to make sense of our own suffering, to find God's will through suffering, and to be utterly sure that by His wounds we are healed and by our own wounds we are healed. A Passionist should empathise rather than merely sympathise. Compassion is the one gift people are hungry for and grateful to receive.

I am disappointed that Van Gogh, as far as I am aware, didn't do a painting of the Road to Emmaus. For me, the Gospel story of the Road to Emmaus is another powerful parable. Jesus recognises that the two disciples are lost, disappointed, broken-hearted, and full of grief because, as far as they're concerned, their religion and their Messiah are dead. "We wasted our lives when we gave them to Jesus," – that's what they were talking about.

Jesus happens to join them on their journey and listens to their conversation. "He walks with them" because that is the practical help they need. He accompanied them on their journey of lostness. They told him his story. What an incredible turnaround! He didn't contradict them but He allowed them tell him his story.

Then he asked, "Do you not remember in the Scriptures why it had to happen this way?" And they were obviously so grief-stricken that they couldn't understand him, didn't take it in, and didn't advert to it. He didn't jump in and say this is what you must do.

Eventually, they came to the crisis, the crossroads – another powerful image. Crisis is a Greek word for opportunity, so crisis is an opportunity to choose. The choice not to choose is the real failure. The value of crisis is that it confronts us with a choice.

They chose to rest for the night. Their own basic decency caused them to ask, "Would you like to stay with us tonight? It's late; don't be travelling on your own." That was the invitation He needed. They invited Him into their lives and, at that point, He broke bread so that they could recognise who was walking with them, but only after they invited Him into their lives.

It is a powerful story of journey as well as a powerful story of being lost. There were no dictates, just little hints. They should have been able to recognise Him. But He knew that, in grief and in loneliness, we don't recognise Christ walking with us and encouraging us to choose a way. Once we choose, He'll sanctify it and bless the road; bless the journey.

If we as a Church are to be true to the call of Jesus, we will have to be people of compassion. We need to understand that we have to love, hope and bring hope. Otherwise the Resurrection is meaningless. We have to show welcome and forgiveness to the lost within and without the Church. There is no other way.

Dickens said the best short story ever written was the story of the Prodigal Son. Look at the familiar phrases it has given to our everyday language: "prodigal son", "fatted calf", "he came to his senses", "lost and found". No story tells us more about God or makes us feel better about ourselves. It tells us what sin is and what God's forgiveness is.

The younger son is typical of most of us. He wanted pleasure and he wanted it immediately. He was bored waiting for life to happen. He wanted his inheritance before his father died, which really meant he wanted his father dead now. His attitude was "to hell with the future, enjoy life now". Be happy today, no matter whom you hurt.

Life teaches a different lesson. When your fortune runs out, so do your friends. Peace of mind disappears quicker than either of them. At least the younger son showed some maturity. He came to his senses. He was willing to change and he was repentant. Hunger also played a huge part in his conversion.

His father's servants were better fed than he was. He would go back to his father, cap in hand, prepare his list of sins and be willing to be a servant rather than an heir. Now that's real repentance. "I no longer deserve to be called your son: treat me as one of your hired men" (Luke 17:19).

Time to introduce the father, who represents a patient God. He knew his son wanted him dead. Yet the Gospel shows a beautiful side to him. "While he was still a long way off he saw his son and he ran out to meet him." Is there a better image of God in the whole world? That's the God of compassion, not the small-minded meanness of so many of our rules and regulations. It's not just a story about a father and a son on a farm. This is about how we treat God and how God treats us. Even though we may be only a dot on the horizon God is still looking out for us. He doesn't smugly wait to humiliate us. He runs out to meet us. If we make any move God makes the rest of them. Each of us matters to God.

Nor do we have to wring forgiveness out of God. There is no need for our childish list according to this story. No jumping through hoops. The son has the list ready, but the father throws his arm around him and starts the rejoicing: "Kill the best calf. Have a feast. My child who was dead is alive again."

St Luke's Gospel tells us in another place: "There will be more rejoicing in heaven over one sinner repenting than over 99 upright people who have no need of repentance" (Luke 15:7). Remorse and repentance lead to rejoicing not only in the sinner, but for God too.

I have great sympathy for the next player, the elder son. He never did much wrong. When the wild one ran off, he kept the show on the road. Was he harshly treated? He certainly was angry. Angry that the calf he reared was being killed to feed the waster. He huffed. He wouldn't even come into the house. He called one of the servants, who did little to help things but rather stirred it even more. The Gospel quotes him: "Your brother was lost and your father is killing the calf that we have fattened."

The servant is probably the most destructive person in the whole story. He fed the brother's anger when he could have taken time to point him in the right direction. He was a coward and a menace. That sad servant has much to say to us today.

Anyway, the elder brother doesn't deal with his anger; he becomes a sad, old begrudger. He is not content that God's goodness allows him into Heaven. He wants to decide who else gets there. The father recognises his meanness but treats him with sympathy too. However, he does make the point: what is yours you will get; you have no need to worry about my generosity to others; there is plenty of room in God's kingdom for us all.

Sometimes we in the Church use our energies and power to drive people out of it. Compassionate priests have to "steal people" into Heaven despite the efforts of the leaders and the fundamentalists who have hijacked God's mercy, like the begrudging son.

All's well that ends well and God has his party anyway.

I'd love to think that we could some day allow God to be God when it comes to reconciliation. There is nothing as healing as the experience of forgiveness. Do we really need these irrelevant rituals of the sacrament? Is it theologically necessary or is it just a pathetic holding onto an outdated Council of Trent canon that some still insist on a list of sins? Why do we continue, needlessly, to demean good people who have a right to God's mercy?

Here's another thought: is not the penitential rite at the beginning of Mass a form of welcome and forgiveness to sinners anyway? Open the gates of compassion and the people will not be found wanting.

The Prodigal Father has shown us the way.

CHAPTER 31

ALL HEART AND ALLSTARS

The Jimmy Magee Allstars was the brainchild of the well-known broadcaster and memory man. The original name was The Jimmy Magee Radio and TV Allstars, which is typically 1960s. It was a mixture of journalists, broadcasters, showband stars, politicians and those famous for being famous. Their first gig was on 6/6/66 in Ballyjamesduff, Cavan. Forty years to the day, we went back to Ballyjamesduff for a Mass, a meal and a show just to prove there's life even in the wandering stars.

This unique and slightly crazy group are the best friends I have in life. They're the people who understand me, accept me without question, and know when I need support. I recorded a television documentary recently, a difficult retrospective of 20 years of change in the Church in Ireland. Six of the most encouraging text messages I got were from showbusiness friends who understood implicitly the point I was making. One of the most helpful notes came from Christy Moore: "What you said on Wednesday night was really inspiring."

I know Christy from football as much as music. We've met in Croke Park over the years. He's a Kildare supporter and I support anything in Croke Park. When I was in Mount Argus they used to say I went to Croke Park every Sunday whether there was a match on or not. I knew Christy's few lines were sincere. That's why they meant so much.

If I was ever wrong, showbusiness friends would be the first to point that out. Maybe it's the struggler in me that they understand. Artists who have to search and are often in the wilderness themselves understand another who's not always right but continues the search for truth anyway.

The Jimmy Magee Allstars travelled the length and breadth of Ireland in the name of charity. Every Monday night, in summertime, we played a team well known in their local area. A team of local personalities played a team of national personalities. We travelled at our own expense and never took a fee. The local committee gave us a meal, as well as doing all the organising on the ground. We just turned up, usually late! Then, after playing a match – that's loose terminology – of Gaelic football, we gathered in a local venue and put on a night of cabaret and entertainment. All the money stayed local.

Over the years (in today's money) we raised about € 6 million. We even went to England, Europe and Las Vegas to raise money, and to have fun too. As well as being good for the charities, it was also a reminder to the "stars" that they ought to give something back to the community.

As it turned out we ourselves became a community of free-and-easy fellow travellers. Many members have died, some have been failures and many have been successful in other careers, but all of us resemble Walter Mitty. It doesn't matter because when we come together, we are just a group of friends, held together by the cement of humour. Jimmy Magee is the centre of everything because, as he says himself, he bought the jerseys and owns the ball.

That first night in Ballyjamesduff in 1966 set the pattern for the rest of our Allstars gigs. Present were some of the top showband names including Larry Cunningham, who played for his native Longford, Brendan Bowyer, Joe Dolan and Dermot O'Brien and their bands. Also present on the night were broadcasters like Seán Óg Ó Ceallacháin, Liam Campbell, Paddy O'Brien and Bill O'Donovan. Not to mention politicians such as Jim Tunney and journalists like Michael Hand, who was starting out on a career which took him to editorship of both the *Sunday Independent* and the *Sunday Tribune*.

I often wonder if they realised how Michael actually started writing. He had an equally famous identical twin, Jim Hand, who was a showband manager. It was a case of "on the one Hand and on the other Hand". At least that's what they always said.

As a teenager Michael worked in Bachelors on Bannow Road in Cabra.

He wanted to be a journalist but couldn't get a start. His mother rang one Thursday from their home in Drogheda saying that there was a vacancy on the local paper and interviews were to be held the next day. She persuaded him to "go sick" and turn up for the interview. Michael couldn't do it and let slip the chance of a start in journalism.

When he got home on Friday night, his mother announced that Michael would be starting on the *Drogheda Independent* the following Monday morning. A startled Michael couldn't believe he got a job he didn't apply for.

"I sent your twin, Jim, to the interview today. He did well so you can start on Monday and they won't know the difference," his mother told him.

That's how Michael Hand started in journalism and he rose to the very top of his profession. Jim went on to spin even greater yarns as a showband manager. They were marvellous characters with wonderful stories.

We had time for spiritual occasions too. Masses on special occasions are central to the Allstars. They're the most memorable Masses I celebrate because everyone feels free to speak, to share, to ask questions and to discuss. We've celebrated Mass everywhere, except in a church. We've had them in hotel rooms, on the side of the road (when we were down in Cork), and once in a wonderful slate quarry on Valentia Island, one heavenly summer's evening. Mick O'Connell was the organiser.

Mick O'Connell was a famous Kerry footballer – the greatest midfielder of all time. He was a gifted footballer but he also had the reputation for being his own man. I love meeting him because of his hypnotic, storytelling ability.

This is my memory of one such story about when he was captain of an All-Ireland-winning Kerry team. Mick wasn't into "booze-ups", so as captain he took the the train to Killarney and then by car to Caherciveen. There was no bridge to Valentia Island so he had to row across to the island in the dark of night, having played his heart out in Croke Park a few hours earlier. He told me that story in a matter-of-fact way. I have this vivid image of a dark, silent sea with the boat bobbing up and down and sea water spilling into the boat.

The Allstars were concerned about our trip to Valentia. We wondered how Mick would take to this collection of would-be players. Would we be serious enough for him? We needn't have worried. He was marvellous company and he became a great friend of ours.

He was particularly fond of Eddie Masterson and they got on like two old pals. Mick fed Eddie the ball during the match and Eddie fed Mick all the best lines as we travelled around.

Ever after, Mick became a hero in the Allstars, and he and Eddie remained friends – genius loves company. Mick and Rosaleen have my unfailing respect for the way they have given their lives to caring for their beautiful special son, Diarmuid, the light of their lives.

Mick brought us to Valentia and we had a successful and enjoyable night out on the island. We had a Mass in the slate quarry on a beautiful summer's evening. During the Mass I was looking at the next parish – America. The slate quarry is shaped like a loudspeaker. There were 700 people there as I was saying Mass. A statue of Mary was perched impossibly high up as if in the clouds. The silence was awesome. There was no microphone but it was a natural, beautiful amphitheatre with the sound carrying out to the Atlantic. Everyone stood in the evening sun at one with God and nature. That was one of the most memorable Masses I had with the Jimmy Magee Allstars. We sang, we prayed and we played the game.

Sadly, Eddie suffered a brain haemorrhage at the age of 47, on his way home from a dance in the Ierne Ballroom in Dublin, in April 1982. I was on my way to anoint him in hospital after Mass next morning at the Richmond Hospital in Dublin. Albert Reynolds was being interviewed, as Minister, on the RTÉ News. I rang Albert and told him his old friend Eddie was dying. Albert drove to be with him and never left his bedside until he died the next morning. Eddie was really loved by those in showbusiness and politics.

When Eddie Masterson died so tragically and so young, I said his funeral Mass in Mount Argus. It was the biggest funeral I ever saw in our church. People from showbusiness, politics, sport and law were spilling into the car park. As I said the prayers over the coffin outside the church after Mass, a quiet man slipped through the crowd to shake my hand. It was Mick O'Connell.

For 40 years this ever-changing group of friends stayed loyal to one another and even though their showbusiness careers are no longer thriving, they still enjoy the odd night walking the boards for a good cause.

If I wanted to travel the world with good friends, there would be two people I would want on either side of me. One would be Jimmy Magee and the other would be Frankie Byrne, who played for Meath over three decades and was also a teacher. I could listen to interesting conversation for an eternity from both these men, and if I listened I'd be educated.

As well as raising money we created our own fun. On one occasion, we were thrown out of a restaurant in Las Vegas for making too much noise laughing. The source of the laughter was the brother of Daniel O'Donnell. Daniel never played for the Allstars but his brother Jamesy is the centre of the Allstars. Daniel is well dressed, proper, well spoken, and totally professional. Jamesy has three days' growth on his beard and a belly bursting out of his shirt. Jamesy tells yarns, most of them bad, but all of them funny, 24 hours a day. He has the art of storytelling off to perfection. He knows exactly how to grab and hold an audience. He knows precisely what not to say and then says it anyway, so that everybody is embarrassed. That's how he knocks you off guard.

In the Las Vegas restaurant he was telling us one of his storytime specials, egged on by Jumpin' Johnny Peters, which I dare not repeat here. He was working his captive audience, acting out the joke, with larger-than-life arm swings.

It was about an elephant; more accurately, the peculiar parts of an elephant. He was on his knees on the floor of the restaurant as if under the elephant, when we were asked to leave to protect the sensitivities of the paying customers. We all left the restaurant immediately and congregated on the sidewalk. Jamesy got down on the street to bring his story to a fitting climax.

By now all the people in the restaurant wanted to hear the end of the story too. The hilarious part was that they also left their meals and joined us on the street, where Jamesy played his audience perfectly. Remember, this was Las Vegas, the home of showbusiness, yet a barman from Donegal on his knees on the sidewalk was a bigger attraction than the multi-million dollar shows in the themed hotels.

Las Vegas is built on gambling, yet has a strict code of practice about gambling. There are millions of one-armed bandits, thousands of acres of casinos, every imaginable card game and every form of mind-numbing bingo for breakfast, dinner and supper. But you cannot gamble in bedrooms. It's a crime, with severe sanctions, for ordinary punters to organise a simple game of 25 in a bedroom.

It was not something I or any of the Allstars was aware of, except Jimmy Magee. He knew that Frankie Byrne, as safe a person as ever God made, Fr Michael Cleary and Liam Campbell, another solid citizen and headmaster, were having an innocent poker session for pennies in Fr Mick's room.

Jimmy gathered the rest of us in the foyer and then "bribed" one of the security officers to help us. He knew for sure nothing bad would happen his three friends.

The security officer phoned up to the room as we were all gathered around him, barely able to contain our laughter. In his best macho voice and using legal jargon brilliantly, he informed the three that they had been captured on camera in the room breaking every law in the book in the State of Nevada. They were not to dare move as he was on his way to arrest them. We could hear Fr Mick making all kinds of excuses and promises.

The guard went up to their room and marched them down to the foyer, where we all greeted them with a loud cheer. It was only then that they realised it was just another "Jimmy Magee special". Mind you, for three respectable men, they knew a wide range of curses and swear words. Mass that day had general absolution!

We've become so close to one another that every Allstar would say exactly what I'm going to say now; the closest people I have outside family are the Jimmy Magee Allstars – this weird club of oddballs who find a reason to be in a good cause.

Through them, I got to play against all the legendary footballers who were my boyhood heroes. I've often said that if my native Fermanagh could win an Ulster title I would die happy. And so I would. For someone like me to meet and play with the greatest Gaelic footballers ever was heaven in itself.

One night I played midfield with the Jimmy Magee Allstars and if my father, who was an outstanding footballer, had seen me he would have been very proud. Mick O'Connell and Jack Quinn were the midfielders on the other team. Jack Quinn, the mighty Meath full back: I couldn't even jump to his belly button, but I played on him. I can also say I played with and against Mick O'Connell. Not many can share that boast.

The Jimmy Magee Allstars played 274 games and had 274 draws. Forty years playing and we never won a single game. That's a parable in itself.

CHAPTER 32

THE ROAD TRAVELLED

One of my favourite pastimes is walking. I used to jog, but now every morning I get my boots and woolly cap and head off round the roads of Fermanagh. At one time I thought giving up running would be the start of my senility. In fact, taking up walking is the best decision I ever made. I have time to think, to notice nature and to pray. When I was young I ran at life and through life. At 60, walking is helpful and appropriate.

I like to think I'm fit, but what's more important is time to myself. Fermanagh is perfect for walking, with its estates, waterways and breathtaking scenery. On special days I may even head off to Glendalough, Achill or Donegal.

One hot, sunny day on Achill, struggling up the mountain at the end of the island, I learned something helpful for the journey. The mountain near the ancient Mass rock is difficult to climb for aging legs like mine. I was bent over, struggling, head down, breathing from the pit of my lungs. I was using every ounce of my energy to conquer the last section before the summit. And all I could see were the sunken holes from the hooves of the cattle, and sheep dung. And I thought, what am I climbing this for? I could see sheep dung in Fermanagh.

I stopped to rest and looked back on the journey I had made. I saw a heavenly vision below. I wasn't conscious of that vision behind me when I was battling on. It was only when I stopped to look back at where I'd come from that I recognised the beauty of the journey. That gave me confidence and the will to tackle the next part of the climb, knowing that the reward at the end of the journey was going to be even greater. And so it was. The awesome vision from the summit made the journey worthwhile.

In the daily struggle of life, the journey can become overpowering – so much so that it is necessary to step back occasionally and look at the road we've just travelled. This book has become a stop along that way.

At The Graan we have a group – called Anam Cara – interested in spiritual development. One day we went on a pilgrimage. To call it a pilgrimage is overstating it because there was time for chat, food and fun as well. At half-past-eight, 13 of us were in cars heading off to a mountain in Donegal for the day.

We arrived in Killybegs before 10 o'clock to enjoy a "full Irish". Killybegs was beautiful in the morning sunshine. Fresh fish was on sale along the streets, there was a summery atmosphere about the place and the huge fishing boats in dock reminded me of how professional fishing has become.

We then headed off around the coast to the village of Carrick and from there towards Slieve League, up narrow roads and then narrow lanes where we had to open and close gates. Eventually we arrived at a bit of a quarry which was the car park. The sun was still shining high in the sky and we were sure we were preparing to be scorched alive.

We started up the mountain. In the beginning we were all together but slowly the pace determined that we'd climb in small groups. Some put their heads down and went on up the side of the mountain, which was steep at all places, and very steep in some.

Gradually the climbers began to string out. Those who wanted to get to the top ploughed relentlessly on. Others stopped and looked back as they climbed, every half mile or so. Still others chatted on the way up and were more interested in conversation than scenery. About half-past-one everybody reached the top of Slieve League. It was a surprise when we got there, because the top wasn't the top at all. There was another 20-minute slog to get to the real top. Yet we all got to the summit of Europe's highest sea cliff in our own good time.

When we reached the summit people reacted in different ways. You could see some were thinking, "Now that we have got to the top let's get back down again." Others wanted to stay there. Others explored what else was available on the top of the mountain. All of these reactions are perfectly legitimate. But they are an indication of how we behave on the journey of life.

We crouched behind a stone cairn that protected us from the cold breeze and began to celebrate Mass. During the Mass we reflected on what it was like coming up the mountain. It was interesting to hear. We reminded ourselves that in biblical terms mountains are where God lives. And clouds are where God speaks. Now that we were on the highest cliff in Europe, looking out at the Atlantic Ocean, we realised what a privileged position we were in.

A few reflected on their journey. They had been so anxious to get to the top that they missed the beauty of the journey. Is that typical of life's journey too? Others realised how unfit they were and had spent their time worrying if they'd make it to the top or not. They were completely caught up in the journey itself.

Almost all agreed that they would not have got to the top without the help and encouragement of others, spurred on by personal pride. As a team all achieved more than they thought they were capable of. That's about life and team spirit.

Most of us admitted that we don't reflect on life often enough, though a few realised they looked back far too often to make any progress. Another little bit of wisdom.

No matter how you get to the top of the mountain, you have to come down. So we need to be careful that the mountains in life we climb are worth the effort. The tasks we dedicate ourselves to in life need to be worth it.

By now it was raining. The brave said it was only a little shower and a little shower never stopped us before. But as the Mass progressed all the lovely plans we had, including music and singing, had to be shelved. We got through the Mass before we were soaked to the skin.

At the end of the Mass we came down the mountain. That's when the rush began. Some people hurried down the mountain without any stops at all. Others had brought heavy bags. Now I knew why. The rain gear appeared. They had come well prepared for every eventuality. They carried a lot of baggage – some of it worthwhile, some of it a waste of energy.

All of us got safely down the mountain even though it was slippery and treacherous. By now we were wet through so it didn't matter. Once you're wet, you're wet. You might as well enjoy it. To be honest, most of us enjoyed the soaking we got on the journey down, as much as the journey up in the sun.

All 13 got to the bottom and now I noticed something different. We'd all been brought closer by our plans going wrong. People swapped T-shirts and even trousers. One man had a couple of towels in the back of his car. Everybody shared to ensure all had something clean and dry to change into. It was amazing how many of us came prepared with a change of clothes. I admit I had a second shirt myself because I thought I'd be too sweaty. Later we all agreed that, despite adversity, the day was one of the most enjoyable we ever had.

We learned another lesson. No matter how well we plan things, and no matter how much we take for granted, God has His own special plan for us. Now as I end my book I realise that unless I reflect on life I'm like the out-of-breath climber – caught up in the journey itself, without fulfilment, purpose or peace.

I took part in a significant TV programme in April 2006, which looked at how Ireland has changed in the past 20 years. *The Time of Our Lives* encompassed all strands of society – politics, sport, economy, art and religion. I was asked to compose a seven-minute television essay on the changes in religion in Ireland. It was filmed over two miserable days on Lough Derg, or St Patrick's Purgatory, as it is better known. It seemed an impossible task which had be to realistic on the one hand and leave some room for hope for the future of religion on the other.

The changes that have taken place between 1986 and 2006 have been phenomenal. In 1986 I looked down at a very different congregation from the one I see now. Then, our churches were full. It was a young congregation and a trusting congregation; a congregation beginning to question some outdated rules and customs, but still respecting priests and trusting them implicitly.

The last 20 years have seen the Church's influence wane dramatically in Ireland because of scandals and because of an increasingly ageing group of clergy growing even more out of touch with modern Ireland.

Not only is there a greying priesthood, but the sparse congregations are predominantly in the over-50 age bracket. The Catholic Church in Ireland today is in crisis and contrary to what many in the clerical circle think, it's not desirable and not possible for things to return to the way they once were.

For the first time in our history, fewer than half the Catholic population of Ireland attend Mass on Sundays.

Some say it's too late for the Church in Ireland; that the Church is already dead. I hope the Church of sex abuse and abuse of power is dead and good riddance to it. But there is hope for the future if we clergy can empower the laity and use all our gifts for the good of society.

Church attendance has dropped significantly but the number of people still declaring themselves Catholic has barely altered. That tells me people need to feel they belong to some religion, that faith is part of the Irish psyche. However, what we are providing in our churches and parishes now is not necessarily what people want or need anymore. It is my duty as a priest and as a member of the Church to wrestle with the direction the Church needs to go, so that trust in the Catholic Church can grow again. Because of the sins of the past, trust in the clerical Church is broken. Trust once broken cannot be restored. The old relationship is dead; the only hope is a new relationship built on a foundation of rock, not sand.

It's not easy and there is no quick fix. It will take decades to lay the foundations. In 50 years' time the seeds of our insecurities may come to fruition. The gift we leave to our successors is the dismantling of the human elements of Church which strangled God's Spirit. There is a time for building and a time for tearing down.

History tells us we need religion, beliefs and rituals.

Over 5,000 years ago in Ireland people had their own system of burials, graveyards, superstitions and prayers. Human nature seems to need a higher power. Even today when people have stopped going to church they indulge in séances, black magic, gurus – all of which are a replacement for religion, according to sociologists.

We need ways of understanding the world. We need reasons for living. We need to understand what the point of our existence is.

The French existentialist philosopher Teilhard de Chardin said, "We are not human beings on a spiritual journey; we are spiritual beings on a human journey."

We are always searching, reaching. The heart doesn't rest until it finds its lasting love.

Religion should provide us with a way of being together. The Church should provide a structure so that a compassionate God can save the lost. But from the several thousand letters a year I receive, it is obvious that most people think the present Church structures and strictures are at best irrelevant.

I agree with them. It will take courage and leadership to launch into the future, trusting God's Spirit more and canon law less. It will take enough humility to let go of the strangling power structures of the present. Some of the unmentionables we should be discussing I have already outlined.

> Our preaching is out of date and keeps good people away from Mass.
>
> Priests don't have to be single and celibate. Compulsory celibacy is a countersign.
>
> Listen to the people. Give them real power. Trust them. Trust their commitment.
>
> Welcome women to genuine leadership roles including priesthood, if possible.
>
> Learn a new sexual morality from married people. Sex is good and a gift from God.
>
> Let the laity have a say in who they want as their priests/leaders and let priests and laity discern who their bishops should be.

There was a poll carried out in America recently and I believe the results would be the same if it were done here. It tried to discover why the Church had lost its influence. There were many options to tick, such as lay involvement, lack of knowledge of the essentials of our religion, no women priests, and celibate priests – all the issues which keep recurring.

What came out overwhelmingly as the main reason why the Church has lost its influence were the sex-abuse scandals. In second place was the feeling that most bishops knew about the abuse and not only allowed it to continue but facilitated it. The Church was saying loud and clear that its image and reputation were more important than the welfare of innocent children. That's the unforgivable sin. If our basic principles are so wrong, how can the Church be trusted in anything?

There are days, and they seem to multiply with age, when I wonder if I should go on. Yet somehow, the grace comes. The call to strive to bring hope, to be a better human being, maybe even a better priest, cannot be dismissed easily.

In the last 20 years our whole society has got sidetracked by wealth, scandals, new religious movements and hostility to religion, but this isn't the first time in history that faith has been challenged here. This is a cycle repeated throughout history, an evolution of salvation. We believe in God, He helps us; we grow proud and think we can go it alone. We make a mess of things. Then we come running back to ask for God's help. It's each of our personal histories and if you read the Old Testament, it's the history of salvation.

The Church can never again hold the powerful, oppressive position it did in Ireland. But we need religion because without it, life, death, and suffering become meaningless.

The only choice for the Church is to reform. We need another Reformation from the bottom up. The deeply ingrained evil of clericalism destroyed the credibility of our beautiful Church. Because of it, one essential point has been missed and no amount of rearranging the deck chairs will camouflage it. The point: the Church will be saved by its laity or it will not be saved at all.

Clerics need to be redeemed by the very laity whose talents we have trifled with for centuries. A dedicated and committed laity is the only hope for the future of the Church. It is the laity who will determine if we clerics are serious in our efforts to accept responsibility for the sex-abuse scandals. The most hopeful sign in the Church today is that many lay people are still willing to throw us a lifeline. Are we humble enough to grasp it?

In return lay people will demand a share in decision-making in every aspect of Church life, which is their right. After centuries of the laity being accountable to the clergy, true balance will be restored when Catholics demand greater accountability from their leaders. Respect and authority have to be earned; that's the only fruitful way forward. Power corrupts, absolutely, because it is imposed by bullies.

So why do I stay a priest? I have not sorted that question out yet. I'm still on the journey. And I doubt if it should be sorted out. Who said I should be spared confusion just because I'm a priest and Religious?

Is there any answer other than that I still believe this is where God wants me to be? That is how He wants me to serve, however uncomfortably.

George Herbert's poem *The Collar* contains prophetic lines:

> *But as I raved and grew more fierce and wild / At every word,*
> *Methought I heard one calling, Child! / And I replied, My Lord.*

I think the explanation of hope is in Van Gogh's remarkable painting *The Sower*. And I don't think it was an accident that I ended up in Van Gogh's museum in the second week that I was struggling to write this book. The works of Van Gogh that I should have seen before, but never did, jumped out at me. It brought home to me something which has been fermenting in my mind for a long time.

I see my vocational role in life now as keeping enough faith alive so that when things change there will be a seed of faith which will mature in God's good time. I will never see it mature, but hopefully by the life I live, I will be able to pass on some seeds of hope to others. I see that as the purpose of religious life as well.

The religious life we're involved in is dying with the Church structures of which it is a part. We need to hold on to some forms of dedicated life so that a new generation will be able to discern their own way of religious life around the concepts we have left. We leave an ember in the ashes which they will use to kindle their own fire.

The same is true for the wider Church.

The kind of Church we're involved in is dying. That doesn't mean the Church is dying. If we can compassionately nurse this model of Church through death without actually committing euthanasia, there will be faith enough to give birth to a new, vibrant community.

As I come to another stop on my journey, I am enthused more than ever by the goodness of other, more experienced, searchers. The singer, the artist, Merton the Monk and most of all "poor Charlie" helped me to bring a dignified closure to the struggles of life so far.

I mentioned earlier that after the thought-provoking *Time of Our Lives* documentary one of the people who contacted me was the singer and writer of searching songs Christy Moore. He showed his care in the form of a brief, handwritten card: "I'm in the Slieve Russell on Friday night. You'll probably be there anyway. Come back and we'll have a chat afterwards."

I know the trials of singers well enough now never to impose myself after a show, when those who perform as intensely as Christy does are simply exhausted. But I timidly accepted his invitation to join him and some of his crew for tea and brown bread backstage.

We talked, not so much in the context of religion, but more about holding onto integrity whilst honestly searching for the right path through life. In a quiet sort of way he wondered why I remained a priest. His personal image of priesthood did not sit easily with my lifestyle and views.

The only way I could explain was to go back to the image of *The Sower*. Christy came to Van Gogh from a different source, namely singer Don McLean's song *Vincent*. He wasn't familiar with Van Gogh's 30 or more attempts to interpret the parable of *The Sower* through art.

I tried to paint word pictures of the frustrated sower walking, head down, into barren darkness, while scattering seeds in a vain belief that they'd take root. By now even the tree trunk is dead, except for barely distinguishable green shoots. It's a hopeless task, but he keeps on doing it despite the deathly darkness.

I told him I believed the hope was in the harvest field behind him, which was the fruit of his labour even though he knew nothing about it. I'm not sure Christy was convinced that the little I was doing would bear fruit in the way I hoped.

Maybe you're not, either.

It's enough for me, though. I don't have to see what the future holds. I simply do my best to speak truthfully and know God will take care of the future. I refuse to choose death for its own sake. I want to go on planting the green shoots and following the advice of Charles of Mount Argus: "Pray, pray, pray."

This is how I pray. Thomas Merton, the prophetic Trappist monk who seems to have journeyed through these pages with me, wrote a consoling prayer which I say every day of my life. It keeps me focused on Hope in a faithful way:

My Lord God, I have no idea where I am going,
I do not see the road ahead of me.
I cannot know for certain where it will end.
Nor do I really know myself, and the fact that I think I am
following Your will does not mean that I am actually doing so.
But I believe that the desire to please You does in fact please You.
And I hope that I have that desire in all that I am doing.
I hope that I will never do anything apart from that desire.
And I know that if I do this, You will lead me by the right road,
though I may know nothing about it.
Therefore I will trust You always though
I may seem to be lost and in the shadow of death.
I will not fear, for You are ever with me,
and You will never leave me to face my perils alone.

(Thoughts in Solitude)

So be it.